RISING
STAR

RISING STAR

China's New Security Diplomacy

BATES GILL

BROOKINGS INSTITUTION PRESS
Washington, D.C.

Copyright © 2007
THE BROOKINGS INSTITUTION
1775 Massachusetts Avenue, N.W., Washington, D.C. 20036
www.brookings.edu

Library of Congress Cataloging-in-Publication data
Gill, Bates.
    Rising star : China's new security diplomacy / Bates Gill.
        p.   cm.
    Summary: "Analyzes the transformation in China's security diplomacy and
makes the case for a more nuanced and focused policy toward Beijing. Focuses
on Chinese policy in three areas—regional security mechanisms, nonproliferation
and arms control, and questions of sovereignty and intervention. Concludes with
recommendations for future U.S.-China relations"—Provided by publisher.
    Includes bibliographical references and index.
    ISBN-13: 978-0-8157-3146-7 (cloth : alk. paper)
    ISBN-10: 0-8157-3146-9 (cloth : alk. paper)
    1. China—Foreign relations—1976– 2. National security—China. 3. Nuclear
nonproliferation—China. 4. China—Foreign relations—United States. 5. United
States—Foreign relations—China. I. Title.
    JZ1734.G56 2007
    355'.033051—dc22   2006039013

9 8 7 6 5 4 3 2 1

The paper used in this publication meets minimum requirements of the
American National Standard for Information Sciences—Permanence of Paper for
Printed Library Materials: ANSI Z39.48-1992.

Typeset in Minion

Composition by Cynthia Stock
Silver Spring, Maryland

Printed by R. R. Donnelley
Harrisonburg, Virginia

Contents

Preface

Few would argue with the proposition that China has now at last "arrived" on the international scene. Of course, China had never really departed and has remained a crucial player in the evolution of international relations throughout living memory and for many, many centuries before. Nonetheless, it was only a few years ago that the respected journal *Foreign Affairs* published a seriously considered article asking the question "Does China Matter?"

Times have surely changed. Today, China attracts flocks of investors, political leaders, and cultural icons, from Bill Gates to Kofi Annan to Mick Jagger. President George W. Bush has met with his Chinese counterparts more than any other American president. In purchasing-power terms, China is the world's second largest economy, is the largest holder of foreign exchange reserves by far, and is the largest foreign creditor to the United States. A day does not go by when events and decisions in China do not resonate in capital markets and political capitals. Every week, it seems, major media outlets carry China stories front and center.

China plays a critical role on global issues, from nonproliferation to climate change, and is at the heart of contentious national debates on such issues as job losses, trade deficits, and human rights. And China's impact goes well beyond elite business and politics: some 120,000 foreign students now study in China (excluding those from Taiwan, Hong Kong, and Macau), more than triple the number from a decade ago. In contrast to the *Foreign Affairs* article noted above, James Kynge, a reporter for the *Financial Times* in China, draws from Napolean Bonaparte's famous admonition and declares in his recent book that *China Shakes the World*. How true.

With China's burgeoning importance, there is a thirst in the United States and throughout the world for a better understanding of China, its prospects, and the impact its rise will have on global affairs, on regional, national, and community interests, and on our personal lives.

That is where this book comes in. This volume is not a personal account of my experiences living and working in China—though those experiences surely inform what is written here. The book is also not a paean to the China market and how to make it rich there—or at least avoid getting ripped off.

Instead, this is a book written primarily for practitioners, policy analysts, students, and other informed observers who want to dig deeper into the motivations, achievements, and implications of China's increasingly proactive—and increasingly effective—foreign and security policy. Remarkably, the subject of much discussion and debate in recent years, this topic has received relatively little book-length treatment.

Three volumes—Michael Swaine and Ashley Tellis's *Interpreting China's Grand Strategy* (2000), the book edited by Deng Yong and Fei Ling Wang, *China Rising* (2004), and Avery Goldstein's *Rising to the Challenge* (2005)—illuminate broad motivations behind China's grand strategy, but spend less time detailing how that strategy has played out in terms of Chinese diplomatic activity and security-related behavior on the ground. Robert Sutter's 2005 book, *China's Rise in Asia,* and the edited volume by David Shambaugh, *Power Shift* (2006), do much more in providing such details, but stay focused predominantly on China's impact within Asia.

The present volume builds from these works to offer a more detailed and policy-oriented look at the impact and meaning of China's security policies at both regional and global levels. It first offers a concise framework for understanding the goals of Beijing's "new security diplomacy." From there, the book describes and explains how China seeks to realize these goals through active policies across a range of specific security-related issue areas: regional and global security mechanisms and confidence-building measures, bilateral "partnerships," military-to-military relations, views toward alliances, nonproliferation and arms control measures at multilateral, bilateral, and domestic national levels, changing views on sovereignty and intervention, and approaches to such issues as counterterrorism and international peacekeeping. The book recognizes throughout that China's new security diplomacy presents significant challenges as well as opportunities to other players in the international system, and devotes concluding chapters to what those are and how the United States and the international community can respond.

This book should both inform and spur further a much-needed debate about how best to deflect the challenges and leverage the opportunities posed by China's new security diplomacy. For the long-term stability and prosperity of East Asia and the world, the United States, China, and countries around the globe may have no greater interest than to see China emerge as a fully contributing partner to the international community, at peace with its neighbors, with a more open and just society at home. But getting there is by no means easy or certain. By clearly understanding and judiciously responding to China's new security diplomacy, we can all have greater expectations of realizing that important objective.

Acknowledgments

This book culminates several years' work and results from the generous encouragement, assistance, and support from a number of individuals and institutions all along the way. I am grateful to Mike Armacost, Richard Haass, and Jim Steinberg (formerly of the Brookings Institution) and John Hamre (President and CEO of the Center for Strategic and International Studies), who, as leaders at the institutions where I worked in completing this book, created the kind of positive atmosphere—intellectual, collegial, and professional—that makes such an endeavor both possible and pleasurable.

China watchers in the United States and abroad remain a collegial bunch, and I have benefited enormously over the years from their wisdom. Most works of this kind build upon what has gone before, and this book is no exception. I am especially grateful to Jim Steinberg, David Shambaugh, Evan Medeiros, Taylor Fravel, J. D. Yuan, Michael Glosny, and six anonymous reviewers, who generously provided their insights and constructive criticism on drafts of this book. Thanks too go out to the participants in the Council on Foreign Relations Task Force on China's military modernization, and especially to Andrew Scobell and Alastair Iain Johnston of that group, for their very helpful comments when I presented the task force with parts of an early version of this manuscript.

I have benefited from the research assistance of several very talented persons in recent years—James Reilly, Jennifer Chang, Drew Thompson, Matthew Oresman, Jennifer Feltner, Melissa Murphy, Chin-hao Huang, and Eve Cary—who made great contributions toward the completion of the book. Working with such intelligent and dynamic young people confirms for me that the future of China watching will be in very good hands indeed. Tirelessly reliable and good humored, Virginia Quintero Rosell and Savina Rupani also supported this work in innumerable ways.

Sarah Palmer, my wife, has been an ever-encouraging partner for more than twenty years, and her constant love and support make all things possible.

Finally, I would like to gratefully acknowledge the generosity of the Smith Richardson Foundation and the United States Institute of Peace, which supported the completion of this volume in its early stages. The Freeman family—and especially Houghton "Buck" Freeman and Doreen Freeman—established the Freeman Chair at CSIS in 1992, and their generosity and vision support and inspire all the work I do. In thanking these individuals and institutions, I would add that, while they should surely take credit for the book's strengths, its remaining faults and weaknesses are entirely my own.

1

The New Security Diplomacy

Only by developing a new security concept and establishing a fair and reasonable new international order can world peace and security be fundamentally guaranteed.

China's National Defense in 2000, Information Office of the State Council, October 2000

Since the mid-1990s, China's global and regional security diplomacy has dramatically changed. Overall, China is pursuing positions on regional and global security matters that are far more consistent with broad international norms and practice than in the past. China's approach to regional and global security affairs has become more proactive, practical, and constructive, a pattern that looks likely to continue for years to come.

Through a combination of pragmatic security policies, growing economic clout, and increasingly deft diplomacy, China has established productive and increasingly solid relationships throughout Asia and around the globe, to include new partnerships in Southeast Asia, Central Asia, Europe, Africa, and South America. While these developments predate September 11, 2001, they have unfolded at a time of strategic preoccupation on the part of the United States, both in military operations in Afghanistan and Iraq and in the global counterterrorism campaign. This last, in turn, has opened strategic space for China to expand its influence at both regional and global levels. As present trends continue in the regional and global security dynamic, China may eclipse Japan as the predominant Asian power in the western Pacific, solidify its role as the key player shaping regional diplomatic and political developments around Eurasia, and strengthen China-driven security relationships in the region and around the world.

In short, as a rising star in the constellation of great powers, China and its new security diplomacy present momentous opportunities and challenges for the international community, for the Asia-Pacific region, and for United States. On the one hand, China has increasingly embraced global and regional security policies that vastly improve its image and position within the international system and that are more consistent with international norms, regional expectations, and U.S. interests. At the same time, fortified by this increased political, diplomatic, and military power in both global and regional security affairs, Beijing is in a better position to realize more self-interested security aims over the longer term (such as resolving the Taiwan question on its terms or asserting itself more forcefully as a regional political-military power), which could be disruptive to regional stability and could even lead to confrontation with regional powers. The strategic stakes of China's new security diplomacy and its outcome are very high. Unfortunately, too little attention and analysis is given either to solidifying the opportunities presented by China's new security diplomacy or to recognizing and deflecting its potential challenges.

Given these opportunities and challenges, it is critically important to analyze China's new security diplomacy and its implications. How has China's global and regional security diplomacy changed, why has it changed, and will this new approach last? What are the motivations and outcomes of this new approach at global and regional levels? In what key areas will these changes in Chinese security diplomacy most profoundly affect global and regional affairs and the interests of the world's major powers, including the United States? What are the opportunities and challenges presented by these developments for U.S. influence and security interests, both in Asia and globally, and for future U.S.-China relations? This book seeks to provide answers and policy responses to these questions.

Not a September 11 Phenomenon

China's new security diplomacy can trace its roots to the early 1980s and a single consistent assumption about the nature of international politics and security—that the overall tendency of world affairs is toward peace and development, increased multipolarity and economic globalization, and a general easing of tensions. Despite dramatic shifts in the security environment internationally and for China since the 1980s, Beijing continues to pronounce an adherence to this supposition.

It is important to recognize that this outlook is not merely a result of post–September 11, 2001, changes in the international security environment, a watershed to which far too many analysts understandably, but often too readily, look in gauging other powers' policies and intentions. Rather, while the post–September 11 environment has opened new opportunities for China's evolving security diplomacy to succeed, that strategy has more fundamental antecedents that considerably predate September 11. In that sense, today's Chinese security diplomacy is less tactical and ephemeral than is sometimes assumed and needs to be taken more seriously and analyzed more carefully.

China's new security diplomacy is rooted in the strategic verdict determined by the late Chinese leader Deng Xiaoping, who, in 1982, concluded that the world was tending toward peace and development, the possibility of a world war was remote, and China could expect a stable international environment in which it could carry out its much-needed domestic development. Deng's pronouncement was a major reversal of the Maoist line of war and revolution and preparation "for an early war, a major war, and nuclear war," which during the first several decades of the People's Republic contributed to disastrous economic hardship, ideological struggle, and international isolation.

This broad strategic view was given further impetus in response to major challenges China began to face on foreign and domestic fronts in the late 1980s. The country first was forced to deal with the diplomatic isolation imposed by the West in the wake of the bloody suppression of the Tiananmen demonstrations in the spring of 1989. Later that year, China, as a Communist country, sensed all the more its isolation as one by one the Communist countries of Soviet-dominated Europe broke free from Moscow's orbit, ousted their Communist Party leadership, and established mostly pro-Western governments. Then in early 1991 China stood by while the United States led a UN-sanctioned coalition of countries to repel Saddam Hussein's invasion of Kuwait and decimate Iraq's armed forces (including vast quantities of Chinese weaponry) in an awesome display of high-tech firepower. In the next year, with great trepidation, China witnessed the collapse and break up of the Soviet Union.

Following the end of the bipolar, cold war world, Chinese leaders and strategic analysts were further troubled to find that, contrary to their expectations, the international security situation did not shift to a more multipolar balance of great powers. This commonly held outlook in China included the view that American power would steadily wane and foresaw an expanded role for multilateral institutions—in particular the United Nations—to govern relationships among states. Rather, over the course of the 1990s Chinese analysts became increasingly concerned with U.S. global primacy, even hegemony, and with its ability to mobilize powerful allied force to achieve its security goals. Of particular concern for Chinese strategists was whether the United States and its allies would use force against China or in a way detrimental to Chinese interests. This was especially worrisome to Beijing given the increasing pro-independence tendencies and intentions expressed on the Taiwan political scene from the mid-1990s onward. Official Chinese pronouncements in the 1990s also stressed broader international problems, such as the need to establish a more "democratic international system" and "fair and rational new international political and economic order," in order to narrow the political and economic gap between the developed and the developing world. They expressed strong concerns that "some countries" wrongly exercise "hegemony," "power politics," and policies of preemption, which infringe upon the sovereignty of smaller states and impose the will of the strong upon the weak.[1]

At home, China faced increasing challenges as well. As China's policies of *gaige kaifang* (reform and opening up) took hold, the country experienced increasingly difficult political, social, and economic growing pains. The Tiananmen demonstrations of 1989 were a wake-up call for the Chinese Communist Party regarding the need to maintain its power through a kind of grand bargain with the Chinese citizenry: keep the party in power in return for continuing economic growth and prosperity. But the spectacular economic progress of the 1990s, while helping defer overt political threats to the regime, also brought with it new social and economic challenges. Chinese leaders clearly recognized this dilemma and became increasingly concerned with addressing burgeoning domestic problems, including pervasive official corruption, widening income gaps between rich and poor, widespread layoffs and underemployment in the state sector, extensive environmental degradation, a fragile banking and financial sector, an ailing social welfare and public health system, and frequent localized disgruntlement and unrest. Managing these growing sociopolitical and socioeconomic challenges at home, while also maintaining political leadership and expanding the domestic economy, became priority number one for Beijing.

THE NEW SECURITY CONCEPT

Following Deng's strategic advice, and in response to the challenges on its foreign and domestic fronts over the 1990s, Beijing's security diplomacy cohered into certain *tifa*, or authoritative formulations, emanating from Chinese officialdom and its strategists.[2] These include the notions of a "new security concept," acting as a "responsible great power," and "China's peaceful rise," for example, all of which feed into some emergent "new thinking" about the country's diplomacy within China's strategic and political elites.[3] The new security concept draws from principles formally advocated by the Chinese government since the 1950s, in particular the Five Principles of Peaceful

Coexistence, which date back to the Bandung Conference of developing world nations in 1955.[4] The Chinese have for decades called on nations to observe these principles. However, in 1994–95 the Chinese began making high-profile appeals for the establishment of a "new" system for international order. For example, the November 1995 Chinese white paper on arms control states that with regard to security in the Asia-Pacific region, it is necessary to "establish a new mutual respect and friendly relationship between nations" based upon not only the five principles but also common economic development, peaceful settlement of disputes, and bilateral and multilateral dialogues and consultations. According to the white paper, all nations should "spare no effort to establish a new peaceful, stable, fair, and reasonable international political and economic order."[5]

These early formulations cohered more distinctly into the idea of a new security concept by July 1998, when Beijing's Information Office of the State Council issued a white paper:

> The world is undergoing profound changes, which require the discard of the Cold War mentality and the development of a new security concept and a new international political, economic, and security order responsive to the needs of our times.
>
> The core of the new security concept should be mutual trust, mutual benefit, equality, and cooperation. The UN Charter, the Five Principles of Peaceful Coexistence, and other universally recognized principles governing international relations should serve as the political basis for safeguarding peace, while mutually beneficial cooperation and common prosperity [is] its economic guarantee. To conduct dialogue, consultation, and negotiation on an equal footing is the right way to solve disputes and safeguard peace.
>
> Only by developing a new security concept and establishing a fair and reasonable new international order can world peace and security be fundamentally guaranteed.[6]

In a major foreign policy speech delivered in Geneva in March 1999, Chinese leader Jiang Zemin presented the core of the new security concept, and much of the thinking behind the concept is enshrined in the declaration at the Sixteenth Chinese Communist Party Congress in 2002.[7]

Noting that the first twenty years of the twenty-first century would be a window of "strategic opportunity" in which to pursue its goal of "comprehensively building a well-off society," the document, echoing Deng Xiaoping of twenty years before, states that because a "new world war is unlikely in the foreseeable future," one could realistically "expect a fairly long period of peace in the world and a favorable climate in the areas around China." It continues, "We will continue to cement our friendly ties with neighbors and persist in building good-neighborly relationships and partnerships with them. We will step up regional cooperation and raise our exchanges and cooperation with our surrounding countries to a new height."[8]

Chinese politicians and strategists also began to speak of China as a *fuzeren de daguo* (responsible great power). This term emerged most openly in association with Beijing's decision not to devalue its currency during the Asian financial crisis of 1997–98, a decision that received widespread praise and appreciation from the region and around the world. Since then, the term has been used more broadly both to describe China's changing diplomatic posture and as a longer term foreign policy goal to which China should aspire. Increasingly, the notion of a responsible major power points to a Chinese security diplomacy that is less victimized, less aggrieved, and less alienated and that more actively supports and operates within international norms and multilateral institutions such as the United Nations, the World Trade Organization, the ASEAN Regional Forum, the Shanghai Cooperation Organization, and others.[9]

For example, from the early 2000s, and particularly from 2001, the Chinese approach to the new security concept and to its regional security strategy became less stridently reactive. This trend predates the global shifts brought on by the September 11, 2001, terrorist attacks against the United States but was accelerated by them, as the new strategic concern of terrorism overtook and sidetracked overt contentiousness between the United States and China. China's entry into the World Trade Organization in December 2001 and a stable transition to the new, fourth-generation leadership in Beijing in 2002–03 further strengthened China's more confident approach toward the international and regional security situation.

China's defense white paper of 2002 expresses the view that "peace and development remain the themes of the present era," that a new world war is "unlikely in the foreseeable future," and that multipolarization and economic globalization continue apace, though "amid twists and turns."[10] The Asia-Pacific region is viewed with particular favor as the "most dynamic region economically with the greatest development potential in the world." The white paper adds that "strengthening dialogue and cooperation, maintaining regional stability, and promoting common development have become the mainstream policy of the Asian countries." References to "factors of instability," "hegemonism," and "power politics" are less prominent, while the emergence of "non-traditional security challenges," particularly terrorism, is frequently mentioned as a problem China and the world must face together. Across the spectrum of China's foreign policy elite, new calls emerged in 2001–03 for a more mature, constructive, and responsible great power diplomacy for China. As Evan Medeiros and M. Taylor Fravel found, this new approach seems to abandon China's long-held and reactive "victimhood" complex, puts the country's "century of shame" to one side, and identifies more closely with a "great power mentality" befitting China's larger and more secure position in regional and global affairs.[11]

A "PEACEFUL RISE"

Consistent with Deng Xiaoping's grand strategy and the notion of a new security concept, in the early 2000s senior Chinese leaders and strategists, particularly those associated with China's fourth-generation leadership, began to speak of *Zhongguo de heping jueqi* (China's peaceful rise). The formulation, most closely associated with one of the Chinese leadership's senior advisers, Zheng Bijian, expresses both a confidence and an acknowledgement that China is a rising power but also asserts that China's emergence will not be disruptive.[12] The notion was most prominently asserted with the publication of a major article on China's peaceful rise by Zheng Bijian in the U.S. journal *Foreign Affairs* in the fall of 2005, which further confirmed this approach as the mainstream and dominant foreign policy line within Chinese leadership circles. The approach gained even more solid footing and official blessing with the issuance in December 2005 of the Chinese government white paper *China's Peaceful Development Road*. China's effort to vigorously promote this concept is interesting on many levels and reveals much about China's evolving new security diplomacy.

First and foremost, promoting China's peaceful rise is intended to counter the long-standing concern about a rising China disrupting the global status quo, in a repeat of the rise of Weimar Germany in the late nineteenth century and of imperial Japan in the early twentieth century. Arguing that China's rise will not be a threat to stability is a pragmatic and much-awaited recognition by Beijing of the security dilemma posed by China's increasing weight in world affairs. Second, asserting a peaceful rise is intended to reassure neighbors of China's benign intentions to seek a win-win outcome in their foreign relations. This is especially important in terms of China's relations with key Asian neighbors and partners, such as in Southeast Asia. But even more important is the desire to put relations with the United States on more solid footing and deflect lingering U.S. concerns about China's emergence as a more powerful player.

Third, and often overlooked by outside analysts, Chinese strategists and commentators explicitly link the concept of a peaceful rise to China's domestic situation. The concept acknowledges that even while China is rising it faces continuing difficult social and economic challenges at home. China's overall security strategy requires that it make "sober internal judgments" to ensure that domestic development is relatively smooth and stable so that China's overall security strategy can be successful. As an authoritative *People's Daily* editorial reminded its Chinese readership,

> It remains a basic reality that ours is a big country with a huge population and a poor foundation to start with; restrictions of resources and environment pose severe challenges to us and the task of realizing sustainable development is quite arduous . . . social reform, improvement and coordination [are] still urgent; economic development remains at a low-end level . . . the lack of core technologies and independent intellectual property rights has prevented us from accomplishing much in industrial creation and innovation.[13]

There has been some debate among scholars and strategists in China about the language and suitability of the term *peaceful rise.*[14] Some Chinese analysts argue that use of the term *peaceful* could constrain options vis-à-vis Taiwan, where China continues to reserve the possibility of using force to resolve its claims of sovereignty over the island. Others advise against use of the term *rise,* both because it is not yet clear that China will continue to rise over the long term and because the term may unduly alarm neighbors, who fear a rising China. Hu Jintao, China's president, preferred to employ the phrase "China's peaceful development" in a speech to the Bo'ao Forum in April 2004; and Wen Jiabao spoke of China's "peaceful development path" before a convocation of Chinese diplomats in August 2004, though the overall thrust of these speeches was part and parcel of the overall peaceful rise formulation.[15]

THE "NEW THINKERS"

Parallel to the development of thinking at the official level on such ideas as the new security concept and China's peaceful rise, a number of academic scholars have come forward to provide further theoretical underpinning and analytical support for China's more pragmatic and proactive foreign and security policy. In some cases, these scholars advocated an even more cooperative approach toward the West, and toward the United States in particular, than the official line. Dubbed "the new thinkers" by China analysts in the West, this group of scholars contends that it is in China's strategic interests to establish cooperative and productive relationships with its neighbors, and particularly with major powers such as the United States and Japan, in spite of persistent bilateral difficulties. For example, these Chinese analysts argue the need to accept and to work with unipolar American power, giving these reasons:

—A truly multipolar world might be dangerous to Chinese interests.

—Support for multipolarity equates to confrontational thinking.

—China would be better served by multilateralism, pluralism, and globalization.

—Through a process of "national social learning," China and the United States can achieve an accommodation with one another.

—American hegemony, properly exercised, benefits regional and global stability.

—Chinese interests are best served by finding an accommodation with the Western-dominated international community to develop common interests, norms, and institutions.[16]

Some thinkers in this camp, including in the Chinese Communist Party Central Party School, openly recognize the importance of the democracy issue in U.S.-China relations and argue that China should pursue democratization to defuse tensions with the United States and the West and to improve China's overall security situation.[17]

More broadly, these new thinkers advocate a set of ideas that, if implemented, would help moderate Chinese foreign and security policy. For example, their work recognizes that a security dilemma between China and its neighbors could arise as a result of China's growing strength and that a negative regional reaction to China's rising power would undermine efforts within China to promote a more positive foreign and security policy. These analysts also attach importance to the need for China to reassure its neighbors by exercising self-restraint and by promoting, joining, and actively participating in regional multilateral security mechanisms and initiatives that moderate state behavior, including that of China. With regard to the United States in particular, these analysts argue that the strong U.S. hegemonic presence in the region can play a positive role for Chinese security (as long as core interests of China, above all regarding Taiwan, are preserved).[18]

It is important to note, however, that the views of these new thinkers are not always accepted by policymakers, within academic circles, or by the broader public in China. For example, when such new thinkers as Ma Licheng, a well-known reform-minded journalist with the *People's Daily*, and

Shi Yinhong, a professor at Renmin University, advocated a more pragmatic and less emotional approach to Japan, it sparked a fierce anti-Japan backlash in intellectual circles and among the broader public in 2003–04, foretelling the anti-Japan riots in many Chinese cities in April 2005. In Shi's writings in defense of Ma, he argues that it is in China's long-term national interest to put the history issue aside and expand common ground with Japan as a way to balance against the strategic encroachment of the United States. These views on Japan, while forward-leaning, fell well out of mainstream thinking but may be gaining greater traction.[19]

Putting Principle into Practice

By the late 1990s and early 2000s, while not explicitly stated as such, China's strategic assumptions and principles began to gel more distinctly into recognizable goals. These fundamental goals provide the underlying motivations for China's new security diplomacy. First, the Chinese leadership generally seeks to maintain a stable international environment in order to defuse instabilities, especially around its periphery, so Beijing can focus on critical economic, political, and social challenges at home. The 2002 Chinese defense white paper puts it clearly: "A developing China needs a peaceful international environment and a favorable climate in its periphery."[20]

Second, China's new security diplomacy obviously aims to augment China's wealth and influence, but in a way that reassures its neighbors of its peaceful and mutually beneficial intent. Beijing has come to understand the security dilemma dynamic and wishes to avoid alarming its neighbors; instead it promotes the notion of China's peaceful rise.

Third, the new security diplomacy seeks to counter, co-opt, or circumvent what it perceives as excessive American influence around the Chinese periphery, while avoiding overt confrontation with the United States, all with the aim of shaping its own security environment. According to Wang Jisi, China's leading analyst of U.S.-China relations, China must play a defensive role and does not want the United States to see it as a foe.[21] In pursuing these goals, China puts the principles of its new security diplomacy into action.[22]

This approach can be seen in Beijing's changing policies and practices in three of the most critical developments shaping global and regional security affairs: the changing role of alliances and the expansion of regional security mechanisms and confidence-building measures; the growing significance of nonproliferation and arms control; and more flexible approaches to sovereignty, intervention, and the use of force.

The first development is the changing role of alliances. With the end of the cold war, traditional alliance relationships have undergone profound change, while regional security mechanisms and confidence-building measures of various stripes have proliferated as countries have sought new arrangements to help secure stability, reduce uncertainty, and establish communication and confidence-building channels. These developments have unfolded in spite of (and at times because of) the unilateral predominance of the United States in world security affairs. The U.S. alliance system itself, while still robust, faces a new, challenging, and transformative future in Europe, in the Middle East and the Persian Gulf, in South and Central Asia, and in the western Pacific. On the other hand, Asian nations have been active in establishing other types of security mechanisms, including not only the ASEAN Regional Forum and the Shanghai Cooperation Organization but also ASEAN+3 and the East Asia Summit.

The second major security concern relates to proliferation and arms control. Of particular concern is the proliferation of weapons of mass destruction and their delivery vehicles, especially nuclear weapons, ballistic missiles, and related technologies. Since the late 1990, India and Pakistan joined the nuclear club, North Korea declared its possession of nuclear weapons, and Iran raised international concerns about its nuclear ambitions. The exposure of A. Q. Khan's network of nuclear technology assistance further underscores the shadowy challenges for nonproliferation in the post–cold war era. The increasing possibility that nuclear devices and other weapons of mass destruction will be used by terrorist organizations dramatically raises the stakes for nonproliferation and arms control. At the same time, however, the international community has made important strides in solidifying norms of arms control and nonproliferation, particularly among the major powers, with the conclusion of several key agreements, including the Chemical Weapons Convention (1993), the Comprehensive Test Ban Treaty (1996), and the indefinite extension of the Nuclear Nonproliferation Treaty (1995). Nevertheless, numerous critical arms control issues remain unresolved today and continue to have an impact on international and regional security affairs, including the role of missile defenses, the powers of the International Atomic Energy Agency and other watchdog groups, the weaponization of outer space, and the conclusion of a fissile materials production cut-off treaty.

Third, the norms of sovereignty and intervention have changed significantly in recent years, as globalization and the transnational nature of world affairs have eroded borders. In the late 1990s, UN Secretary General Kofi Annan argued that traditional notions of state sovereignty were being challenged by forces of globalization and international cooperation and that states did not have unlimited sovereignty in their domestic affairs if they are committing fundamental human rights abuses. U.S.-led forces, under the North Atlantic Treaty Organization, intervened on humanitarian grounds against Yugoslavia in 1999 without UN authority. In response to the September 11, 2001, terrorist attacks against the United States, Washington pushed an even more assertive principle of preemptive intervention to justify attacks against Afghanistan and Iraq. These developments are highly controversial, yet it is also clear that the emergence of all manner of transnational threats and challenges—from terrorism, to energy security, to health concerns—demands new thinking within the international community on issues of security.

The core chapters of this book examine China's new security diplomacy, both its positive and negative aspects, in each of these important areas of global and regional security and then consider the challenges and opportunities China's new security diplomacy presents to the world, and to the United States in particular.

Chapter 2 details how, as part of its new security diplomacy, Beijing has shed much of its traditionally skeptical, reluctant, and often contrarian approach toward regional security mechanisms and confidence-building measures to adopt more proactive and constructive policies. This chapter outlines these developments by examining China's more active role within such organizations as the ASEAN Regional Forum, in fostering and sustaining such organizations as the Shanghai Cooperation Organization and ASEAN+3, in building a range of key bilateral "strategic partnerships," in playing a critical role in the six-party talks for Korean peninsula security, and in taking part in an unprecedented number of multilateral and bilateral security dialogues, military-to-military activities, and other confidence-building measures.

Chapter 3 describes and analyzes China's new security diplomacy toward issues of nonproliferation and arms control. For much of its history, the People's Republic of China was skeptical and openly defiant of international nonproliferation and arms control norms and generated serious concerns about its role as a proliferator of sensitive weapons and technologies. However, as detailed in chapter 3, since the mid-1990s to the late 1990s, and as part of its new security diplomacy, Beijing's approach toward nonproliferation and arms control has substantially changed, to include a leadership position on certain arms control and nonproliferation initiatives, dramatic reductions in its weapons exports, and the implementation of its commitments to stem the flow of destabilizing weapons and technologies. To be sure, many concerns remain about China's approach to nonproliferation and arms control. But China's new policies and practices on these issues represent some of the most striking aspects of China's new security diplomacy.

Chapter 4 examines China's new security diplomacy and its approach to questions of sovereignty and intervention. While it is true that Chinese leaders and strategists have strong views supporting traditional definitions of state sovereignty and opposing foreign interventionism, especially regarding the Taiwan question, nevertheless, Chinese views on sovereignty and intervention display signs of greater flexibility and pragmatism across a range of security-related questions. This chapter looks into the important policy changes in Beijing by contrasting its past and current approach to questions of sovereignty and intervention and by detailing Chinese policy and practice regarding peacekeeping and counterterrorism. While not as proactive or constructive as China's policies toward regional security mechanisms or nonproliferation, Beijing's changing approach to sovereignty and intervention merits closer scrutiny.

It is important to recognize that Beijing's changing views and policies in each of these aspects of international and regional security are motivated by its aim to achieve the three fundamental goals of its new security diplomacy: alleviate external tensions in order to address challenges on the domestic front, reassure neighbors about China's peaceful intentions, and find ways to quietly balance the United States. Because these three goals are so fundamentally important to China's long-term security and stability, the new security diplomacy is likely to be an enduring and increasingly irreversible aspect of China's grand strategy for years to come.

The U.S. Response

Few would disagree that, for better or for worse, China is one of the world's most important powers in economic, political, and military terms and is likely to become even more powerful and influential in the years ahead. Yet in spite of China's strategic importance, Beijing's new security diplomacy has only belatedly begun to receive the sustained attention it deserves by strategists and policymakers in the United States. To the degree China's new security diplomacy has generated attention, it is too often in the negative sense, expressed in overly simplistic ways about China's threat to U.S. interests. But a more nuanced, coherent, and focused U.S. policy response is called for.

On the one hand, China's new security diplomacy presents a potentially difficult and sophisticated set of challenges. China's ability to challenge U.S.

interests concerns not only issues related to Taiwan. The two countries face a number of other unresolved security-related differences, including over missile defenses, nuclear nonproliferation, humanitarian intervention, the role of alliances, the pursuit of energy resources, and the American political-military presence in Asia. As Beijing's new security diplomacy results in a more powerful and influential China in Asia and around the globe, including stronger relations between China and many of America's friends and allies, the United States may be increasingly constrained in its ability to manage and shape outcomes on issues where the two countries continue to differ.

Chapter 5 goes into greater detail on this point, describing the potential challenges and uncertainties China's new security diplomacy presents to the international community, the Asian region, and the United States. The chapter describes how China's new security diplomacy may challenge U.S. interests in three broad areas: the role of alliances and regional security mechanisms, Chinese nuclear proliferation activities and U.S.-China differences over the bilateral and global arms control agenda, and China's approach to sovereignty and intervention.

On the other hand, the proactive, pragmatic, and productive aspects of China's new security diplomacy offer opportunities for constructive and cooperative Chinese policies consistent with U.S. interests. In some cases, the United States has sought to leverage such opportunities, as in efforts to cooperate with China to resolve the North Korean nuclear standoff. But far more can be done to work with China: many opportunities presented by China's new security diplomacy have largely been overlooked or too readily dismissed.

Chapter 6 lays out an ambitious but practicable and "opportunistic" agenda to take fuller advantage of China's new security diplomacy in ways that deepen positive aspects of China's approach, give China a greater stake in global and regional stability, defuse the potential for U.S.-China confrontation, and promote a more open, constructive, and responsible China in the future. These opportunities fall into three categories. First, regarding alliances and regional security mechanisms, the United States should intensify bilateral discussions on mutual regional security concerns, increase bilateral military-to-military relations, deepen U.S. and U.S.-China interaction within regional security mechanisms, strengthen coordination with regional allies on issues related to China, and realize a long-term, nonmilitary resolution to differences between China and Taiwan. Second, regarding nonproliferation and arms control, Washington should seize all opportunities to resolve persistent Chinese proliferation cases, work to improve China's own arms export control capability, establish a stable, long-term framework for bilateral strategic nuclear relations, improve cooperation on global arms control issues, and expand upon past nonproliferation successes with China. Third, and finally, U.S. policy should leverage China's changing approach to questions of sovereignty and intervention by intensifying U.S.-China dialogue regarding objectionable and threatening regimes, reaching common ground in defining and addressing new transnational threats, and encouraging greater Chinese support and participation in peacekeeping and nation-building operations.

In short, the United States needs to formulate and sustain a more balanced, forward-looking, realistic, and strategic China policy, one that more clearly recognizes and meets the challenges and opportunities of China's new security diplomacy. Unfortunately, and to the detriment of U.S. interests, American China policy has been hamstrung from more effectively pursuing such an approach. Four important reasons stand out for this.

AN UNFAMILIAR SITUATION

First, the rise of China and its more proactive security diplomacy present an unfamiliar situation for policymakers in Washington, one for which there is little to no good parallel in living memory. In the recent past, when faced with challenges from rising powers, the American response could be relatively straightforward. In the cases of imperial Japan and Nazi Germany, for example, the necessary American response eventually became clear, culminating in unconditional surrender for those powers. In the face of the challenge of the Soviet Union, a long "twilight struggle" and policy of containment, contributing over time to the collapse of the regime and the eventual end of the cold war, were widely accepted to be the necessary American course. The challenge of an economically rising Japan in the 1980s was more easily moderated by the friendly and stable U.S.-Japan alliance and eventually by the changing economic fortunes of Japan and America.

China presents an altogether different and unfamiliar set of challenges. Unlike Nazi Germany, imperial Japan, and the Soviet Union, on the one hand, and "Japan, Inc." on the other, China cannot be so clearly distinguished as friend or foe. China is unlikely to seek aggressive territorial gains into areas of core American strategic interest, such as the heart of Europe, or seek to extend imperial dominion across vast areas of Pacific Asia, or attack American possessions to meet those aims. Beijing does not seek to spread Communist ideals, establish global networks of ideological client states, or foment revolution in the developing world. Chinese companies have been slow to invest aggressively in the United States, unlike the case with Japan. Moreover, unlike Japan of the 1980s and 1990s, the China market is vastly more open to foreign direct investment, imports, and foreign ownership.

Rather, Beijing's approach seems to be subtle and long term, seeking to avoid open confrontation while quietly pursuing its interests and aspirations for great-power status. Under these conditions, the American response will likewise require subtlety to manage the increasing complexities of U.S.-China relations, characterized by elements of both cooperation and competition.[23] This prospect becomes all the more difficult in the absence of relevant previous experience from which to draw.

POST–SEPTEMBER 11 PRIORITIES

Second, U.S. strategic priorities after September 11, 2001, hamper a more effective policy response to China's new security diplomacy. One factor is that the U.S. strategic focus is predominantly on Southwest Asia and the Middle East: the conflicts in Afghanistan and Iraq, the unstable governments in those countries, America's plummeting image among Muslims, and the Israel-Palestine conflict. Moreover, the post–September 11 environment has uncovered new tensions in U.S. relations with its allies, such as in the transatlantic relationship. China's new security diplomacy, by comparison—particularly as it has unfolded in Asia and Europe—has not garnered sufficient attention in Washington.

The September 11 effect also skews U.S. analysis of Chinese foreign policy, as American political leaders and strategic analysts understandably gauge other powers on the basis of their post–September 11 actions. However, it is mistaken to interpret China's new security diplomacy as driven predominantly by a counterterrorism agenda or as a tactical accommodation of American interests. It is neither. While the current global security environment opens opportunities for China to pursue its new security diplomacy, the strategy itself is rooted in decisions and actions taken well before September 11, 2001. Ignoring this point complicates Washington's ability to effectively recognize, interpret, and respond to the opportunities and challenges of China's new security diplomacy.

INTERNAL DIVISION

Third, an effective U.S. response to Beijing's new security diplomacy is seriously encumbered by the divisive and often politically charged nature of American views toward China. As an unfortunate result, American reactions to China's increasingly proactive global and regional security policies are tentative, uncertain, and muddled, reflecting a persistent tension between two well-established camps.[24]

One of these camps, the "engager-hedgers," is comparatively hopeful about the future of U.S.-China relations, emphasizing the common interests the two countries share—especially in the realms of economics, business, and trade—while recognizing the persistence of certain difficult issues. This camp recognizes the limits on Chinese power and that through political, economic, and security-related engagement with Beijing, it is possible to embed China more firmly in the international system while also generating greater social, economic, and political openness for China's domestic scene. The engager-hedgers point out that by and large U.S. and Chinese security interests have converged over the past two decades and that—especially since September 11, 2001, and in spite of lingering differences—the United States and China have an opportunity to open a new chapter in their relationship, based on a mutually recognized interest in combating terror and other transnational threats to global, regional, and domestic security.

This approach expects the two countries to see the new global threat environment in much the same way they did other common enemies in the past (Japan in the 1940s and the Soviet Union in the 1970s) and join together, mutually constrained from heading purposefully into conflict, in order to pursue their shared security interests. It also recognizes that the two sides still differ over critical issues, especially over Taiwan, and that as a result the United States should continue to hedge, pursuing a strategy of aiming for the best, but being prepared for the worst. But overall, such an approach sees the value in intensified, comprehensive, and sustained cooperation between the United States and China.

"China hawks," on the other hand, hold a darker view, envisioning an inevitable conflict between the two countries. Basing their claim in history and a realpolitik understanding of world affairs, some argue that a rising and revisionist China, eager to establish a more prominent place in regional and international affairs, will ultimately confront the established power of the United States, leading to conflict. Others would add that China, as an authoritarian state, is less accountable than the United States in its foreign policy and hence more prone to adventurism; because of this, it will seek to aggrandize its power and influence as a matter of course, even if only as a last-ditch means to maintain flagging party legitimacy at home. Conflict over Taiwan is most often cited as the flashpoint where the United States and China will come to blows in the near term as a part of the larger, longer-term confrontation between these two powers. With a U.S.-China conflict not a matter of if but when, this view advocates a curtailment of interaction with Beijing, especially those ties that would strengthen China and make it a more formidable adversary in the future. It also calls for a more active effort to contain Chinese power and weaken its government, with the aim of establishing a more benign and friendly China. In recent years, economic, trade, and financial problems have become more prominent in U.S.-China relations, further bolstering the concerns of the China hawk camp.

Both of these approaches have valid points and concerns. But they both have serious flaws in their approach. Engager-hedgers tend to downplay some of the serious and persistent security-related differences between the United States and China and may place too much confidence on the positive effect of "engagement" on China. China hawks, however, are overly wedded to the inevitability of conflict and dismiss too quickly the positive and substantive convergence of U.S. and Chinese security interests in a number of key areas, such as combating terrorism, disarming a nuclear North Korea, ensuring a stable U.S.-China bilateral relationship, and maintaining stability and fostering prosperity across Eurasia. Most important, neither of these views adequately accounts for the proactive, productive, and pragmatic security diplomacy put forward by China. China hawks tend to overlook the opportunities for American interests, particularly at the level of global and strategic issues and with regard to Chinese domestic developments; they see only threats in China's rise. Engager-hedgers on the other hand tend to overlook the challenges of China's new security diplomacy to U.S. interests, especially with regard to China's growing influence in regional affairs and with American allies. Perhaps worst of all, the two camps are often highly polarized, undermining the possibility of a well-crafted, coherent, and sustained U.S. strategy toward China.

VOLATILE PAST RELATIONS

Fourth, and finally, these factors are made more complicated by the volatile nature of U.S.-China relations, which keeps Washington's policy focus on the near-term ups and downs in U.S.-China relations rather than on strategic trends in Chinese security diplomacy. U.S.-China relations have swung from poor to good every couple of years since the mid-1990s. Relations seriously deteriorated in the wake of the visit of Taiwan's president, Lee Teng-hui, to the United States and China's subsequent show of force between July 1995 and March 1996, when China conducted missile tests into the waters adjacent to Taiwan and held large-scale military exercises opposite Taiwan. China's coercive diplomacy culminated in missile firings into the waters north and south of Taiwan in the week just before the Taiwan presidential election of March 1996 and prompted the dispatch of two American aircraft carrier battle groups toward the Taiwan area.

U.S.-China relations went through a brief period of improved relations from late 1996 to late 1998, witnessing two important summits between Presidents Clinton and Jiang. But this period was followed by another serious downturn, with allegations of Chinese high-tech espionage and attempts to influence the U.S. presidential election. Relations further plummeted when, owing to calamitous intelligence errors during Operation Allied Force against Yugoslavia in the spring of 1999, a U.S. B-2 bomber dropped five 2,000-pound precision-guided munitions onto the Chinese embassy in Belgrade, killing three Chinese and injuring some twenty others.[25] In outrage, citizens across China took to the streets in demonstrations, which the government could channel but could not stop. The American embassy building in Beijing was besieged for days by rock-throwing protesters. U.S. consulate property in Chengdu was set afire. The Chinese media attacked the United States. At its harshest, the Communist Party mouthpiece, *People's Daily,* issued an article denouncing American "hegemony" and comparing the United States to Hitler's Germany.[26] Going into the 2000 presidential campaign, the challenger, George W. Bush, referred to China as a "strategic competitor," language repeatedly employed by some of his senior advisers once in the White House in early 2001. The April 1, 2001, collision between a Chinese fighter jet and an American EP-3 reconnaissance aircraft near Hainan Island and the resultant twelve-day standoff for the release of the American crew further fueled suspicions between the two sides.

Beginning in spring 2001, and especially in the wake of the September 11 terrorist attacks against the United States, the pendulum of U.S.-China relations took a dramatic, positive swing. Visits to China by State Department Director of Policy Planning Richard Haass and then by Secretary of State Colin Powell in mid-2001 helped the two sides overcome the EP-3 incident and put the bilateral relationship back on track. Chinese President Jiang Zemin, having watched the terrorist attacks on the World Trade Center on television in Beijing, was among the very first world leaders to telephone President George W. Bush to express condolences and solidarity. Over the year from October 2001 to October 2002, Presidents Bush and Jiang held three summits, twice in China (October 2001 and February 2002) and once at President Bush's home in Crawford, Texas (October 2002).

By the end of 2001 and in 2002, the two sides spoke of "constructive and cooperative" ties (the U.S. side added "candid" to the phrase). In September

2003 Secretary of State Powell declared that "U.S. relations with China are the best they have been since President Nixon's first visit." Quoting from the *National Security Strategy of the United States*, Secretary Powell stated that the United States welcomes "a strong, peaceful, and prosperous China. And we seek a constructive relationship with that China."[27] In a speech two months later, Secretary Powell reiterated U.S. support for a strong, peaceful, prosperous China, adding, "We welcome it. We do not feel threatened by it. We encourage it."[28] Deputy Secretary of State Robert Zoellick remarked in September 2005, "We now need to encourage China to become a responsible stakeholder in the international system. As a responsible stakeholder, China would be more than just a member—it would work with us to sustain the international system that has enabled its success."[29] Considering these extraordinary swings in U.S. policy toward China over just the past several years, with official American views shifting so dramatically from one extreme to another—from dire predictions of strategic competition to welcoming China's rise to a "responsible stakeholder"—the United States has been slow to fully acknowledge, assess, and respond to China's new security diplomacy.

Looking Ahead

Washington's often incoherent response to China's new security diplomacy cannot be sustained and, for the sake of U.S. interests, cannot continue. In the years ahead, the U.S. policy leadership must take a more careful and critical look at China's new security diplomacy so as to develop a response that addresses both its opportunities and its challenges. There are some signs that more reasoned, judicious, and coherent sets of understandings and policies are in the works for Washington's China policy, but it remains too early to predict their effectiveness and sustainability.[30] Washington can and must chart a course in response to China's new security diplomacy that defuses potential challenges; that reaps significant benefits for global stability, regional security, and improved U.S.-China relations; and that helps realize a more open and constructive China for the future. The following chapters are intended to help chart a course toward those critically important goals.

2 | Regional Security Mechanisms

Hegemonism and power politics remain the main source of threats to world peace and stability; cold war mentality and its influence still have a certain currency, and the enlargement of military blocs and the strengthening of military alliances have added factors of instability to international security.

—*China's National Defense*, Information Office of the State Council, July 1998

China pursues a foreign policy of building a good-neighbor relationship and partnership with its neighbors, trying to create an amicable, secure, and prosperous neighborhood and vigorously pushing forward the building of a security dialogue and cooperation mechanism in the Asia-Pacific region.

—*China's National Defense in 2004*,
Information Office of the State Council, December 2004

In reviewing China's experience of misfortune with alliances and other security-related institutions—both as a partner in them and as a target of them—it is easy to understand the country's traditional ambivalence and suspicion toward such arrangements.

However, since the mid-to-late 1990s China has altered its approach and, as a core aspect of its new security diplomacy, has fostered and strengthened an expanding range of bilateral and multilateral political and security-related ties and confidence-building measures throughout the region and around the globe. Beijing's more proactive approach to regional security mechanisms is motivated by the three overarching goals of its new security diplomacy: defuse tensions in its external security environment to better focus on domestic challenges, reassure neighbors about China's rise, and cautiously balance the power of the United States to more effectively meet Chinese security interests. These important developments deserve much greater attention than they have been given and present both opportunities and challenges for regional security and stability in the years ahead.

China's Traditional Approach

For most of its postwar history as the People's Republic, China has eschewed the entanglements of alliance relationships and other security arrangements, on the one hand, questioned their motives, on the other, and maintained as much freedom of action as possible to manage its bilateral relationships with powers great and small around its periphery.

ALLIANCES AND SECURITY MECHANISMS

Until recently, China's experiences as a member of alliances or other security arrangements had not been positive. Over most of the twentieth century, it is difficult to identify a major alliance, quasi-alliance, or other security-related arrangement in which China participated that ended well for the country.

At the Paris Peace Conference of 1919, China was one of twenty-seven countries gathered to help build the post–World War I international system, but it could only look on helplessly as, in order to gain Japanese participation in the League of Nations, the conference acceded to Tokyo's demands for Japanese authority over former German holdings on China's Shandong peninsula, in blatant disregard for Chinese sovereignty. The international community was later powerless to respond to Chinese calls to invoke the Nine Power Pact of 1922 or the Kellogg-Briand Pact of 1928 (China was a signatory to both) as a means to resist Japanese aggression in China.[1] Moreover, China's status as a founding member of the League of Nations made no difference in repelling the encroachments of Japan in Manchuria and its all-out war against China by the late 1930s. The most "successful" alliance for China in the twentieth century was in concert with the United States and other powers in opposition to the Axis powers in World War II and, in particular, in defeating imperial Japan. But even this experience proved bitter for the Communists, who came to lead mainland China by 1949. Following World War II, the United States ultimately threw its support behind Chiang Kaishek and the Chinese Nationalists; the United States did not accept Chinese Communist claims to legitimately represent China internationally and even wound up establishing an alliance with Japan. This move on the part of the United States was designed in part to contain and roll back Chinese communism.[2]

The only two post–World War II alliances China formally established were with the Soviet Union and North Korea. China's most high-profile alliance in the latter half of the twentieth century, the Sino-Soviet Treaty of Mutual Friendship, signed February 4, 1950, was never an especially trustworthy affair and ended bitterly a mere ten years later. For China the treaty carried with it an abiding sense of humiliation and promises broken. The treaty began poorly (Mao cooled his heels for two months in Moscow while he waited for Stalin to act) and ended in animosity, with the expulsion of Soviet advisers from China in 1960. The treaty was never formally abrogated by either side; instead, it quietly expired, as stipulated by the document, thirty years after it went into force. According to article 1 of this treaty, the two parties agreed that if one or the other were "attacked by Japan or States allied with it . . . the other High Contracting Party will immediately render military and other assistance with all the means at its disposal." In practice, the relationship resulted in massive transfers of Soviet economic and military assistance in the early and mid-1950s, but such assistance amounted to little in the political-military sense. By the end of the 1960s, the two treaty partners were engaged in intensive military skirmishes along parts of their disputed border and vitriolic exchanges of political rhetoric.

The Chinese alliance with North Korea was informally established in late 1950, when Chinese troops surged across the Yalu River to push U.S.-led United Nations forces back across the thirty-eighth parallel on the Korean Peninsula.[3] Chinese forces remained on the peninsula until the latter half of the 1950s. In the early years of this military relationship, China provided generous support to North Korea, including significant transfers of military equipment in the late 1950s and early 1960s, as well as possible assistance to North Korea's nuclear weapons and ballistic missile programs as late as the 1970s. In July 1961, as the Sino-Soviet relationship deteriorated, Beijing and Pyongyang signed a Treaty of Friendship, Cooperation, and Mutual Assistance.[4] The treaty envisioned that the two sides would "adopt all measures to prevent aggression against either of the Contracting Parties" and that if either were subjected to aggression by any state or group of states, the other would "immediately render military and other assistance by all means at its disposal." The treaty also stipulated that "Neither Contracting Party shall conclude any alliance directed against the other Contracting Party or take part in any bloc or in any action or measure directed against the other Contracting Party."[5]

Nevertheless, this alliance was constantly fraught with tension as Pyongyang sought advantage by playing Moscow and Beijing off one another. While professing eternal fealty to North Korea, the Chinese leadership steadily weaned itself away from an overtly supportive position toward Pyongyang and, from the late 1980s, built a "two-Korea" policy. The culmination of this process was the August 1992 establishment of diplomatic relations between Beijing and Seoul, bringing a practical and peaceful end to decades of cold war animosity between China and South Korea and effectively ending China's one-sided, pro-Pyongyang approach to the Korean peninsula. It is true that China continued to provide considerable material and financial support to prop up the economically faltering North throughout the 1990s and into the early 2000s, portraying itself as a useful political and economic model for Pyongyang. But what had begun in the 1950s as an alliance hallowed in blood and joint sacrifice had, by the early 2000s, turned into a close relationship for many of the wrong reasons in Beijing: China's North Korean ally became a potentially disastrous burden rather than a positive military asset.

China also provided considerable political and military-related support for Vietnam in its war against the United States in the 1960s and early 1970s. China's contributions included tens of thousands of soldiers and engineers, mostly as anti-aircraft artillery support. But by 1978 the Sino-Vietnamese friendship had collapsed: China launched its punitive invasion against Vietnam in early 1979 to retaliate for Hanoi's Soviet-backed war in Cambodia; Sino-Vietnamese border clashes lasted into the mid-1980s.

China's political alliance with Albania in the mid-1960s—based on bilateral joint statements issued in 1964 and 1966—fell well short of a traditional alliance and ultimately collapsed. At the time, the two sides shared opposition to "imperialism" (the United States) and "revisionism" (the Soviet Union) but maintained only an informal and unstructured relationship to pursue this agenda. As China's foreign policy in the 1970s became more pragmatic, and the Sino-U.S. relationship warmed, the tenuous links between Tirana and Beijing strained to the point where China cut off all economic, technical, and military aid by 1978.[6] Even China's short-lived strategic alignment with the United States in the late 1970s and into the mid-1980s (involving intelligence sharing, U.S. arms sales to China, and close cooperation to defeat the Soviet Union in Afghanistan and the Vietnamese in Cambodia) was a fleeting and ultimately fragile expediency, which collapsed entirely with the Tiananmen Square crisis of 1989 and the fall of the Soviet Union in 1991.

The other relationship that comes close to—but still falls short of—a formal alliance for China is its ongoing political and military-related ties with Pakistan. This relationship, with roots in the mid-1960s in the wake of the

1962 Sino-Indian War, has included an extensive military-technical component, including the transfer of both nuclear- and missile-related technology and systems and a range of conventional weapons. Forged in joint opposition to Indian power on the subcontinent, the Sino-Pakistani connection also proved useful to the two sides (and to the United States as well) in the late 1970s and early 1980s as the parties worked together to support the mujahideen in their struggle against Soviet aggression in Afghanistan. However, Beijing and Islamabad have never formalized this association into an alliance. China's close connections with and military assistance to Pakistan came back to haunt Beijing by the late 1990s as the India-Pakistan rivalry escalated to new heights with the detonations of nuclear weapon tests by both countries. Resulting in part from its long-standing quasi-alliance with Islamabad, Beijing faces a potentially destabilizing nuclear weapons buildup on its borders with South Asia. China's long-standing relationship with Islamabad proved helpful in 2001 by bolstering Pakistan's decision to lend support to the U.S.-led counterterrorism fight in Afghanistan. However, at the same time, Beijing watched from the sidelines as U.S.-Pakistan political and military ties steadily revitalized as a result.

AS TARGET OF ALLIANCES

At the very outset of the twentieth century, during the Boxer Rebellion of 1900, China declared war on and was in return assailed by a loose coalition of foreign powers seeking to expand their influence over the decaying Qing dynasty. In response to a months-long siege by the nationalist Boxers against the diplomatic legations in Beijing, a multinational force of 20,000 foreign troops was landed to lift the siege. Fighting in and around Tianjin and Beijing ensued, and the conflict ended in Chinese defeat by mid-1901. The Qing government was forced to pay an indemnity of 450 million ounces of silver, equivalent to nearly twice the government's yearly revenues, to be paid over several decades.

Later in the century, before the newly established People's Republic was a year old, Beijing found itself the target of American military relationships around its periphery, especially with the outbreak of the Korean War in June 1950. The decision to insert American naval forces into the Taiwan Strait to protect Chiang Kaishek's government on Taiwan was quickly followed by the steady advance of U.S.-led forces, under a UN mandate, toward the Chinese border in pursuit of North Korean forces on the Korean peninsula. In entering the war in November 1950 to defend its North Korean neighbor, China found itself at war with the international community, with bloody clashes between the Chinese "People's Volunteers" and UN forces under U.S. command. By the mid-to-late 1950s, with the steady establishment of the U.S. alliance structure in Asia, China was increasingly surrounded by neighbors with bilateral military relationships with Washington: Japan (1954), Republic of Korea (1953), Republic of China (Taiwan, 1954), the Philippines (1951), Australia (1951), New Zealand (1951), Thailand (1954), Southeast Asia (Southeast Asia Treaty Organization, or SEATO, 1954), and Middle East countries (Central Treaty Organization, or CENTO, 1959).[7]

As the United States waged its war against North Vietnam in the 1960s and early 1970s, Beijing and Washington were more cautious to signal one another to avoid a repeat in Indochina of their Korean conflict. Nevertheless, tens of thousands of Chinese forces served in North Vietnam against the Americans and South Vietnamese. Later in the 1970s, China found itself the target of another set of alliances, this time led by the Soviet Union. Hanoi and Moscow signed a twenty-five-year Treaty of Friendship and Cooperation in November 1978, an agreement that emboldened Vietnam to resist China's putative regional dominance and spread Soviet-backed Vietnamese power throughout Indochinese Southeast Asia. Vietnam's invasion and occupation of Cambodia prompted China's attack into northern Vietnam in the early months of 1979; low-level border clashes and heated political rhetoric were exchanged between the two sides until the mid-1980s.

More recently, Chinese political leaders and strategists appear ambivalent at best about American alliances. They continue to voice concern over the role of American alliances in the Asia-Pacific region, fearing that China is considered a target for "containment" by these alliances. Over the 1990s, most Chinese strategists only grudgingly accepted the presence of American military alliances in the region, with the expectation that over time they would weaken and eventually depart from the scene, particularly in East Asia. For these analysts, the best that could be said about American alliances is that they helped keep the peace in Asia, a situation that has greatly benefited China. In addition, Chinese analysts acknowledged that in some cases—such as with Japan and with Taiwan—the U.S. alliance system can restrain the junior partner from creating trouble in the region: keeping Japan from returning to its militarist past, for example; or preventing Chiang Kaishek from launching an attack from Taiwan to retake the mainland; or restraining Taiwan's pro-independence leanings.

But by and large, Chinese analysts in the 1990s and into the early 2000s saw U.S. alliances as outdated cold war relics, potentially troublesome factors for instability in the near term and a potential threat to China over time, and realized that regional stability and Chinese security interests might be best served by their demise, sooner rather than later. In 1997, while visiting Asian capitals, high-level Chinese officials went so far as to call for the complete abrogation of alliances.[8] Such views were also powerfully and authoritatively expressed in Chinese defense white papers of the time. The 1998 Chinese defense white paper notes that "the enlargement of military blocs and the strengthening of military alliances have added factors of instability to international security." The 2000 defense white paper highlights the increasing factors that may cause instability and uncertainty in the world, including the NATO intervention in Yugoslavia, the pursuit by certain big powers of "neo-interventionism" and "neo-gunboat diplomacy," and the development and introduction of missile defenses. The 2000 defense white paper added with concern that "some countries have continued to enlarge military blocs, strengthen military alliances, and seek greater military superiority. This has seriously affected world security and stability."[9] A Pentagon assessment of Chinese strategy in 2000 put it this way:

> Senior [Chinese] leaders are concerned primarily that the United States wants to maintain a dominant position in the Eurasian balance of power by containing the growth of Chinese power and preventing a resurgence of Russian power. Beijing assesses that Washington is trying to sustain a "unipolar" balance of power by strengthening its security alliance with Tokyo and by expanding NATO's reach beyond Western Europe. . . . Moreover, Beijing suspects that new U.S.-Japan Defense Guidelines Review measures authorize Japanese military action beyond Japan's previous defense posture and prompt Tokyo to improve its regional force projection capabilities. Beijing also calculates that U.S. efforts to develop national and theater missile defenses will challenge the credibility of China's nuclear deterrence and eventually be extended to protect Taiwan, a move that China would consider a gross intervention in Chinese affairs and that would complicate China's efforts to establish an intimidating conventional theater missile capability opposite the island.[10]

When the George W. Bush administration came into power in 2001, Chinese strategic commentators warned of the growing American presence and strategic interest in Asia and how this might exacerbate regional conflict and increase pressure on China.[11] However, with the advent of China's more proactive security diplomacy and improvements in U.S.-China relations, Chinese rhetoric on the U.S. alliances took on a slightly different tone. Beginning in the summer of 2001, senior Chinese officials conveyed to their American counterparts that China did not seek to oust the United States from East Asia and that it recognized that the U.S. presence served a stabilizing role. President Jiang Zemin also delivered this message to George Bush during their summit meeting in Shanghai in October 2001.[12]

Nevertheless, as the United States strengthened ties to Japan and improved military cooperation with Taiwan, Chinese concerns about U.S. alliances were never far below the surface. The conclusion in September 1997 of new U.S.-Japan defense guidelines—which for the first time noted that U.S.-Japan defense cooperation would also include joint efforts in response to "situations in areas surrounding Japan"—prompted agitated Chinese concerns that the alliance was expanding its mandate to encompass contingencies in the Taiwan Strait or against China.[13] More recently, China voiced "serious concern" over the U.S.-Japan Security Consultative Committee's February 2005 joint statement, which for the first time overtly expressed a joint concern about the Taiwan issue and the transparency of Chinese military affairs. In swift reaction to the statement, Foreign Ministry spokesman Kong Quan said the Chinese government and people "resolutely oppose the United States and Japan incorporating the Taiwan issue . . . in their joint statement." He added that "the U.S.-Japan military alliance is a bilateral arrangement that took shape under the special historical conditions of the Cold War" and that it "should not exceed a bilateral scope."[14]

In March 2005 China warned that a military pact between Australia and the United States should avoid being concerned with Taiwan. He Yafei, head of the Foreign Ministry's North American and Oceanian Affairs Bureau, stated, "We all know Taiwan is part of China, and we do not want to see in any way the Taiwan issue become one of the elements that will be taken up by bilateral military alliances, be it Australia-U.S. or Japan-U.S."[15] Chinese Foreign Ministry spokesman Liu Jianchao added: "China always held that bilateral military alliances in the world should not go beyond the bilateral scope and that the countries concerned should fully take into consideration the interests and concerns of other countries in the region when dealing with alliance relations and do more things that are beneficial to peace and stability in the whole region."[16]

The New Security Diplomacy

From the mid-to-late 1990s, and in part as a response to concerns about U.S. "hegemony" and alliance-strengthening, Chinese officials and analysts began to more openly embrace and foster alternative security structures as part of a broader effort to promote Beijing's new security concept. Emerging from diplomatic isolation following the Tiananmen Square crisis of 1989, seeking stable international footing with the collapse of European and Soviet communism at the end of the cold war, and facing the daunting prospect of an increasingly powerful and potentially hostile United States, Beijing gave practical effect to the new security concept by establishing a host of new and productive political and security relationships with partners around its periphery and across the globe. Fostering at first a series of bilateral partnerships, most prominently with Russia, China then came to increasingly embrace multilateral security arrangements, such as the Association of Southeast Asian Nations (ASEAN) Regional Forum in the mid-1990s, and to help found new multilateral security mechanisms, such as the Shanghai Cooperation Organization in the late 1990s. By the mid-2000s China had proactively participated in a broadening range of bilateral and multilateral security mechanisms, including hosting multiparty negotiations to resolve the North Korean nuclear standoff, addressing disputes in the South China Sea, opening new security dialogues, and carrying out military-to-military confidence-building measures with partners around the world.

These steps are driven by the three key factors that motivate China's new security diplomacy. First, by proactively embracing multilateral security mechanisms, Chinese leaders hope to dampen tensions in its external security environment so they can focus on domestic economic, political, and social reform challenges. Second, active engagement in multilateral security mechanisms helps China extend its influence and power but in a way that reassures its neighbors about the country's "peaceful rise" and "peaceful development." Third, China's active involvement in multilateral security mechanisms contributes to countering, co-opting, or circumventing U.S. influence and "hegemony" around the Chinese periphery, while avoiding overt confrontation with the United States.

THE ASEAN REGIONAL FORUM AND ASEAN

The ASEAN Regional Forum (ARF), first discussed seriously in the early 1990s, held its first formal meeting in the July 1994.[17] The ARF began with eighteen members, has since grown to twenty-three members, and encompasses virtually all the major countries of the Asia-Pacific region from India eastward and includes Canada, the European Union, and the United States.[18] The group's principal meeting is the annual foreign ministers' gathering in the summer, which is preceded by one senior official meeting in May. In addition, intersessional meetings are held throughout the year to work on specific issues of interest to the ARF; the intersessionals are co-chaired by one ASEAN and one non-ASEAN country. The ARF operates in the "ASEAN way": the highest priority is given to consultation and consensus, where, through dialogue, the goal is to create a high degree of "comfort" for all participants. The organization has no permanent secretariat, and security is to be strengthened not through collective security or formal defense structures but rather through the consultative and "socialization" process. The group has set out three phases for its work, developing first confidence-building measures, then preventive diplomacy mechanisms, and then conflict resolution arrangements. So far the organization has not developed the last two phases to any meaningful degree (in part because of China's resistance to movement in that direction).[19]

In spite of these comparatively modest arrangements and goals, China was not particularly supportive of the ARF idea when it was first proposed in the early 1990s, offering only vague support for the concept of a regional security mechanism. China first became more involved in what would become the ARF process when, in July 1991, it attended for the first time the ASEAN Post-Ministerial Conference (ASEAN PMC) as a "consultative partner." According to one prominent Chinese strategic analyst, China's original plan for the ARF in February 1993 envisioned minimal confidence-building measures, restrictions upon the extent of the ARF, and a limited role for Russia and the United States in the region.[20] Other analysts expressed deep reservations about the ARF's goals and sought to restrict them. For example, a leading analyst with China's largest government-run think tank stated that not only do the "guiding principles" of the ARF (confidence building, enhanced trust, reduction of hostile activities) "still need further discussion and study," but if the ARF was to begin acting more proactively, "the Forum would undoubtedly become a highly systematic security organization that would be involved in regional conflicts on its own initiative and might interfere with the internal affairs of other states."[21] Reflecting China's early concern with the ARF, this think-tank specialist argued that the group should refrain from initial involvement in regional conflicts, try to foster a consensus among regional states, and only then coordinate with global-level organizations, such as the United Nations, to deal with local crises. But even that view was not fully shared by others in

China, particularly with regard to preventive diplomacy and conflict resolution mechanisms. For another analyst, the ARF should be "retarding" conflict and decreasing tension but not addressing more fundamental national security concerns in the region through interference or intervention.[22]

The highest levels of decisionmaking in China shared this more narrow view of the ARF's mandate. As the Chinese vice premier and foreign minister, Qian Qichen, emphasized at the inaugural ARF meeting in Bangkok (July 1994), a slowly evolving, lowest-common-denominator approach was required:

> The Asia-Pacific nations have different historical traditions, cultural origins, political systems, religious beliefs, and even value systems and development levels. Naturally they have different views and proposals on the security situation and cooperation. . . . We should fully consider the above historical and, at the same time, current characteristics of this region. . . . Only if it is based on the common interests and needs of all members, can the forum succeed in promoting healthy development in this region. . . . Different values and norms [among ARF members] could best be overcome by strengthening bilateral relations with other states and by rigidly observing the principle of equality in all negotiations.[23]

Speaking again before the ARF in 1997, Qian Qichen pointed to the "diversity" and "different security experience in history in this region" as reasons why confidence building (as opposed to more ambitious undertakings in preventive diplomacy or conflict resolution) "should be the central task of the Forum for a considerable period of time."[24] Qian's successor to the foreign minister post, Tang Jiaxuan, argued in 1999 that the forum should maintain its focus on confidence-building measures and not move into preventive diplomacy arrangements. Tang stated that the ARF should "first discuss fully the concept, definition, principles, and scope of preventative diplomacy in the Asia-Pacific region so as to reach a basic consensus."[25] The very term "conflict resolution" was one the Chinese could not accept as an official goal of ARF deliberations. Originally set out to characterize the third phase of the ARF's work, at Chinese insistence the term was changed in official ARF deliberations to "elaboration of approaches to conflicts," because Beijing feared that the organization was moving too rapidly toward an institutionalized security structure.[26]

What went largely unspoken in these analyses and statements were the deeper concerns China had about the ARF. First and foremost, Beijing was worried that the Taiwan issue and South China Sea disputes would become a part of ARF discussions. Indeed, Chinese analysts were quoted as saying in 1994 that such multilateral forums were "largely irrelevant" and "potentially damaging" for the resolution of what should be bilateral disputes.[27] Second, Chinese strategists were also worried that the ARF would become a forum dominated by powerful states such as the United States and Japan, which would shape the organization to meet their interests, to China's detriment. Finally, Beijing was also apprehensive that the forum would become a venue for others to gang up on China (a classic concern of China is that it might be "encircled" and "contained") and to criticize, for example, its military modernization program and human rights record.

Nevertheless, the Chinese did not wish to be the odd man out and realized that nonparticipation in multilateral security mechanisms was riskier than involvement, however selective and carefully considered.[28] Indeed, Beijing took a number of steps outside the ARF to strengthen and improve its relations with its ASEAN neighbors. For example, China and ASEAN established the Joint Committee on Economic and Trade Cooperation and the Joint Committee on Science and Technology in July 1994; China joined the ASEAN PMC as a full dialogue member in July 1996; and China helped found the ASEAN+3 summit beginning in July 1997 (involving the ten ASEAN members plus China, Japan, and South Korea), which led to the associated annual ASEAN-China summit meetings.[29]

Still, Beijing remained throughout most of the 1990s a reluctant player within the ARF itself. Chinese representatives read strictly from prepared texts and tried to deflect discussions on issues on which it stood alone. But gradually China's approach began to change as it was able to see in its participation a number of opportunities to achieve Chinese interests, including possibly constraining the role of Japan and the United States in the region, reassuring and establishing improved relations with its Southeast Asian neighbors, and helping to foster a more stable regional environment conducive to Beijing's overall goal of economic development. By 1997, one observer of the ARF noted, China had become a much more active participant in the ARF, and in March 1997 China even co-chaired (with the Philippines) an intersessional meeting on confidence-building measures in Beijing. It was the first time China hosted an official multilateral conference on regional security issues. Later, in 2003–04, China and Myanmar co-hosted two intersessional meetings on confidence-building measures.[30]

China took a number of other small steps in the late 1990s and early 2000s to more deeply engage with the ARF, an engagement that likely contributed to the issuance of its first white paper on defense and arms control matters in November 1995 and the subsequent publication of four more defense white papers in 1998, 2000, 2002, and 2004. China supported the development of "softer" confidence-building measures within the ARF framework, such as mutual naval ship visits, high-level visits by senior military officers, information exchanges, and the exchange of personnel from defense universities and colleges. For example, China hosted the ARF Seminar on Tropical Hygiene and Prevention and Treatment of Tropical Infectious Diseases in November 1998, the ARF Professional Training Program on China's Security Policy in October 1999, the Fourth ARF Meeting of Heads of Defense Colleges in September 2000, the ARF Seminar on Defense Conversion Cooperation in September 2001, the ARF Seminar on Military Logistics Outsourcing in September 2002, and the ARF Workshop on Drug-Substitute Alternative Development in September 2004. Annual meetings of the ARF also offer regularized channels for Beijing to reiterate its official commitment to the peaceful resolution of disputes and the maintenance of regional stability. Without the ARF, discussion and debate regarding the scope, relevance, and utility of transparency and dialogue probably would not have entered official Chinese policymaking circles as early as they did.

In another interesting development, at the July 2002 meeting of the ARF, the Chinese delegation submitted a formal position paper, which provided a detailed explanation of the new security concept, the first time China had submitted such a position paper to the ARF. The position paper broke no new ground in describing the new security concept but more explicitly linked the concept to the work of the ARF: "The line of thought of the [ASEAN Regional] Forum in promoting security through dialogue among equals suits the idea of the new security concept."[31]

At the June 2003 ARF meeting in Phnom Penh, the Chinese foreign minister proposed the establishment of an ARF security policy conference, to be attended by senior-level defense and military personnel from the member states, and intended to open new channels of dialogue and increase confidence and trust among regional military and defense personnel. The proposal was further fleshed out at the November 2003 ARF intersessional meeting on confidence-building measures, held in Beijing. Topics proposed for discussion by China included challenges to Asia-Pacific security, security and military strategies of ARF members, and such professional topics as the revolution in military affairs, defense modernization, defense conversion, and civil-military relations.[32] This was remarkable for the fact that gatherings of ARF military personnel, once strongly supported by the United States, had been opposed by China and many of the ASEAN states in the past. China's proposal was approved during the 2004 ARF ministerial meetings, and the first ARF Conference on Security Policies, attended by all twenty-four ARF member delegations, was held in Beijing in November 2004. During the meeting, the Chinese hosts also staged a counterterrorism exercise for ARF attendees.[33] At the 2004 ARF ministerial meeting, China proposed the continued consolidation of regional confidence-building measures, more work on preventive diplomacy, increased participation of military and defense officials in ARF activities, and greater focus on transnational crime and counterterrorism.[34]

But most interestingly for China's approach to multilateral security-related mechanisms in Southeast Asia, Beijing moved in the late 1990s and early 2000s to establish a number of confidence-building measures and dialogue channels outside the ARF process, emphasizing "nontraditional" and "transnational" issues, all under the rubric of the new security concept. For example, the ongoing ASEAN+3 process and the related ASEAN-China summit have led to a number of important developments. In November 1999 the ASEAN+3 group issued its Joint Statement on East Asia Cooperation and appointed a task force, the East Asia Vision Group, to draft a report outlining ASEAN+3 cooperation for the future. The report presented a range of cooperative activities for ASEAN+3, including in political-, economic-, security-, and energy-related fields, and called for an annual East Asia leadership summit.[35] In addition, as part of the ASEAN+3 process, China, Japan, and South Korea have begun holding regular leadership summits. At their fifth tripartite summit meeting, in October 2003, the leaders of the three nations issued their Joint Declaration on the Promotion of Tripartite Cooperation among the People's Republic of China, Japan, and the Republic of Korea. This document affirms their intention to increase security-related exchanges and military-to-military confidence-building measures and to work together on arms control and nonproliferation questions, including the denuclearization of the Korean peninsula.

Building from the ASEAN+3 process, ASEAN leaders agreed to establish a new mechanism, the East Asia Summit (EAS). The inaugural meeting of the group was held at the conclusion of the ASEAN summit in December 2005. The EAS will meet on a regular basis in an ASEAN capital, and ASEAN will be in the "driver's seat" at the forum.[36] In both public and private, Chinese officials have been at pains to emphasize the ASEAN and, in particular, Malaysian role in forming the EAS. But the forum obviously serves China's strategic interests, and Beijing is an enthusiastic supporter. Some controversy swirled around this meeting, as the United States was not invited to join.

ASEAN members agreed on three conditions for membership: invitees must have substantive relations with ASEAN, be full dialogue partners, and sign onto the Treaty of Amity and Cooperation in Southeast Asia. According to a U.S. Department of State official, "the United States has no current plans to sign the agreement" owing to "concerns about the text, including the rights of non-ASEAN members."[37] These "concerns" probably allude to limitations that would be placed on signatories' military options in the region (for example, limitations on unilateral strikes against terrorist targets).[38]

In a move that was largely viewed as an attempt to reduce Beijing's influence at the EAS, in addition to the originally intended participants (the ten ASEAN countries, China, Japan, and South Korea) Australia, New Zealand, and India were invited to attend the first EAS summit, held in Kuala Lumpur. An article in *People's Daily* commented that the United States had taken an "opposing attitude towards the summit" but that with the inclusion of Australia and New Zealand "the United States has turned itself from an opponent to an audience," noting that "it is hopeful that the U.S.–East Asia relations be relaxed through the platform of the East Asia Summit."[39] In the declaration issued at the end of what was more of a geopolitically symbolic than a substantively meaningful meeting, it was also made clear that while the EAS "could play a significant role in community building in this region," ASEAN would remain firmly "as the driving force" in what would be an "open, inclusive, transparent, and outward-looking forum."[40]

Meanwhile, direct China-ASEAN security-related cooperation intensified in the early to mid-2000s. In October 2000 China and ASEAN established a mechanism known as the Cooperative Operations in Response to Dangerous Drugs, which has included ministry-level meetings among China, Laos, Myanmar, and Thailand to deal with the challenge of drug smuggling in their shared border regions.[41] During the China-ASEAN meeting of November 2002, a number of important agreements were reached. First, it was announced that China and ASEAN would seek to establish an eleven-party free-trade area by 2012. The November 2002 summit also unveiled a joint declaration of cooperation on "nontraditional security issues." This agreement commits China and ASEAN to work jointly in combating "trafficking in illegal drugs, people smuggling, including trafficking in women and children, sea piracy, terrorism, arms smuggling, money laundering, international economic crime, and cyber crime."[42]

The most important agreement to come out of the November 2002 China-ASEAN summit was the Declaration on the Conduct of Parties in the South China Sea. This statement is intended to govern the activities of claimants to various parts of the South China Sea and to reduce the potential for tension and conflict in the disputed areas. Critically, the parties committed to "resolve their territorial and jurisdictional disputes by peaceful means, without resorting to the threat or use of force . . . in accordance with universally recognized principles of international law, including the 1982 UN Convention on the Law of the Sea" and "to exercise self-restraint in the conduct of activities that would complicate or escalate disputes and affect peace and stability."[43] To achieve these objectives, the parties agreed to establish consultations addressing the disputed claims, provide voluntary notice of military exercises in the area, and undertake joint cooperation in marine science, environmental protection, search and rescue, and crime prevention. The South China Sea agreement with ASEAN was a critical step forward from previous Chinese positions. Before 2002 China had insisted that South China Sea disputes be dealt with strictly on a bilateral basis and that outside parties should not be involved.

A year later, at the China-ASEAN summit in October 2003, additional agreements further solidified China's relations with its Southeast Asian neighbors. China acceded to the 1976 ASEAN Treaty of Amity and Cooperation in Southeast Asia, which, among other matters, commits China and other signatories to "foster cooperation in the furtherance of the cause of peace, harmony, and stability in the region," to "not in any manner or form participate in any activity which shall constitute a threat to the political and economic stability, sovereignty, or territorial integrity" of the other parties, and to "refrain from the threat or use of force and . . . at all times settle such disputes among themselves through friendly negotiations."[44] At the October 2003 China-ASEAN summit, the two sides also signed the Strategic Partnership for Peace and Prosperity agreement, committing the eleven countries to cooperation on global and regional issues. The purpose of the partnership is to "foster friendly relations, mutually beneficial cooperation, and good neighborliness between ASEAN and China by deepening and expanding ASEAN-China cooperative relations in a comprehensive manner in the 21st century, thereby contributing further to the region's long-term peace, development and cooperation."[45]

At the eighth China-ASEAN summit meeting, held in November 2004, the two sides "agreed to further strengthen cooperation in the nontraditional security field" and also adopted an action plan to implement the Strategic Partnership for Peace and Prosperity agreement, in order to "accelerate all-dimensional cooperation between the two sides with a view to consolidating and deepening the ASEAN-China strategic partnership." A number of priority areas were identified, including energy cooperation, especially alternative clean energy, biofuels, and hydroelectric power; public health; science and technology; and quarantine inspection. The ASEAN chairman's statement issued at the conclusion of the meeting also "acknowledged the increasingly important role China has been playing in regional and global affairs."[46] In November 2004 the China-ASEAN Five-Year Action Plan was unveiled, providing a political framework for closer, more cooperative relations between Beijing and its Southeast Asia neighbors. In January 2005 China hosted the ASEAN Workshop on Earthquake-Generated Tsunami Warning, during which an action plan was adopted.[47] Participants agreed to set up an integrated Asian Regional Seismographic Network, to which the Chinese government agreed to provide assistance in the form of technical support, training, research on earthquake forecasting and prediction, disaster assessment, and emergency response, in coordination with the United Nations. The China Earthquake Administration will also alert ASEAN and other interested parties as soon as events are detected by the China National Seismic Network.

THE SHANGHAI FIVE PROCESS AND THE SHANGHAI COOPERATION ORGANIZATION

The Shanghai Five process and it successor, the Shanghai Cooperation Organization (SCO), are explicitly cited by Beijing as examples of China's new security diplomacy. With its creation in 2001, the SCO provides a regularized channel for China to strengthen political, economic, and security relations among its major Central Asian neighbors, including, in the words of a senior Chinese official, the opportunity to "depend on cooperation in the fight against terrorism, separatism, and extremism and tap the potential for cooperation in the economic and trade fields."[48]

The Shanghai Five originally consisted of China, Kazakhstan, Kyrgyzstan, Russia, and Tajikistan. While the original five participants held working meetings in the early 1990s, the group was more formally launched when it held its first summit in April 1996 in Shanghai. Interestingly, the formal establishment of the Shanghai Five came shortly after the 1994 initiation of NATO enlargement and the creation of its Partnership for Peace program in the same year.[49] The 1996 Shanghai Five summit was followed by summits in Moscow (1997), Almaty, Kazakhstan (1998), Bishkek, Kyrgyzstan (1999), and Dushanbe, Tajikistan (2000). At the 2001 summit in Shanghai, the group expanded to include Uzbekistan and institutionalized itself more formally under the name Shanghai Cooperation Organization. A formal charter for the organization was issued at the group's summit meeting in St. Petersburg in the summer of 2002. Summits have subsequently been held in Moscow (2003), Tashkent, Uzbekistan (2004), Astana, Kazakhstan (2005), and Shanghai (2006).

The relatively brief history of the organization has been marked by a steady intensification of multilateral contact, dialogue, and the institutionalization of relations among its members. The joint border between China and its Central Asian neighbors extends some 7,000 kilometers (about 4,000 miles), from the Sino-Afghan border in China's Himalayan far southwest around to Mongolia in the north and beginning again in China's northeast, where the Sino-Russian border extends all the way to the sea south of Vladivostok. Settling lingering territorial disputes along that lengthy border and transforming the border from the militarized hostility that characterized much of the postwar Sino-Soviet relationship were primary motivations for China to push ahead in the Shanghai Five process in the mid-1990s. The most significant early accomplishments of the group include its package of military confidence-building measures, including a pullback of some troops and equipment to 100 kilometers (about 60 miles) off the common borders, verification procedures along the border, and prenotification of exercises and other military activities. These steps were largely achieved by the mid-to-late 1990s, as border talks eventually led to the 1996 Shanghai Five Agreement on Confidence-Building in the Military Field along the Border Areas and its 1997 Agreement on Reducing Each Other's Military Forces along the Border Regions. The 1996 agreement stipulates that military forces in the border regions will not be used to attack one another, military exercises will not be aimed at one another and will be limited in frequency and scale, major military exercises within 100 kilometers of the border require notification and an invitation to the neighboring Shanghai Five participants to send observers, and friendly military-to-military exchanges will be established. The 1997 agreement took steps to implement these measures more fully.[50]

By the July 2000 Shanghai Five summit, the five parties announced that implementation of the 1996 and 1997 agreements had "helped build for the first time, in the border belt of more than 7,000 km., a region of trust and transparency where military activities are predictable and monitorable."[51] In addition, the group made strong statements of its opposition to a range of illegal activities in their jointly affected region, such as terrorism and arms smuggling; established a joint antiterrorist center in Tashkent, Uzbekistan;

and agreed to step up cooperation on these issues among their security, customs, and military forces.

Since the late 1990s, the group also began to comment more explicitly on developments in the international arena beyond the immediate scope of Central Asia. For example, on international security issues, the Bishkek statement of 1999, issued shortly after the NATO campaign against Yugoslavia, declared that the five countries "oppose the use or threat of force, unsanctioned by the U.N. Security Council, in international relations." In the Bishkek statement, as well as the Dushanbe statement the following year, the Shanghai Five noted that "multipolarity is the general trend for the development of the present-day world and promotes lasting stability of the international situation" and called for the "construction of just and rational new international political and economic order."[52] The Dushanbe statement, signed by the Shanghai Five on July 5, 2000, is a far-reaching and ambitious statement of principles and goals (see box 2-1).

Consistent with the new security concept, the Dushanbe statement also reaffirmed that the forum's activities embody "a new security view that is built on mutual trust, equality, and cooperation"; that its activities be "conducive to enhancing mutual understanding and good-neighbor relations"; and that they contribute "in a constructive manner to ensuring stability in this extensive region."[53] According to a Chinese interpretation of the Dushanbe document, the Shanghai Five also agreed that "every state has the right to choose its own political system, economic model, and path of social development, affirming that the five countries will support each other to safeguard their state sovereignty, independence, territorial integrity, and social stability."[54]

In addition, the five countries established the Joint Monitoring Group to oversee the implementation and verification of their various military confidence-building measures, especially the 1996 and 1997 agreements. In December 1999, in Bishkek, the Shanghai Five held their first joint meeting of officials concerned with public and state security, convening under the name Bishkek Group. In the 2000 Dushanbe declarations, the five parties also called for the establishment of various joint, interdepartmental groups among the countries to combat such cross-border criminal activities as drug trafficking, arms smuggling, and illegal immigration; and declared their intention to establish high-level working groups aimed at promoting trade and other forms of beneficial economic interaction.

The 1999 Bishkek and 2000 Dushanbe statements also supported regularized meetings between the countries' defense chiefs, foreign ministers, and other top leaders. The first Shanghai Five defense ministers meeting was held

Box 2-1. *Key Principles and Goals of the Dushanbe Statement*

Acknowledging the trend toward multipolarity.

Cooperating in the political, diplomatic, economic and trade, military, military technological, and other fields to consolidate regional peace and stability.

Opposing the use or threat of force internationally without the UN Security Council's approval.

Opposing any country's or group of countries' attempt to monopolize global and regional affairs.

Supporting the one-China principle and the Russian Federation's position on the Chechen Republic.

Supporting the 1972 Anti-Ballistic Missile Treaty, which "must be unconditionally upheld and strictly complied with."

Opposing a "bloc-based, closed-theater missile defense system in the Asia-Pacific," which would "undermine stability and lead to an arms race."

Opposing the inclusion of Taiwan in a theater missile defense system.

Strengthening the Joint Monitoring Group, which implements and oversees verification of military confidence building measures along their borders.

Establishing a regional antiterrorist agency in Bishkek.

Holding regular meetings of military, law enforcement, border defense, customs, and internal security personnel, including joint antiterrorist and counterviolence exercises and peacekeeping experiences.

Conducting annual meetings of foreign affairs ministers and defense ministers.

Supporting the establishment of a Central Asia Nuclear Free Zone.

in March 2000 in Astana; the first foreign ministers meeting was held in July 2000 in Dushanbe; and the first heads-of-government (prime ministers) meeting was held in September 2001. The Dushanbe document also called for the creation of a National Coordinators' Council and the adoption of a "five-nation constitutional document," a step toward a more formal institutionalization of the Shanghai Five in the future.[55] At the July 2000 summit, the parties agreed to "transform the Shanghai Five into a regional structure for multilateral cooperation in various fields."[56]

This drive toward greater institutionalization of the Shanghai Five process resulted in the establishment of the SCO at the June 2001 summit meeting of the group in Shanghai. At this meeting, the Shanghai Five welcomed Uzbekistan as a new member, and the six countries together formed the charter membership of the new organization. The group issued two important documents at this meeting. The first was the Shanghai Convention on the Fight against Terrorism, Separatism, and Extremism, which commits the six to intensifying their cooperation in the area of counterterrorism, setting this as a high priority. A part of this convention included a reiteration of the group's intention to establish a regional counterterrorism center.

The other document was the Declaration on the Creation of the Shanghai Cooperation Organization. This statement takes favorable note of the Shanghai Five's past achievements, and on the basis of those achievements, the six governments declared the creation of the new SCO. The statement sets out the goals of the group and the principles and mechanisms by which it would operate. The document declares the group will "firmly adhere to the goals and principles of the Charter of the United Nations, the principles of mutual respect of independence, sovereignty and territorial integrity, equality and mutual benefit, the solution of all issues through mutual consultations, noninterference in internal affairs, non-use of military force or threat of force, renunciation of unilateral military superiority in contiguous areas."[57]

The declaration goes on to state that the organization is not directed against any third party and is open to new members if they meet the principles of the organization. The declaration also recognizes the challenges of terrorism and other transnational threats, stating that the SCO "assigns priority to regional security and will work to combat terrorism and separatism as well as illicit trafficking in weapons and narcotics, illegal migration, and other criminal activities." In addition, a Council of National Coordinators for the SCO was established at the 2001 meeting. This body was tasked with developing a charter for the organization. The Council of National Coordinators held meetings during the remainder of 2001 and into 2002, preparing a charter for signature at the 2002 heads-of-state meeting in St. Petersburg.

At the June 2002 St. Petersburg summit, several key documents emerged. One key document was the group's annual political declaration, which offered the leaders' views on a range of timely topics. The declaration stated the SCO's opposition to terrorism, but consistent with official Chinese positions, the document urged that counterterrorist activities be conducted in accordance with the UN Charter and other international norms. It also welcomed the U.S.-Russia agreement on reducing strategic nuclear forces, endorsed a call to establish a nuclear-weapons-free zone in Central Asia, and urged political dialogue to resolve the Indo-Pakistan, Israel-Palestinian, and Korean peninsula disputes. The declaration also focused on efforts to step up economic cooperation among SCO members in Central Asia.

Another key document issued at this summit was an agreement announcing the formal establishment of a permanent regional counterterrorism center. This agreement established the legal mechanisms by which the member states can coordinate their national security and law enforcement agencies to combat the "three evils": "international terrorism, national separatism, and religious extremism."[58] The agreement originally called for the center to be established in Bishkek, Kyrgyzstan; however, the center was later built in Tashkent, Uzbekistan, and was formally opened in early 2004.

Most important, the June 2002 SCO summit highlighted the completion of the twenty-six-article SCO charter. Commenting on the signing of the charter, Chinese President Jiang Zemin said that it "laid a firm legal basis for the building of the organization for it explicitly states the aims, principles, structure, and operating rules."[59] Among the "aims and objectives" outlined in the charter are the development of "multi-profile cooperation" for the maintenance of peace and security in the region; "joint opposition to terrorism, separatism, and extremism in all their manifestations"; and fighting "illicit traffic in narcotics and weapons and other types of transnational criminal activity." Further development of political, trade, defense, and other areas of common interest were also encouraged. Making clear that the SCO was not aimed at any other country or international organization, article 1 of the charter emphasized the development of relations with other states and "interaction in the prevention of international conflicts and their peaceful settlement" in the "joint search for solutions of problems that arise in the twenty-first century." In addition, the charter designated the regional antiterror office as a "permanent institution of the SCO" and established a secretariat in Beijing to oversee the coordination of SCO activities.[60] SCO members also engaged in joint military exercises (see box 2-2).[61]

In January 2004 the SCO formally opened the organization's secretariat, based in northeast Beijing. China built the secretariat building and provides it to the SCO free of charge. The first secretary-general of the SCO, who served for a three-year term, 2004–06, was Zhang Deguang, an experienced Chinese diplomat and former ambassador to Russia. The secretariat is staffed

---

Box 2-2. *SCO Joint Military Exercises*

One of the more substantive steps to emerge from Beijing's engagement with its SCO partners was the joint China-Kyrgyzstan counterterror military exercise held during October 2002 and the "command post" exercises among China, Kazakhstan, Kyrgyzstan, Russia, and Tajikistan in August 2003. The October 2002 exercise was relatively small in size and scope, involving about a hundred soldiers from each side, plus observers from the other four SCO states. Operating at high elevations in southern Kyrgyzstan, using light weapons, antitank guns, helicopters, and armored personnel vehicles, the exercise simulated the capture and eradication of terrorists operating within the mountainous region that forms the countries' border. The command post exercises of August 2003 took place in two parts. The first half was held in the Taldy-Qoorghan region of Kazakhstan's Almaty Oblast and involved mostly Kazakh, Kyrgyz, and Russian troops. The second part took place near the town of Inyin, in China's Xinjiang Uighur Autonomous Region, and involved mostly Chinese and Kyrgyz troops.

These exercises highlighted China's intention to strengthen its security-related relations with its Central Asian neighbors and underscored Beijing's expectation that member states of the SCO work jointly to combat "terrorism, separatism, and extremism" along their common borders. The October 2002 exercise marked the first joint military exercise that China is known to have conducted in decades. It signaled a small but significant change in the way China views multilateral military-to-military security cooperation and confidence-building measures. Since those SCO exercises, China has stepped up its joint exercises with other countries as well.

The description of this exercise is drawn from "China Ends War Games with Kyrgyzstan," Associated Press, October 11, 2002; "China, Kyrgyzstan Hold Joint Antiterror Military Exercise," Xinhuanet, October 12, 2002; "Joint War Games Boost Terror Fight," *South China Morning Post*, October 12, 2002.

---

by an additional thirty persons, drawn from the diplomatic corps of SCO member states: China and Russia have the largest number of billets, comprising about half of the secretariat staff. The secretariat coordinates and oversees the implementation of the expanding agenda of SCO activities and offers policy and budget recommendations for SCO work.[62]

The SCO also opened its Tashkent-based Regional Antiterror Structure in January 2004. The first executive director of the Antiterror Structure was an Uzbeki, C. T. Casymov. It is staffed by thirty persons drawn from the six member states, with China and Russia both providing seven persons each. The seven Chinese are experts on counterterrorism from the Ministry of Public Security. China and Russia are also the largest supporters of the Antiterror Structure, with each providing a quarter of the necessary financing for its operation. As the only antiterror center in Central Asia, its goal is to coordinate the member states' counterterrorism activities, monitor terrorist activities in the region, recommend counterterror activities for the member states, and exchange information with other international organizations.[63]

At the Astana summit in 2005, Chinese President Hu Jintao called on member states to "make joint efforts to turn, as quickly as possible, the organization's cooperation potential into practical results in order to properly cope with the challenges brought about by the complicated changes in the international and regional situations."[64] With an emphasis on improving the practical functioning of the organization, the member states agreed to set up an institution made up of permanent representatives in order to further the aims of the Shanghai Convention on the Fight against Terrorism, Separatism, and Extremism and to facilitate the work of the Regional Antiterror Structure. The summit also discussed concrete plans for economic integration with the formation of the SCO Business Council and establishment of the SCO Development Fund. Of particular significance for the region, the member states granted Pakistan, Iran, and India observer status in the SCO.

What garnered most attention, however, was the request for outside forces to set a timetable for withdrawal from Central Asia. While avoiding mention of the United States by name and couching the request in diplomatic language, the declaration issued at the conclusion of the meeting stated:

We support and will support the international coalition carrying out an antiterrorism campaign in Afghanistan. We have taken note of the positive dynamics and the stabilization of the political situation in Afghanistan.

A number of SCO member countries offered their land-based infrastructure for temporary location of military contingents of coalition members as well as their territory and airspace for military transit in the interests of antiterrorist coalition. As the active military phase in the antiterror operation in Afghanistan is nearing completion, the SCO members consider it necessary that relevant members of the antiterrorist coalition determine a deadline for the temporary use of the said infrastructure and for their military contingents' presence in SCO member countries.[65]

The declaration indicates a strengthening of relations and a recognition of common interests among SCO member states, in particular a shift on the part of Kazakhstan and Uzbekistan, which have faced destabilizing unrest from what is largely viewed in the region as U.S.-inspired democratic movements. With this in mind, the declaration states: "Every people . . . have the right to choose its [sic] own way of development," and in "the area of human rights it is necessary to respect . . . the historical traditions and national features of every people, the sovereign equality of all states." Against the "backdrop of a contradictory process of globlization" (and in line with China's new security diplomacy), the declaration calls upon the international community to "form a new concept of security based on mutual trust, mutual benefit, equality, and interaction" and for the establishment of relations upon "true partnership with no pretence to monopoly and domination in international affairs."

In November 2005 Beijing hosted the SCO Defense and Security Forum, a ten-day event attended by twenty-six high-ranking military officers from SCO member nations as well as from Mongolia, Pakistan, Iran, and India. According to China's official news agency Xinhua, the theme of the forum was "China's peaceful development and regional security cooperation."[66] In a speech, the deputy director-general of the Chinese Ministry of National Defense Foreign Affairs Office, Jia Xiaoning, emphasized that "military cooperation among the SCO member states and countries with SCO observer status is not meant to build a military alliance. . . . It will not threaten any other countries and organizations." Jia added that China's "new concept of security" is the "base on which the SCO is founded."[67]

The June 2006 SCO summit, convened in Shanghai and marking the fifth anniversary of the group, also generated some international controversy. Despite protests by the United States and Europe, the Iranian president, Mahmoud Ahmadinejad, was invited to participate as an observer at the summit, even though the former were attempting to bring pressure on Iran to roll back its nuclear ambitions. But the Chinese and other participants gave little notice to these concerns. Achievements announced from the meeting included the conclusion of a joint statement on international information security, the release of a new cooperation program for 2007–09 in combating "terrorism, separatism, and extremism," and a plan to hold an SCO joint counterterrorism exercise in Russia in 2007 involving armed forces from all six member states. The leaders of the SCO also emphasized that countering drug trafficking would be elevated to a "top priority" along with combating the "three evils" of terrorism, separatism, and extremism. Increased intra-SCO commerce and improved rail and road transportation routes and energy development all figured prominently in the summit discussions. The parties agreed to begin work on the conclusion of a "multilateral legal document of long-term good-neighbor relations, friendship and cooperation." China also formally made available US$900 million in the form of preferential buyer's credits for SCO members seeking to purchase Chinese exports.[68]

In another indication of China's influence in shaping the official direction of the SCO, the Joint Declaration of the 2006 summit made a point of emphasizing the "Spirit of Shanghai," including "discarding the Cold War mentality and transcending ideological differences":

> The SCO owes its smooth growth to its consistent adherence to the "Spirit of Shanghai" based on "mutual trust, mutual benefit, equality, consultations, respect for the diversity of cultures, and aspiration towards common development." This spirit is the underlying philosophy and the most important code of conduct of the SCO. It enriches the theory and practice of contemporary international relations and embodies the shared aspiration of the international community for realising democracy in international relations. The "Spirit of Shanghai" is therefore of critical importance to the international community's pursuit of a new and nonconfrontational model of international relations, a model that calls for discarding the Cold War mentality and transcending ideological differences.[69]

Looking ahead, it appears that the SCO will make steady gains in certain areas. To begin with, its geographic and demographic breadth (the six-party group now represents some three-fifths of the Eurasian landmass, about one-quarter of the world's population, and straddles some of the globe's most volatile regions) makes the organization unique and potentially important for regional security. The SCO grasps that this is particularly true with regard to efforts aimed at combating cross-border crime and terrorist activities, where the group's members have the strongest joint interest. In the wake of America's counterterrorism campaign launched in September 2001, the role of the SCO in this particular security arena could enlarge, if managed well. For example, China hosted an ad hoc meeting of the SCO's foreign ministers in January 2002 to specifically address the future of Afghanistan and the war on terrorism. The joint statement from this meeting expressed full support for relevant UN resolutions and activities in the counterterror effort, welcomed "the deliverance of the Afghan people from the Taliban regime, [which is] closely connected with international terrorism," urged close cooperation with the International Security Assistance Force in Afghanistan, and called for the "speedy elaboration of a Comprehensive Convention against International Terrorism and a Convention for the Suppression of Acts of Nuclear Terrorism."[70] At a minimum, the SCO will undoubtedly continue to serve Chinese interests in the counterterrorism area, while also providing Beijing a relatively prominent multilateral channel to express its concerns over international security affairs.

However, it may be more difficult for the group to evolve beyond these important benefits for Beijing. First and foremost, the two principal powers in the group, China and Russia, have a number of differing views and interests, which would limit a much deeper commitment to solidify the Shanghai grouping. If additional members eventually come into the group over time, this would complicate its mission and interests: analysts point to the tensions between Russia and Uzbekistan, as well as between Moscow and the other three former Soviet republics in the group.[71] Differences over geopolitics, proposed oil pipelines from Central Asia through China, turbulence in Afghanistan, U.S. military relations with Central Asian states, and tensions over the treatment of Muslim minorities all have the potential to limit the SCO's progress as a truly influential regional player. Nevertheless, the SCO will continue to strengthen its cooperative activities and will likely remain a platform from which Chinese leaders can advance their new security diplomacy in Asia.

CHINA-RUSSIA RELATIONS AND THE FRIENDSHIP TREATY

China and Russia announced their intention to establish a "strategic partnership of equality, mutual confidence, and mutual coordination" at the summit meeting of Chinese President Jiang Zemin and Russian President Boris Yeltsin in Beijing on April 25, 1996. The joint summit statement notes significant progress in resolving remaining border disputes; supports the establishment of military confidence-building measures along the border; and calls for increased bilateral trade, increased science and technological cooperation, and more "friendly exchanges between their military forces at various levels and [to] further strengthen their cooperation on military technology." Most important, China supported Russian policy to "safeguard national unity" with regard to Chechnya, while the Russian side reiterated its adherence to a one-China policy. On international issues, the new partnership also declared solidarity by noting that "the world is far from being tranquil" and that "hegemonism, power politics, and repeated imposition of pressures on other countries have continued to occur. Bloc politics has taken up new manifestations. World peace and development still face serious challenges." In agreeing to cooperate to enhance disarmament, peacekeeping, and the role of the United Nations in maintaining international security, they also called for "the establishment of a new international economic order." Given that the two sides only a decade before were engaged in diplomatic and military struggles for influence in Indochina and Afghanistan, the 1996 statement marked a high-water mark in the rapprochement between Moscow and Beijing.[72]

Regularized, high-level summitry between the leaders of Russia and China date to the early 1990s. These meetings have also led to regularized exchanges of foreign and defense ministers. Statements from the presidential summits gain the most attention and, over time, have come to increasingly address international issues. The Sino-Russian statements of partnership in the late 1990s and early 2000s, for example, favorably contrast China's new security concept with the U.S. alliance-based approach. The 1997 declaration modified the bilateral association, calling it a "strategic cooperative partnership [*zhanlue xiezuo huoban guanxi*] of equality and mutual trust that is oriented towards the 21st century." Of primary importance in the 1997 statement, however, is reference to the international situation: the first paragraphs of the document state that the two sides will "strive to promote the multipolarization of the world and the establishment of a new international order," that the "establishment of a just and equitable new international political and economic order based on peace and stability has become the pressing need of the times and the inevitable necessity of history," and that both sides support "the establishment of a new and universally applicable security concept, believing that the 'Cold War mentality' must be abandoned and bloc politics opposed."[73]

Following upon the U.S.-led NATO operations against Yugoslavia, U.S. President Clinton's announced intention to proceed with national missile defense, the U.S. Senate rejection of the Comprehensive Test Ban Treaty (CTBT), and the finalization of strengthened U.S.-Japan defense guidelines, the joint Sino-Russian statement in December 1999 was especially critical of Washington and its security policy. The statement began with a call for "all the nations to set up a democratic, balanced, and multipolar world" and went on to censure "a negative momentum" in international security affairs. The United States was rebuked for seeking to modify or dismantle the Anti-Ballistic Missile (ABM) Treaty, for seeking to deploy with its allies and friends (including Taiwan) a missile defense system in the Asia-Pacific region, and for rejecting the CTBT. Without naming them directly, the statement criticizes the United States and NATO for their action against Yugoslavia, particularly as this action circumvented the authority of the United Nations, demonstrated the reinforcement of "military blocs," and attempted to force "the international community to accept a unipolar world pattern and a single model of culture, value concepts, and ideology."[74] This statement followed on the heels of a resolution jointly sponsored by China, Russia, and Belarus that supported the ABM Treaty and that easily passed in the UN General Assembly over U.S. opposition (Russia, China, and Belarus went on to sponsor and gain General Assembly approval for similar resolutions in 2000 and 2001). At the July 2000 summit the following year, the two sides issued a joint statement to uphold the ABM Treaty as well as a more comprehensive statement reaffirming their support for forces that "oppose hegemonism, power politics, and bloc politics."

The July 2000 summit also declared that the two sides would "conduct negotiations on preparations for a Sino-Russian treaty on good-neighbor friendship and cooperation."[75] The results of those negotiations were issued in the form of a twenty-five-article "treaty" the following year, during the Jiang-Putin summit of June 2001.[76] Replete with mutual confidence-building measures, the treaty was achieved at China's insistence and sought to codify the steadily improved Sino-Russian partnership. Beginning with the Five Principles of Peaceful Coexistence, the treaty goes on to disavow the use or threat of the use of force in Sino-Russian relations, to pledge that neither will be the first to use nuclear weapons, and to state that they do not aim nuclear weapons at one another and there are "no territorial demands between them." The treaty also promises that neither party will participate in an alliance or bloc nor allow an organization to be established on their soil that would threaten the sovereignty, territorial integrity, and security of the other. The agreement sets out the many areas of cooperation that the two sides will seek to achieve. The long list of cooperative efforts features, most prominently, "military and military technology cooperation" but also includes disarmament; supporting the United Nations; cooperating in the fields of science and technology, energy, transport, nuclear power, finance, aviation and space, and information technology; and bolstering a range of exchanges related to culture, education, public health, information, tourism, sports, and legal work.

The treaty twice states that its declarations are not aimed at any third party, and the closest the document comes to anything resembling a "mutual defense treaty" is in chapter 9, which reads, "If one party to the treaty believes that there is a threat of aggression menacing peace, wrecking peace, and involving its security interests and is aimed at one of the parties, the two parties will immediately make contact and hold consultations in order to eliminate the threat that has arisen."[77]

Since the release of the friendship treaty, the two sides have continued to carry out regular exchanges between their leaders and working-level officials. Summit meetings between the two countries have reaffirmed their "strategic partnership," put forward plans to strengthen their relationship, particularly in economic and technological fields, and pronounced their solidarity on a range of international security issues. For example, during the Putin-Hu summit in Moscow in May 2003, the two sides agreed to expand practical cooperation in trade, atomic energy and other energy-related areas, finance, space exploration, aviation, and military-technical spheres, as well as in dealing with a range of transnational crime challenges they face on their common border. They also expressed their concern with the "logic of force and the policy of unilateral actions [which] introduce new factors of instability in an already unstable world." They stated their support for a "multipolar, just, and democratic world order" and advocated for the central role of the United Nations in addressing international security challenges, such as the postwar reconstruction of Iraq.[78]

In September 2004 Premier Wen Jiabao traveled to Russia to meet his counterpart, as well as President Vladimir Putin, in the ninth heads-of-government summit between China and the Russian Federation. The two sides issued a far-ranging statement at the conclusion of the summit, which, if fully implemented, would mark a significant deepening of relations between Beijing and Moscow. Among other items, the two premiers announced the establishment of a secure hotline between their offices; a series of agreements for strengthening economic and trade relations; cooperation in science and technology, energy development, and space flight; and a Chinese education aid package for Chechnya. They also agreed on a number of issues on the international security agenda, including support for a "UN-dominated global system to deal with today's challenges and threats" and a ban on "weapon deployment in outer space and the use or threat of use of force against targets in outer space."[79] A month later, during the Putin-Hu summit in October 2004, the two countries announced the final resolution and demarcation on all outstanding territorial disputes along their 4,300-kilometer (about 2,700-mile) border, bringing some forty years of negotiation on this issue to an end, defusing a hot-button issue between the two sides, and—particularly for China—demonstrating the practical value of the new security concept.[80]

In 2005 Hu Jintao became the first Chinese president to visit Russia twice in one year, first in May to attend ceremonies marking the sixtieth anniversary of the end of World War II and then again in July for a state visit. China's state news agency Xinhua quoted President Hu as saying "both sides agreed . . . that the China-Russia strategic partnership has continuously achieved new progress and has reached an unprecedented high level," with an additional agreement regarding the eastern part of the Sino-Russian border.[81] The two sides began a dialogue on state security and opened up a "new channel for high-level strategic dialogue." Hu said that the two countries "support each other on the major issues of Taiwan and Chechnya that are related to their respective key interests." In a joint communiqué issued after the summit, the two sides pledged to strengthen economic ties, with a goal of boosting bilateral trade to between US$60 billion and US$80 billion by 2010. Trade volume reached a record US$21.23 billion in 2004. Of special importance to China, in light of its growing energy needs, cooperation deals on oil, natural gas, and electric power were signed, although few details were made public.[82] In the communiqué, the two countries also "vowed to promote their strategic and cooperative partnership steadily and continuously and to boost military cooperation and exchanges," noting that the "strategic and cooperative partnership between the two countries has entered a new stage of development, with bilateral political mutual trust reaching a new level and cooperation expanding in various fields."[83] The communiqué stressed that the two sides "will take mutual support on the major issues of national sovereignty, security, and territorial integrity as an important character of their strategic partnership."

Presidents Hu and Putin also signed a joint statement calling for "the international order of the twenty-first century," in which the "central task for mankind" is "to safeguard peace, stability, and security for all of mankind and to achieve comprehensive and coordinated development under conditions of equality, [while] safeguarding sovereignty." The statement calls for "mutual respect, mutual benefit, and ensuring the development prospects of future generations." The statement calls for "the right of countries to choose their development paths in light of their own conditions, equally participate in international affairs, and seek development on an equal footing," adding that "differences and disputes must be settled peacefully without the adoption of unilateral action and coercive policy and without resort to the threat of force or the use of force." In line with China's new security diplomacy, the statement says that "the United Nations is the world's most universal, representative, and authoritative international organization, and its role and functions are irreplaceable. The United Nations should play a leading role in international affairs and serve as the core for establishing and executing the basic norms of international law. UN peacekeeping operations should be in compliance with the aims and principles of the United Nations Charter." Moreover, the statement says, "the new type of state-to-state relationship between China and Russia is making a major contribution to building a new international order," and "the practice of Sino-Russian relations attests to the vitality of the principles enunciated in this statement. At the same time, it shows that good-neighbourly, friendly, and cooperative relations can be effectively developed and various problems solved on this basis."[84] Chinese analysts note that the statement was issued in part as a critique of U.S. unilateralism.[85]

However, while China and Russia maintain their strategic partnership, a number of problems and differences remain. Both sides remain wary of one another politically and harbor memories of difficult relations in the past. In Russia the body politic remains divided over the long-term wisdom of a close relationship with China, while discussions in Beijing reveal continued concerns about Russian stability on the one hand, and its trustworthiness as a China-leaning (as opposed to Western-leaning) partner on the other.[86] The most important area of practical cooperation is in the military-technical realm, where China imports significant amounts of weapons, technical assistance, and know-how from Russia's ailing military-industrial complex. Even here, big questions arise as to the sustainability of this aspect of the relationship owing to concerns of dependence in China and strategic implications of a more powerful China in Russia. A revitalization of U.S.-Russia ties would also call into question how committed Russia will be to a strategic partnership with China. Nevertheless, such questions do not appear to affect the long-term motivations for China's approach with Moscow. As a result, barring a significant falling out between Moscow and Beijing and assuming certain U.S. allied activities in the future (such as further expansion of NATO, strengthened U.S.-Japan alliance ties, the continued presence of U.S. and allied troops in Central Asia, the deployment of regional missile defenses in the Western Pacific, and progress in U.S. strategic missile defense plans), China will continue to see the benefits of maintaining a strategic partnership with Russia.

SECURITY ON THE KOREAN PENINSULA

China has an enormous stake in the outcome of the evolving situation on the Korean peninsula. China and North Korea share a lengthy border (at 1,416 kilometers, or about 880 miles, it is North Korea's longest border, as opposed to only 238 kilometers [148 miles] with South Korea and 19 kilometers [12 miles] with Russia). The China–North Korea political-military relationship, while more troubled in recent years, has functioned much like a formal alliance for significant periods over the past fifty-plus years, including transfers of military equipment to North Korea in the late 1950s and early 1960s as well as assistance to Pyongyang's nuclear and ballistic missile programs as late as the 1970s and early 1980s. Neither side has formally withdrawn from their Treaty of Friendship, Cooperation, and Mutual Assistance, signed in July 1961, and the two sides continue to carry out official party-to-party and military-to-military exchanges.[87] Quoting Chinese Defense Minister Cao Gangchuan, North Korean sources report that Beijing and Pyongyang will continue to expand military cooperation.[88] Cao also said that while "maintaining the special and long-standing friendly ties . . . the friendship provided by President Kim Il-song and the leaders of the elder generation of China is unbreakable as it stood all tests of history."[89] Until other Chinese security concerns in the region are fully resolved to its liking—such as the future of the U.S.-Japan and U.S.–South Korea alliances and the role of the United States on the Korean peninsula—Beijing's relationship with Pyongyang, if carefully managed, can be a useful buffer and leverage point to help ensure outcomes favorable to Chinese interests.

To be sure, the relationship comes at a cost, as North Korea depends heavily on China for its economic well-being: China is North Korea's largest trading partner, with two-way trade reaching US$1.386 billion for 2004 and US$1.580 billion in 2005. North Korea's exports to China in 2004 were around US$586 million but dropped to US$499 million in 2005. Since the early 2000s, China–North Korea trade has grown from 28 to 39 percent of North Korea's total trade; by some estimates, about 70 percent of North Korean imports come from China, largely critical, basic commodities such as foodstuffs, fertilizers, and energy supplies.[90] Beijing also has shown the limits of its patience with its often troublesome neighbor and certainly does not wish to see an openly nuclear-armed North Korea on its doorstep. China must also balance its remaining support for North Korea and the maintenance of a stable situation on the peninsula against its interest to preserve a constructive relationship with the United States.

Under these often contradictory circumstances, and consistent with its new security diplomacy, China since the late 1990s has displayed increased support for regional security mechanisms aimed at resolving differences between North Korea and its neighbors over its nuclear weapons program and other security concerns. China's more active involvement in North Korea–related regional security mechanisms is a pronounced shift from previous policy, as throughout much of the early to mid-1990s Beijing preferred to keep a low profile and let others, such as the United States, Japan, and South Korea, engage Pyongyang. With the onset of the first North Korean nuclear crisis in 1993, Beijing played an important, but still behind-the-scenes, role in encouraging North Korea to reach a negotiated solution with the United States. Later, Beijing abstained from participation in the Korean Peninsula Energy Development Organization, which became the key multilateral mechanism through which major powers—including the United States, South Korea, Japan, and the European Union—aimed at bringing North Korea's nuclear weapon ambitions to an end.

With strong encouragement from Washington and Seoul, China participated in the short-lived four-party talks with North Korea, South Korea, and the United States. Six sessions were held between December 1997 and August 1999. These talks were intended to foster dialogue between North and South Korea, with Beijing and Washington working to resolve their differences. These talks became increasingly difficult as North Korea sought the benefits of a more direct bilateral dialogue with Washington. China remained quietly on the sidelines as bilateral negotiations with North Korea gained momentum, highlighted by the historic North-South summit meeting between President Kim Dae-jung of South Korea and President Kim Jong-il of North Korea in June 2000 and by the October 2000 visit to Pyongyang by U.S. Secretary of State Madeleine Albright.

As Beijing more clearly recognized the troubling course of developments on the Korean peninsula and the threats they posed to Chinese interests, it began to more actively seek a regional security dialogue to diffuse tensions. Irritants in the Beijing-Pyongyang relationship included North Korea's reluctance to adopt Chinese-style economic and social reforms; Pyongyang's enduring economic mismanagement; the increasing flow of North Korean refugees into China in 2001 and 2002 (and the embarrassing public efforts of some of them seeking asylum in foreign diplomatic compounds in Beijing and other major Chinese cities); and the North Korean effort in 2002 to open the Sinuiju Special Economic Zone opposite the Chinese border town of

Dandong and have it run by an errant Chinese businessman, Yang Bin. All of these happened without consultation with Beijing. In addition, with the advent of the Bush administration in 2001, it became clear to Beijing that Washington was not prepared to negotiate bilaterally with North Korea and that it might take unilateral military action.

As concern about North Korea's nuclear weapon ambitions mounted during 2002 and 2003, and U.S.–North Korea relations deteriorated further, China became more supportive of a multilateral security dialogue to diffuse the impending crisis. In October 2002 North Korea reportedly acknowledged to U.S. officials that it was carrying out a clandestine uranium enrichment program, admissions that led to the disintegration of the Korean Peninsula Energy Development Organization and the U.S.–North Korea Agreed Framework process. At the end of December, North Korea shut down monitoring equipment and ousted the remaining International Atomic Energy Agency inspectors from the Yongbyon nuclear facility; and in January 2003, citing a "grave situation where the national sovereignty and supreme interests of the state are most seriously threatened" by the United States, the North Korean government declared its immediate withdrawal from the Nuclear Nonproliferation Treaty and from its obligations under article 3 of the treaty to allow inspections of its nuclear facilities.[91] In April 2003 North Korean Deputy Foreign Minister Li Gun told American counterparts that North Korea had nuclear weapons and threatened to prove their existence or possibly export them.[92] Li Gun also declared that North Korea completed the reprocessing of 8,000 spent fuel rods, which had been stored in cans in a cooling pond awaiting removal from North Korea as envisioned by the Agreed Framework. A month later, in May 2003, North Korea announced its withdrawal from the Joint Declaration of the Denuclearization of the Korean Peninsula, a 1992 agreement with South Korea in which the two sides pledged they "shall not test, manufacture, produce, receive, possess, store, deploy, or use nuclear weapons."[93]

In the midst of these troubling developments, China encouraged the United States and North Korea to meet at the negotiating table. China initially sought bilateral discussions between Pyongyang and Washington and was willing to serve as host in talks in Beijing. However, at Washington's insistence, and as China grew increasingly frustrated with its North Korean neighbor, Beijing came to support a multilateral approach. By the end of 2006 Beijing had hosted several sets of multilateral talks aimed at resolving the North Korea nuclear standoff. The first, involving China, North Korea, and the

United States, was held in April 2003. The second set of talks was held in August 2003 and was expanded by an additional three parties: Japan, Russia, and South Korea. Second, third, and fourth rounds of unsuccessful six-party talks were convened in Beijing in February 2004, June 2004, and July 2005. However, in September 2005 China received high praise for its role in facilitating a breakthrough during resumption of the fourth round of talks, in particular the drafting of a joint statement in which North Korea agreed to halt its nuclear weapons programs and allow international inspections in exchange for economic cooperation, aid, and security assurances from the United States. South Korea's chief negotiator Song Min-soon said China was "outstanding" in creating favorable conditions for progress, adding that "China has demonstrated patience and wisdom to push forward the talks, and the [South Korea] delegation appreciates China's efforts," sentiments echoed by U.S. officials in private.[94] Throughout 2006, however, the six-party mechanism stalled in spite of China's efforts to urge parties back to the table. Prospects for reconvening the talks worsened when, in July 2006, Pyonyang test-fired ballistic missiles and, in October 2006, detonated a small nuclear device.[95]

China's efforts to promote a regional security mechanism to address North Korea security issues are complicated by a number of challenges. One of the greatest difficulties concerns China's ability to influence North Korea in a way that encourages Pyongyang's cooperation but does not result in instability on the peninsula or prompt a complete breakdown of relations with North Korea. A good example of this dilemma for China was Beijing's inability to dissuade North Korea from going forward with its multiple missile tests, including a test of the longer-range Taepodong-2 in July 2006, or from testing a nuclear weapon in October 2006. China–North Korean bilateral relations have chilled considerably since the 1980s and the introduction of market reforms in China, especially since China opened diplomatic relations with South Korea in 1992. China's more reform-minded, outward-looking, and growth-oriented leaders viewed its isolated and recalcitrant neighbor with concern at best and alarm at worst. By the mid-1990s China halted officially sanctioned barter trade, no longer accepted payment in nonconvertible North Korean currency, cut off regularized direct subsidies, and required foreign currency for trade payments. In response, North Korea returned some snubs of its own, especially under the leadership of Kim Jong-il. Unlike his son, Kim Il-song spent his formative years in China, spoke Chinese, studied in Chinese Manchuria, participated in pre-1945 Chinese Communist political and guerilla movements, and was indebted to China for intervening in the

Korean War. Kim Jong-il does not have such personal, political, and security ties to China.

In addition, Beijing's interests vis-à-vis North Korea's nuclear weapons program are likewise complicated. To begin, China itself is partially responsible for North Korea's nuclear pursuits, having provided some assistance to North Korea's nuclear development program beginning in the late 1950s. By 1987 China apparently halted such official nuclear-related training and assistance for North Korea, but reports persisted of other forms of cooperation, mostly involving Chinese enterprises exporting various technologies and components to North Korea that could have applications for Pyongyang's nuclear weapons and ballistic missile programs.[96] Moreover, China should be considered at least indirectly responsible for the recently revealed enriched uranium bomb program: this pathway to nuclear weapons is similar to the program Pakistan pursued with Chinese assistance; Pakistan in turn is believed to have assisted Pyongyang in the development and design of a uranium-triggered weapon beginning in the late 1990s.

While China's precise role in North Korea's nuclear and ballistic missile programs is unclear, it is still the case that North Korea may be the fourth nuclear-armed state on China's border, joining Russia, India, and Pakistan. Many Chinese strategists and scientists discount the nuclear threat from North Korea, either expressing skepticism that Pyongyang's program could advance to weaponization and operational deployment, or noting that even if North Korea can successfully deploy nuclear weapons, China would probably not be a target. On the other hand, Chinese strategists and scientists also recognize that North Korean nuclear and ballistic missile development helps drive military modernization programs elsewhere in the region, notably in Japan. More broadly, North Korean nuclear- and ballistic-missile-related provocations strengthen the case for a more robust and ready Japanese defense and military modernization program, including a stronger U.S.-Japan alliance and, in some Japanese circles, a discussion of a more offensive conventional and even nuclear capability, all moves that are not in Beijing's interests. Similarly, provocative North Korean steps with regard to its missile and nuclear programs have already sparked an escalated American military response, most prominently including the development of more advanced missile defenses.

In spite of these many challenges, China is likely to continue its active support for a regional mechanism to resolve the North Korean impasse. Through such efforts, Beijing has managed to keep the parties focused on a negotiated outcome and avoid conflict on the peninsula. The process has also given

Beijing a more prominent role in the region and burnished its claims to be a responsible power. Beijing's support for the talks includes the appointment of a special ambassador for the North Korea issue in its Foreign Ministry and its open promotion of the talks.[97] Well-known Chinese strategists have even gone so far as to call for a permanent Northeast Asian security mechanism, building on the six-party framework now in place.[98]

BILATERAL PARTNERSHIPS

Since 1993 China has worked to establish bilateral partnerships with many of the world's major powers, including Brazil, the European Union, France, India, Japan, Russia, the United Kingdom, and the United States—as well as countries in China's immediate region (see box 2-3). David Finkelstein writes that these arrangements are a way for Beijing to debunk "China threat" theories, demonstrate China's "forward-leaning approach to foreign policy," and substantiate China's aspirations to regional and global leadership.[99] In the 1990s such bilateral arrangements appealed to Chinese strategists, as they promoted China's new security concept on the one hand but also avoided entangling Beijing in more complicated multilateral security mechanisms.[100] In addition, these bilateral partnerships were seen as an important way for China to diplomatically demonstrate an alternative approach to security, especially in contrast to U.S. alliance-based frameworks.[101]

One of the most high profile of these partnerships is the October 1997 U.S.-China declaration to "build toward a constructive, strategic partnership for the twenty-first century." In the United States, such an approach foundered by the end of the 1990s, as the bilateral relationship took a turn for the worse. Indeed, by 2000 presidential candidate George W. Bush stated that the United States and China were not "strategic partners," but rather were "strategic competitors." This kind of rhetoric was later toned down once the Bush team entered office, but the notion of a strategic partnership between China and the United States was quietly dropped from the official lexicon in Washington. In the case of the partnership declared during Jiang Zemin's diplomatically disastrous visit to Japan in November 1998, Tokyo declined to establish a "strategic" partnership with China due to the military connotations. Instead, the two sides opted for "friendly, cooperative" partnership, which, as in the American case, was later set aside.

But beyond these more contentious relationships, China has actively courted a range of key partners, including many friends and allies of the United States. In Southeast Asia, China has been particularly active, establishing a strategic partnership with ASEAN as well as setting up ten separate

Box 2-3. *China's Bilateral Partnerships, 1993–2005*

November 1993
Long-term and strategic partnership with Brazil

March 1996
Strategic cooperative partnership with Russia

November 1996
Constructive partnership of cooperation with India, oriented toward the
twenty-first century

December 1996
All-round cooperative partnership with Pakistan, oriented toward the
twenty-first century
Good-neighbor and friendly partnership with Nepal, oriented toward
the twenty-first century

May 1997
Long-term, comprehensive cooperative partnership with France

October 1997
Partnership with the United States to build toward a constructive, strategic partnership for the twenty-first century

November 1997
Cross-century comprehensive partnership with Canada

December 1997
Cross-century partnership of all-round cooperation with Mexico
ASEAN good-neighbor partnership of mutual trust

April 1998
Long-term, stable, and constructive partnership with the European
Union

(continued)

Box 2-3. *(continued)*

October 1998
Enhanced comprehensive partnership with the United Kingdom

November 1998
Cooperative partnership with the Republic of Korea
Friendly, cooperative partnership with Japan

April 1999
Strategic cooperative relationship with Egypt, oriented toward the twenty-first century

November 1999
Strategic partnership of equality, mutual benefit, and common development with South Africa

October 2003
ASEAN strategic partnership for peace and prosperity
All-round strategic partnership with the European Union

January 2004
Comprehensive strategic partnership with France

April 2005
Strategic partnership for cooperation with India
Strategic partnership for cooperation with Pakistan
All-round cooperative partnership with Bangladesh
All-round cooperative partnership with Sri Lanka
Strategic partnership with Indonesia

November 2005
Comprehensive strategic partnership with Spain

bilateral agreements with all ASEAN member states over the course of 2003–05, ranging from basic statements to more complex arrangements. In April 2005 China and Indonesia went further, formally declaring a strategic partnership. According to the Indonesian defense minister, this relationship could include Chinese assistance in reviving his country's short-range ballistic missile program. In reference to a U.S. ban on exporting fighter jets to Indonesia, the Indonesian defense minister said that Chinese assistance in missile development would be "cheaper to offer some kind of deterrence rather than relying on fighter planes."[102]

One of the most important "bilateral partnerships" China has forged is with the European Union. In 2004 the European Union became China's largest trade partner, surpassing Japan and the United States; China was the EU's second-largest trade partner in 2004.[103] This political and security relationship has also considerably deepened in recent years. China and the European Union initiated annual summit meetings in the mid-1990s, which have become a cornerstone of more deeply institutionalized channels across a range of issues, including security-related questions.

For example, at the Ninth EU-China Summit in 2006 the two sides agreed to launch negotiations to realize a formal partnership and cooperation agreement to govern their relations and to update their 1985 trade and economic agreement, which has long since been passed over by events. At the same meeting the two sides declared that a China-EU science and technology year would start in October 2006 to build greater cooperation in these fields, and that China would begin a five-year program to provide a hundred scholarships a year to European students to study China and the Chinese language. At their summit in 2004 the two sides signed a Joint Declaration on Nonproliferation and Arms Control and agreed to recognize one another as strategic partners in this area of international security affairs. The 2004 summit also reached an agreement to allow for greater cooperation in the peaceful use of nuclear energy between China and the European Atomic Energy Community (Euratom), including a provision allowing access to research facilities for experts on both sides. The joint statement also touched on a number of pressing security issues, including the joint concern with "promoting peace, security and sustainable development throughout the world, with the United Nations at its core" and "the leading role of the United Nations with respect to counterterrorism."[104]

The 2003 summit reached an agreement to govern Chinese involvement in the Galileo satellite navigation program.[105] The Galileo program is a joint

EU–European Space Agency effort to stand up a global navigation satellite system similar to the U.S. Global Positioning System (GPS) and the Russian GLONASS system; only it will be more accurate than either. According to the agreement, in return for China's commitment to the project of approximately US$230 million (roughly one-fifth of the overall cost of building the twenty-seven-satellite network), it could expect to take part in joint research, development, market development, and training, manufacturing, and technical work. China is the first non-EU country to take full part in this program. In December 2004 the EU also expressed its intention to lift the arms embargo it placed on China following the Tiananmen Square crisis of 1989; it was poised to do so in 2005 but decided against it, in part owing to heavy pressure from Washington to keep the embargo in place. In November 2005 President Hu Jintao paid "fruitful" state visits to the United Kingdom, Germany, and Spain, signing the first-ever joint communiqué and establishing a "comprehensive strategic partnership" with Madrid.[106] In addition to these China-EU ties, China and individual European countries have established various security relationships as well, which are discussed in more detail below.

Beijing has also worked to improve traditionally difficult relationships. For example, Premier Wen Jiabao's visit to India in April 2005 was lauded as "the beginning of a strategic partnership between the two Asian giants" and marked the culmination of a gradual reconciliation between the two traditional foes.[107] The groundwork for Wen's visit was laid in January 2005, when Vice Foreign Minister Wu Dawei led a Chinese delegation to India for the first-ever "strategic dialogue" aimed at broadening "the scope of the blooming bilateral relationship, allowing both sides to exchange notes on global and regional security issues."[108] The highest-level military exchanges between the two sides in almost a decade have also been taking place. Former Indian Defense Minster George Fernandes's visit to China in 2004 broke new ground in the development of military-to-military relations between Beijing and Delhi and paved the way for the joint search-and-rescue exercise between the Chinese and Indian navies in November of that year.[109] Chinese Defense Minister Cao Gangchuan visited India in March 2004 and, during talks with Indian army chief N. C. Vij in Beijing in December 2004, the two sides vowed to expand the relationship between their militaries.[110]

During Wen Jiabao's April 2005 visit, a deal comprising twelve separate agreements was signed, including measures aimed at enhancing trade and economic ties and at increasing two-way trade from the current US$14 billion to

US$30 billion by 2010.[111] Most significant, an agreement was also signed establishing a roadmap for resolving the long-standing border dispute between the two nations, a disagreement that sparked their 1962 war and that has remained a source of bilateral tension. While the dispute remains far from settled, for the first time China formally recognized Indian sovereignty over the Himalayan territory Sikkim, and India reaffirmed its position that Tibet is part of China. The two sides also agreed on a three-phase process for addressing remaining territorial claims along their 3,400-kilometer (2,000-mile) border.[112] A Protocol on Implementation of Confidence Building Measures in the Military Field along the Line of Actual Control (LAC) was signed by Chinese Vice Foreign Minister Wu Dawei and Indian Foreign Secretary Shyam Saran, under which the two countries agreed to avoid holding military exercises involving more than 15,000 troops close to the LAC and to observe self-restraint if the two sides come face to face along the border or if airspace is violated. They also decided to increase the number of border meetings held each year in order to include Spanggur Gap in the Western Sector, Nathula Pass in Sikkim, and Bum La in the Eastern Sector as part of their border discussions.[113]

Although significant sources of tension remain between the two nations, notably mistrust over China's relations with Pakistan and over India's relations with the United States, according to the joint statement issued by the two sides, Premier Wen Jiabao's "highly successful state visit to the Republic of India marked a new level of India-China relationship and opened a new chapter in the friendly relations and cooperation between the two countries."[114] Following the visit, it was reported that China had agreed to support India's candidature for a permanent UN Security Council seat.[115] Later in the year, China was accorded observer status to the South Asia Association for Regional Cooperation (SAARC), a regional security mechanism traditionally led by India.[116] The developments in China-India relations are particularly striking given the historical complexities, lingering differences, and potential rivalry between these two important Asian powers.

OTHER SECURITY CONSULTATIONS

In addition to embracing various forms of regional multilateral security mechanisms and confidence-building measures with neighbors in Southeast Asia, Central Asia, Northeast Asia, South Asia, and beyond, China has also significantly stepped up its military-to-military and defense consultations with other countries since the late 1990s. According to the 2004 Chinese defense white paper, China now has military-to-military relations with more than 150 countries and more than 100 defense attaché offices abroad. More than 1,600 Chinese military delegations have traveled to more than 90 countries over the past twenty years, while China has received some 2,500 military groups. Over the period 2003–04, some 1,200 military personnel representing 91 countries studied in Chinese military colleges and universities, and officers from more than 40 countries took part in the fifth and sixth international symposiums convened by the Chinese National Defense University.[117] In 2003–04 the Chinese military sent senior delegations to more than 60 countries and received 130 senior-level delegations from more than 70 countries. In 2003 the Chinese military dispatched some 120 technical delegations, involving some 6,000 person-trips, to conduct short-term cooperative exchanges with foreign militaries in such areas as equipment, logistics, and visits to defense colleges, and sent almost 200 military officers abroad for training.

In recent years, counterterrorism has been a focus of many of these activities. The joint counterterrorism exercises noted above under the auspices of the SCO, held in October 2002 and August 2003, were among the first joint peacetime exercises held by China with the aim of enhancing confidence among its neighbors. In August 2004 China continued this pattern by holding joint counterterrorism exercises, named Friendship 2004, with Pakistan. The exercise took place in the mountainous Taxkorgan district of far western Xinjiang Uighur Autonomous Region, an area bordering on Tajikistan, Afghanistan, and Pakistan, and involved about 200 soldiers.[118] Later in August 2004, Chinese and Indian frontier troops held joint mountaineering training in Tibet, again, the first time the two armies have carried out such maneuvers with each other.[119] In November 2004, at the First ASEAN Regional Forum Security Policy Conference, held in Beijing, participating officials from the Asia-Pacific region observed an antihijack drill conducted by Chinese Special Forces. In September 2006 several hundred Chinese and Tajik troops carried out a joint military exercise code-named "Co-ordination 2006," which practiced responding to a terrorist hostage-taking scenario in a mountainous area near Kulyab, Tajikistan.[120]

In August 2004 China and Russia carried out their largest joint military exercises ever and the largest joint exercise China has ever conducted with any foreign military; it involved some 10,000 troops from the countries' airborne, naval, army, and air forces. The exercise, known as Peace Mission 2005 (*he ping shi ming 2005*), took place in the Vladivostok region, on the Shandong peninsula, and in the seas off these areas. Peace Mission 2005 involved a number of ships from the Russian Pacific fleet, including amphibious landing ships and a destroyer, Russian Su-27 fighter jets, and long-range transport aircraft. Activities included headquarters and command exercises in Vladivostok, movement of ships from Vladivostok to the Shandong peninsula, the parachuting of Russian airborne forces onto the Shandong peninsula, a joint amphibious landing of marines on the peninsula, and over-water air force exercises. The purpose of the exercise, according to Chinese and Russian spokesmen, was to deepen political and military-to-military relations between China and Russia, to practice joint efforts against "terrorism, extremism, and separatism," and to improve their ability to coordinate and respond to a crisis.

China has also increased joint maritime exercises with foreign militaries since the late 1990s. Russia and China held their first joint naval exercise since the 1950s in October 1999, when two Russian ships sailed to Shanghai to mark the fiftieth anniversary of relations between the two countries. In December 2001 Chinese soldiers took part in a search-and-rescue exercise between the U.S. Coast Guard and Air National Guard and the Hong Kong Government Flying Service. Invited by the Hong Kong government to participate in this annual exercise between the United States and Hong Kong, the Chinese contributed a helicopter and frigate to the four-day drill. China and Pakistan jointly held a naval search-and-rescue exercise, dubbed Dolphin 0310, off the coast of Shanghai in October 2003. The following month, three ships from the Indian navy held joint exercises with Chinese counterparts off the coast of Shanghai. In November 2005 a Chinese destroyer and naval supply ship conducted joint maritime search-and-rescue exercises with ships of the Pakistani navy in the Arabian Sea. The Chinese vessels also made port calls to, and carried out search-and-rescue exercises with, India and Thailand. This was the first time that the Chinese and Thai navies held joint exercises.[121]

In 2004 China held first-ever maritime exercises with three Western countries. The first was the joint naval drills held between China and France in March, followed by exercises between China and the United Kingdom in June, both of them off the coast of Qingdao. Military attachés from fifteen countries were invited to observe the Sino-British exercises. The exercises with France and the United Kingdom involved tactical maneuvers for the ships and shipboard helicopters, communication exercises, and search-and-rescue drills. In October 2004 China and Australia held their first-ever joint maritime exercises. They involved two Chinese and one Australian warship, as well as shipborne helicopters, and carried out fleet formation changes, shipboard helicopter landings, and communication and search-and-rescue exercises.[122] In September 2006, in a shift for U.S.-China military-to-military ties, China and the United States held a basic joint search-and-rescue exercise off the coast of San Diego; the Chinese naval vessels then held similar exercises with the Canadian navy off the coast of Vancouver.

China also broke new ground in the early 2000s by allowing foreign military personnel to observe Chinese military exercises. In August 2003, 27 military personnel from fifteen countries, including Canada, France, Germany, Israel, Pakistan, Russia, Singapore, South Africa, Tanzania, Thailand, Turkey, the United Kingdom, and the United States, were allowed to observe Chinese military exercises, named Northern Sword 0308U, in Inner Mongolia; the exercise involved tanks, armored vehicles, artillery, combat helicopters, and some 5,000 soldiers.[123] In early September 2004 China allowed a small group of military representatives from France, Germany, Mexico, and the United Kingdom to observe an amphibious landing exercise in Shanwei, Guangdong Province. Later in September 2004 some sixty foreign observers, hailing from sixteen Asian countries, including Bangladesh, Brunei, Cambodia, India, Indonesia, Kazakhstan, Laos, Malaysia, Pakistan, the Philippines, Russia, Tajikistan, Thailand, Uzbekistan, and Vietnam, were invited to a live-ammunition exercise code-named Iron Fist 2004. The exercise involved a mechanized infantry division, Chinese military aircraft, and 10,000 soldiers and took place at the Queshan Training Base in Henan Province. The Chinese press noted that this was the largest military exercise ever opened to foreign observers.[124] Members and observers of the Shanghai Cooperation Organization were invited to observe joint China-Russia military exercises in August 2005. In September 2005 some forty foreign military officers, the largest contingent invited to date, observed North Sword 2005 at the Chinese tactical training base in Inner Mongolia.[125]

China has also been increasingly open to participating as an observer of foreign military exercises in East Asia. China was an observer at the Rim of the Pacific exercises in 1998 and at the first Pacific Reach 2000, a joint search-and-rescue exercise for submarine forces hosted by Singapore in October 2000 (and including Japan, South Korea, and the United States). In January 2002 Chinese military officers observed a naval mine clearance exercise in Singapore, and in April 2002 they observed a Japan-sponsored submarine search-and-rescue exercise. In May 2002 China also participated for the first time as an observer of the U.S.-led Cobra Gold military exercises in Thailand, sending six military personnel. China sent observers again in 2003, 2004, and 2005.[126] China sent observers to military exercises in Russia and in Japan in 2003 and 2004.[127]

Since the mid-to-late 1990s, China has established regularized, high-level strategic dialogues and security consultations with virtually all of its principal partners, bringing together senior-level military and defense officials to convey strategic concerns and exchange views on security affairs of mutual interest. Such regular strategic dialogues have been established among China's closest neighbors as well as with major powers further afield (see box 2-4).

Since the mid-1990s, China has stepped up its naval port visits abroad but

---

Box 2-4. *Countries That Have Held Strategic Dialogues with China*

Australia: Seventh Sino-Australian Strategic Defense Consultation held in October 2003; Eighth Sino-Australian Strategic Defense Consultation held in October 2004.

France: Six rounds of strategic consultation held since 1997; counterterrorism dialogue established in 2003.

Germany: First and second rounds of strategic consultation talks held in May 2002 and July 2004.

India: First-ever strategic dialogue at vice foreign minister level held in January 2005.

Japan: Fourth security consultation by PRC Ministry of National Defense and Japan Defense Agency held in January 2004; fifth security consultation held in October 2004; a Sino-Japan strategic dialogue was initiated in May 2005.

Kazakhstan: Second round of strategic consultation held in September 2004.

Kyrgyzstan: Second round of strategic consultation held in September 2004.

Mongolia: First round of defense and security consultation held in April 2004.

Pakistan: Second round of defense and security consultation held in July 2003.

Russia: Strategic consultations by General Staff Headquarters held seventh and eighth rounds in 2003 and 2004; talks on strategic security at the vice foreign minister level held in 2004; "new channels for high-level strategic dialogue" opened in July 2005.

South Africa: Joint defense commission agreed on by Ministries of National Defense in April 2003.

(continued)

Box 2.4 *(continued)*

Thailand: Second defense security consultation held by Ministries of National Defense in September 2003; third consultation held in October 2004.

United Kingdom: First, second, and third rounds of strategic dialogue held in May 2002, October 2003, and March 2004; counterterrorism dialogue established in 2003; Sino-British strategic security dialogue mechanism set up.

United States: Seventh round of defense consultative talks held in January 2005; three rounds of talks on strategic security, multilateral arms control, and nonproliferation held at the vice foreign minister level in 2003–04; third and fourth rounds of counterterrorism consultations held in 2003 and 2004; third and fourth rounds of the Military Maritime Consultative Agreement held in 2003 and 2004; senior officials dialogue established between Department of State and Ministry of Foreign Affairs in August 2005 and December 2005.

---

has kept most of those visits focused on the Asia-Pacific region. These visits included calls in Pakistan, Sri Lanka, and Bangladesh (the Chinese navy's first foreign port visit, in 1985), Hawaii (1989), Pakistan (1993), India (1993), Russia (1994, 1995, and 1996), North Korea (1996), Hawaii, San Diego, Mexico, Chile, Peru, the Philippines, Malaysia, and Singapore (1997), Australia, New Zealand, and the Philippines (1998), Hawaii and Seattle (2000), South Korea, India, Pakistan, Australia, New Zealand, and Vietnam (2001), Guam (2003), Pakistan, India, and Thailand (2005), and San Diego, Vancouver, and Manila (2006). The Chinese navy has also made two sets of port visits to Europe. The first was in September 2001, when Chinese ships paid calls in France, Germany, Italy, and the United Kingdom. The second set of visits was in 2002 during the Chinese navy's first circumnavigation of the globe, a trip that included port calls in Singapore, Egypt, Turkey, Ukraine, Greece, Portugal, Brazil, Ecuador, and Peru.

Conclusions

China's embrace of regional security mechanisms and confidence-building measures engages a broadening array of countries and encompasses an increasing range of unprecedented activities for China. Yet across this diversity of engagement and activity, Beijing exhibits a consistency of motivations and goals. Forming a central pillar of China's new security diplomacy, Beijing's greater appreciation for and activities in support of regional security mechanisms help defuse tensions abroad so Beijing can focus on domestic issues, reassure partners about a "peacefully rising" China, and softly balance against the United States at a regional and global level to shape the security environment more on Chinese terms.

China's proactive approach to regional security mechanisms helps Beijing ensure that it keep its attention first and foremost on its many internal challenges. This appears particularly true with regard to Beijing's efforts to secure the necessary inputs from abroad to sustain economic growth and maintain stability at home. Establishing better relations with its neighbors and beyond not only quells potential tensions with those partners, but significantly improves China's economic prospects at home by ensuring greater access to foreign capital, technology, and know-how as well as to strategic commodities, raw materials, and energy supplies that fuel China's continued growth.

For example, on the Korean peninsula, China seeks first and foremost a peaceful resolution to the nuclear stand-off in order to avoid potential destabilizing effects at home. Beijing places a high priority on a stable North Korea and the avoidance of measures that, in Beijing's view, would escalate tensions, prompt even more reckless behavior from Pyongyang, and destabilize North Korea and the strategic buffer it provides for Chinese interests. In the near term, China faces a growing presence of illegal North Korean economic migrants, who seek better opportunities across the border in ethnic Korean parts of northeastern China. There may be as many as 300,000 North Koreans illegally resident in China, and that number, and the challenges it poses to Chinese local and central authorities, would rise exponentially were North Korea to devolve into deeper economic, social, and political chaos. Beijing has thus far resisted efforts by the UN High Commissioner of Refugees and other UN agencies to fully assess the refugee situation along the China–North Korea border or to openly prepare for the possibility of larger inflows of persons. Military conflict in North Korea could be a major factor for instability and open all kinds of uncertainties for Beijing: refugee flows, political instability, and the possibility of U.S. and allied troops positioned at or near China's border. A rapid alteration of the political situation in Pyongyang and on the peninsula could also stimulate nationalistic responses among China's ethnic Korean population along the Jilin Province–North Korea border.

In Central Asia, Chinese leaders recognized in the mid-1990s the wisdom of defusing tensions with its Central Asian neighbors and the domestic benefits that would accrue as a result. For starters, Chinese strategists understood that the wave of newly independent states in post-Soviet Central Asia would catalyze separatist- and independence-minded activists in China's far west, especially in Xinjiang. From the mid-to-late 1990s, China encouraged the Shanghai Five and later the SCO to cooperate in suppressing terrorist activities, especially among fundamentalist and separatist Muslim populations in the region, which in Beijing's view were gaining increasing influence in Xinjiang. China sought more positive diplomatic, security, and economic relations with Central Asian states that shared concerns about the establishment of a greater "East Turkestan" in their region. As its demand for domestic energy and other raw material surged in the early 2000s, China expanded the range of SCO activity to encompass joint economic development and access to energy and other resources from its Central Asian neighbors. As early as 2000 Chinese leaders openly called for expanded cooperation to help benefit Central Asian and western China development. The benefits envisioned were increased investment and trade as well as joint "construction of highways, railways, airports, major natural gas pipelines, power grids, telecommunications facilities, and other infrastructure in China's western region."[128] Chinese analysts see the vastly improved Sino-Russian relationship during the 1990s and 2000s as a means to stabilize historically troublesome relations with Moscow and to steady a potentially unstable neighbor at China's backdoor.

China's embrace of regional security mechanisms such as in Southeast Asia also helps promote an image of a "peacefully developing" China and provides some tangible evidence of China's new security diplomacy. Similarly, Beijing's support for a regional security mechanism to resolve concerns with North Korea helps it foster more productive relations with its neighbors, reassuring them about China's overarching concern with "peaceful rise" and "peaceful development," while acting like a "responsible great power." This point is particularly important for Beijing with regard to its meticulously crafted two-Korea policy. Since the normalization of Beijing-Seoul relations in 1992, China has carefully, and largely successfully, balanced its relations between both North and South, with the long-term aim of reasserting China's traditional sway over the Korean peninsula. Many near-term benefits have accrued as well, most notably the robust economic and trade relationship between China and South Korea: China replaced the United States as South Korea's largest trade partner in 2004. China also became South Korea's largest export market.[129] South Korea also remains one of

China's major trading partners and one of its largest export markets.[130] Politically, too, Beijing and Seoul have come closer together on a range of regional issues, particularly in seeking a diplomatic solution to problems with North Korea (downplaying tensions in favor of a more gradual and accommodating policy of political, economic, and diplomatic engagement).

Beijing's more nuanced security diplomacy also helps it shape a security environment more on Chinese terms while also avoiding difficult relations with the United States. For example, the six-party process should, in Beijing's view, help achieve peaceful, gradual change in North Korea, to include the introduction of Chinese-style economic and political reforms, the stabilization of North-South relations, and the eventual reconciliation of a stable, nonnuclear Korea within China's sphere of influence. In Central Asia, China promoted the Shanghai Five process and the SCO in part to promote an alternative approach to regional security. For example, in Jiang Zemin's July 5, 2000, speech at the Dushanbe summit he maintained that the Shanghai process is "a way to overstep the Cold War mentality and explore a new type of state-to-state relations, a new outlook on security, and a new mode of regional cooperation."[131] As a participant in the Sino-Russian border agreement talks, the Shanghai Five process "is aimed at promoting the mutual security of the countries concerned and at building confidence and is not directed at a third nation, so that it differs from 'bloc confrontation' or the 'strategy of containment.'"[132] Another Chinese strategist drew the distinction even more clearly when he wrote, "People find such a mechanism [the Shanghai Five process] attractive not only because of its tangible achievements . . . but also its successful efforts to develop a set of new concepts for international security, diametrically contrasting to the out-of-date Cold War thinking and hegemonism."[133] In this sense, the Shanghai Five and SCO process is partly an effort by Beijing to carve out an alternative approach to regional security as compared to the U.S.-led alliance system in the Asia-Pacific region. China's increasing appreciation of closer relations with major European countries and with the EU overall are likewise intended, in part, as a potential counterweight to U.S. influence in world affairs.

In Southeast Asia, China's participation in the ASEAN Regional Forum (ARF) is a way for Beijing to manage and if need be limit region-based security discussions and arrangements that might impinge on China's freedom of movement and strategic interests, while providing a forum where Beijing can reassure its neighbors about its benign intentions. A part of the motivation for joining the ARF was to ensure that the United States and its partners did not use the organization in ways Beijing would find contrary to its interests, such as getting involved more directly in the Taiwan issue. On the other hand, with China's initiation of new security arrangements outside of the ARF structure—an organization China had little hand in creating and in which it must operate side by side with other major powers such as the United States and Japan—Beijing can achieve great political and diplomatic advantage with its Southeast Asian neighbors on terms it has a direct hand in creating. It is also the case that Beijing sees its participation in the ARF and in developing China-ASEAN security mechanisms as a way to promote an alternative approach to Asia-Pacific security as compared to U.S.-led alliances and security arrangements in the region. The ARF model, while still in its nascent stages, at least provides for China (and others) an alternative vision for how regional security can be enhanced beyond an overreliance on the U.S. network of regional alliances and military relationships. Chinese officials have in the past utilized the ARF platform to generate opposition to U.S.-led efforts to strengthen its bilateral alliances in the region, particularly that with Japan and particularly on such issues as missile defenses.[134] A leading Chinese academic specialist on U.S.-China relations made a similar point when he wrote that by advocating multilateralism China may "undermine the political and moral basis of the U.S. efforts to strengthen its bilateral security ties in the region."[135] On this point, Rosemary Foot argues:

> What this campaign against bilateral alliances suggests is that the intrinsic worth of the multilateral security approach has yet to be accepted at the highest levels in Beijing and is primarily valued for its possible contribution to the weakening of U.S. ties with its Asian allies. The hope is that such weakening will lead to a reduction in the American presence in the region and move regional states in the direction of the "new security concept" that China advocates.[136]

Even in the case of Sino-Russian ties, where the two countries still harbor mutual suspicions in spite of remarkable gains in bilateral security relations, the regularized high-level contacts between Beijing and Moscow offer a platform from which Beijing (and Moscow) can consistently deliver their worldview and concerns about the United States:

—that multipolarity is the clear trend of the times;

—that cooperative, strategic Sino-Russian relations represent a new conceptual approach to international security;

—that the partnership is at the leading edge of world opinion demanding a new international political and economic order;

—and that certain activities by "other powers" (that is, the United States) run against the grain of international opinion.

In the late 1990s, in particular, Chinese analysts argued that associating closely with Russia can provide a diplomatic counterweight to the United States and U.S.-led alliances. Writing for a defense intelligence journal of international affairs, Xie Wenqing said in 1999 that the U.S. expansion of alliances with NATO and Japan, and their implicit containment strategies aimed at Russia and China, impelled closer relations between Moscow and Beijing.[137] Another senior international affairs specialist, Li Zhongcheng, pointed out that when NATO began its "eastward expansion" plans in 1994–95 and the United States and Japan "redefined the U.S.–Japan security treaty," it was precisely then that China and Russia took steps to establish their strategic cooperative partnership.[138] In particular, the Kosovo crisis of 1998–99, with American-led NATO military action in an area of traditional Russian influence, was seen in China as another reason to bolster the Sino-Russian partnership in the face of U.S.-allied hegemony.

The United States and other countries need to more clearly recognize the opportunities and challenges presented by these developments. In carrying out its new security diplomacy, China is seeking to establish a greater leadership role in the Asia-Pacific region. While many countries in the region and beyond harbor continuing concerns about Beijing's long-term intentions, China's approach to regional security mechanisms has largely succeeded in allaying near-term fears in the region and in building closer relationships with key partners, including U.S. allies, while also committing China to a deeper stake in regional stability. This does not mean that China has abandoned its views on the importance of realpolitik in great power relations. To the contrary, as a careful study of "engaging China" advises, "institutions merely obstruct non-cooperative behavior, but do not change the interests motivating this behavior."[139] These developments have significant implications for U.S. interests in the Asia-Pacific region and beyond and call for more careful scrutiny and judicious policy responses by Washington and other capitals.

3 | Nonproliferation and Arms Control

> The Chinese government resolutely opposes the attempts of some coun-
> tries to use arms control and disarmament to weaken other countries and
> reinforce their own military superiority for the purpose of seeking regional
> or global hegemony.
>
> —*China's National Defense in 2000,*
> Information Office of the State Council, October 2000

> Nonproliferation is an important link in maintaining international and
> regional peace and security in the new century.
>
> —*China's Nonproliferation Policy and Measures,*
> Information Office of the State Council, December 2003

> The proliferation behavior of Chinese companies remains of great concern.
>
> —*Unclassified Report to Congress . . . ,* Central Intelligence Agency, January 2004

Nonproliferation and arms control have been at the heart of contentious differences between China and the international community, and
especially the United States, since the mid-1980s. More recently, nonproliferation and arms control issues became even more contentious given concerns
over possible terrorist access to weapons of mass destruction, especially in
light of China's proliferation-related ties to such countries as Iran, North
Korea, and Libya.

For much of its history since its founding in 1949, and especially between
the 1950s and 1980s, China expressed ambivalence, skepticism, and active
defiance of mainstream international nonproliferation and arms control
norms. Since 1955 China has actively pursued nuclear weapons, long-range
ballistic missiles, and nuclear submarines and became the world's fifth
nuclear power with the detonation of an atomic bomb in October 1964. During the 1950s, 1960s, and 1970s China is believed to have supported nuclear
weapons and ballistic missile programs in such countries as North Korea and
Pakistan. Beijing scoffed at the nonproliferation and arms control efforts of

the 1960s and 1970s—such as the Threshold Test Ban Treaty (1974), the Nuclear Nonproliferation Treaty (1967), the Anti-Ballistic Missile (ABM) Treaty (1972), and U.S.-Soviet SALT I (1969–72)—as "shams" designed to keep weak countries weak and strengthen the superpower nuclear weapons duopoly. Beginning in the 1980s China became a more active proliferator of advanced and sensitive weapons and technologies, including ballistic missile exports to such recipients as Iran, Pakistan, Saudi Arabia, and Syria, and chemical weapons–related exports to Iran.[1]

However, since the mid-to-late 1990s China's approach toward nonproliferation and arms control has substantially changed. China's positions and practice on nonproliferation and arms control form a key part of the country's new security diplomacy and include a higher profile and even a leadership position on certain arms control and nonproliferation initiatives; dramatic reductions in its exports of weapons and other sensitive technologies; and the implementation of international, bilateral, and unilateral commitments to monitor and stem the flow of destabilizing weapons and technologies.

This more constructive approach to nonproliferation and arms control can be traced to the three overarching goals of the country's new security diplomacy: to defuse tensions in its external security environment to better focus on domestic challenges, to reassure neighbors about China's rise, and to cautiously balance the United States in a way that meets Chinese security interests more effectively. Many concerns remain regarding China's record and commitment to nonproliferation and arms control, but the change in Chinese policy and practice has been dramatic nevertheless. China's new approach to nonproliferation and arms control marks some of the most striking aspects of China's proactive security diplomacy over the past decade and deserves far greater attention and analysis—for the opportunities and the challenges it presents for global and regional stability and security.[2]

Past Positions

China emerged on the international scene in the late 1970s as a relative conceptual newcomer—and a skeptical one at that—to the arms control and nonproliferation framework that had been established over the course of the cold war. Throughout most of the cold war, from the early 1950s through the early 1980s, Beijing was generally unfamiliar with and suspicious of international arms control and nonproliferation efforts, judging them as schemes of the two superpowers to strengthen their relative dominance. Even as Chinese policy in the late cold war and early post–cold war period came to favor certain arms control and nonproliferation efforts, Beijing often argued that the global framework on these questions was largely established without China's involvement, either as part of negotiations between the United States and the Soviet Union or as part of larger multilateral efforts to which China was not invited—or in which China chose not to participate. For example, the Beijing government was initially reluctant to join United Nations disarmament efforts of the late 1970s, such as the Conference on Disarmament, but eventually joined that body in 1980. China joined the International Atomic Energy Agency (IAEA) in January 1984 and acceded to the Biological and Toxin Weapons Convention in November of that year. However, these and similar steps were relatively cost free, as they imposed little restraint on China's own vertical or horizontal proliferation activities.

China also differed in the past with mainstream nonproliferation and arms control over the proper targets of those efforts. Generally, Beijing tended to eschew supply-side approaches: the denial and control of sensitive technology and weapons flows through the establishment of multinational technology control and inspection regimes, through national export control systems, through sanctions policies, through armed interdiction and intervention, and through diplomatic pressures and incentives. Instead, Beijing favored a demand-side approach, which addressed the security threats that drove developing world states to seek advanced weapons in the first place. Indeed, Chinese officials argued that certain elements of a supply-side approach—especially the threats or use of military force—may actually promote rather than limit proliferation. For example, in condemning the specific case of the U.S.-led NATO intervention against Yugoslavia, the Chinese ambassador to the Conference on Disarmament claimed it had larger implications for arms control and nonproliferation: "Under such circumstances, countries outside military alliances will be deprived of basic security, so how can we anticipate any progress in the field of arms control and disarmament? If the many small and weak countries are pushed to the wall, how can they be convinced to support international nonproliferation regimes?"[3]

This view also reflects China's traditional approach to nonproliferation and arms control, which saw such efforts as merely hypocritical attempts by strong countries to keep weak countries weak. This viewpoint has its roots in China's long-held self-perception as an aggrieved party and weak player in the international arena. In the late 1990s, two Chinese military analysts argued that, following the cold war, the United States "used the international strategic structural shift away from the bipolar structure to establish a global arms control and disarmament system with the United States as the center and through cooperation has pulled other states into an international strategic order with the United States at the head. This then became an important tool to establish an American-led international order." They continued, "This so-called cooperation is actually cooperation with the United States as the center, and the so-called arms control is actually arms control with the prerequisite of maintaining U.S. military superiority." They concluded that U.S. nonproliferation and arms control policy in the post–cold war era shifted from "maintaining a strategic balance of power to pursuing strategic superiority."[4] In the Conference on Disarmament, China's ambassador put it this way:

> [While] some countries try every means to limit and reduce the armament of other states under the cover of arms control and disarmament, at the same time they never cease to arm themselves with more advanced military technology and equipment. They interfere with other nations' internal affairs and sovereignty with violent and ruthless military means. On one hand, they exaggerate the so-called "missile threats" from developing countries as a pretext for developing its missile defense system; on the other hand, they are launching their most advanced missiles onto the soil of developing countries.[5]

Chinese analysts also argued that the United States, as the world's largest exporter of weapons by far, could not legitimately promote the benefits of arms control and nonproliferation while at the same time supplying advanced weaponry to allies and other partners around the world. This was, and remains, a particular concern to China with regard to U.S. advanced weapons exports to Taiwan. For China, the U.S. Senate rejection of the Comprehensive Test Ban Treaty as well as Washington's plans to move ahead with strategic defenses, its abandonment of the Anti-Ballistic Missile (ABM) Treaty, and a further militarization of space are also examples of U.S. efforts to talk arms control and nonproliferation while at the same time rejecting restraints on its own military modernization. Chinese strategists also saw hypocrisy in Washington's perceived unwillingness to take forceful measures against such states as Israel and, more recently, India, to roll back their nuclear weapons programs (in favor of friendlier strategic ties with those nations), while at the same time taking active countermeasures in response to proliferation activities by such states as Iran, North Korea, and Pakistan (with which China has closer ties).

In past years, China also did not see certain weapons as all that threatening to its own security, even including nuclear weapons and ballistic missiles, since the would-be proliferant states were typically not seeking such weapons to counter threats from China. In some cases, China's exports of sensitive weapons and technologies were—as was the case for other major powers—part of a broader national security effort to maintain active and beneficial strategic ties with certain states. China's role—particularly in the 1970s and 1980s, as a supplier of sensitive weapons and technologies to such countries as North Korea, Pakistan, Iran, and Iraq—was in part intended to undermine superpower influence while enhancing China's strategic, political, and economic interests.[6]

China's effort to achieve security through military-technical relations can be seen most clearly in China's approach to Pakistan and, to a lesser extent, Iran. The long-standing Sino-Pakistani relationship comes close to a formal alliance relationship for Beijing, dating back more than forty years to China's efforts to counterbalance Indian influence on the South Asian subcontinent. Part of this effort has been the maintenance of Pakistan's military capability through conventional exports of aircraft, armor, artillery, and naval vessels; through the provision of technical assistance in the development of Pakistan's indigenous weapons production facilities; and through critical support for Pakistan's nuclear weapons and ballistic missile programs. Chinese suppliers continue to provide this kind of support to Pakistan today, though at a far lower level than in the past. Similarly, though not as strongly, Beijing has also maintained a close political, economic, and security relationship with the Islamic Republic of Iran, dating back to the early 1980s. Chinese leaders and strategists continue to see value in a strong relationship with Pakistan and Iran, and this may in part explain the difficulty in limiting China's proliferation activities of concern with such partners.

China's commitment to nonproliferation and arms control in the past was also contingent on whether the obligation it made was international, bilateral, or domestic in nature. Chinese commitments clearly distinguished between those reached on an international, multilateral level, those reached at a bilateral level with the United States, and those steps that China undertook at home. China's strongest commitments, in principle and in practice, were to international, multilateral agreements. More questionable were China's commitments (for reasons of principle, politics, and practice) to agreements made on a bilateral basis, such as with the United States, or commitments made in the form of Chinese domestic laws and regulations, such as export controls. This contingent approach to nonproliferation and arms control commitments can still be seen today, though not as obviously as in the past.

The positions described above are amply illustrated by three key cases of past Chinese nonproliferation and arms control policies: Iran, Pakistan, and Chinese views regarding missile defenses.

CHINESE PROLIFERATION TO IRAN

China's military-technical relationship with Iran dates back at least to 1981–82, when, motivated by a mix of strategic, political, and economic aims, China began providing an array of conventional weapons to the newly established Islamic Republic. Over most of the 1980s, China provided several hundred main battle tanks, armored personnel vehicles, heavy artillery pieces, dozens of F-6 and F-7 fighter jets, thousands of antitank missiles, and hundreds of air-to-air and surface-to-air missiles. These and other arms transfers were provided to help Iran in its war effort against Iraq (to which China was also selling vast amounts of conventional weaponry).

The most controversial Chinese arms transfers to Iran involved more advanced systems such as antiship cruise missiles as well as possible Chinese assistance for the development of Iranian weapons of mass destruction and their delivery vehicles, such as ballistic missiles. The United States opposed China's antiship cruise missile sales to Iran because they posed a threat not only to vital commercial oil shipments in the Persian Gulf and Strait of Hormuz—such as during the Iran-Iraq War, when Iran fired Chinese "Silkworm" antiship cruise missiles at oil tankers and platforms—but also to vessels of the U.S. navy patrolling in international waters near Iran. Iran's possession of such weapons was also disconcerting to many of its neighbors in the Persian Gulf region. In spite of these concerns, however, China's cruise missile trade and technology cooperation with Iran continued throughout the Iran-Iraq War and intensified over the 1990s.

China was also believed to have assisted Iran in other important areas, including ballistic missiles and missile production technology. For example, some observers determined that missile-related cooperation was included in the January 1990 Sino-Iranian ten-year memorandum of understanding on military technical assistance and in a US$4.5 billion arms trade deal between Beijing and Tehran in 1996.[7] A 1995 CIA report leaked to the press reveals that in 1994–95 China transferred dozens, and possibly hundreds, of missile guidance systems and computerized machine tools destined for Iran's indigenous missile development programs.[8] Another CIA report, leaked to the *Washington Times* in August 1996, stated that the China Precision Machinery Import and Export Corporation, the trading arm of the China Aerospace Corporation, sold Iran missile technology and components, specifically gyroscopes, accelerometers, and test equipment.[9] China also allegedly provided Iran with a range of nuclear-related assistance from the late 1980s to the late 1990s, including cooperation in uranium mining, uranium enrichment and conversion technologies, research reactors, production facility blueprints, and technical training and assistance.[10]

The United States has also tried to monitor and limit China's chemical exports to Iran, with an eye to curbing China's assistance to Iran's alleged chemical weapons program. The best known instance—and for Beijing, the most notorious—was the early Clinton administration effort in July and August 1993 to monitor and force ashore a Chinese ship bound for Iran, which U.S. intelligence agencies claimed contained chemical precursors. The so-called *Yinhe* incident—named after the ship in question—resulted in embarrassment for the United States, as no weapons-related chemicals were identified after the ship was pressured to land in Saudi Arabia and submit to inspection. This incident continues to negatively color Chinese views of American nonproliferation practices.

From the late 1980s through the early 2000s, Washington maintained its pressure on China and sought to curtail or prevent Chinese exports in a number of sensitive areas, including cruise missiles, ballistic missiles, nuclear technologies, and chemical weapon–related precursors and technologies. In May and July 2002 the U.S. government levied sanctions against Chinese firms pursuant to the Iran-Iraq Arms Non-Proliferation Act of 1992 and the Iran Nonproliferation Act of 2000, in part over concerns of missile-related transfers from China to Iran. At present, the United States continues to sanction Chinese individuals and companies for their trade in missile and chemical weapons–related exports with Iran. (U.S. nonproliferation sanctions against China from 1987 to June 2006 can be found in the appendix to this book).

CHINESE PROLIFERATION TO PAKISTAN

China's military-technical relationship with Pakistan is far more extensive than that with Iran, dating back to the mid-1960s and China's efforts to bolster Pakistan to counterbalance India in South Asia.[11] The Sino-Pakistan relationship is as close to an alliance as it comes for Beijing, though no treaty formalizes the relationship as such. With regard to arms transfers, no other Chinese client has received more weapons from Beijing than Pakistan. Even during years when Pakistan maintained friendly and strategic relations with the West, China remained its most dominant weapons supplier.[12] Over nearly four decades China has helped maintain Pakistan's military capability through conventional exports of aircraft, armor and artillery, and naval vessels; through the provision of expertise, technical assistance, and development of indigenous weapons production facilities; and through critical support for Pakistan's nuclear weapons and ballistic missile programs.

The greatest concerns about Sino-Pakistan military-technical cooperation have revolved around China's active support for Pakistan's nuclear weapons and ballistic missile programs. China has long been suspected of assisting Pakistan's nuclear weapons development program, particularly in the 1970s and 1980s; according to American intelligence sources, China "provided extensive support in the past to Islamabad's nuclear weapons . . . programs."[13] Such assistance may have included acquisition of highly enriched uranium, assistance in highly enriched uranium production, and confirmation of Pakistani nuclear weapons designs. For example, China reportedly assisted Pakistan in the construction of a fifty-to-seventy-megawatt plutonium production reactor at Khushab, including the provision of a specialized furnace and advanced diagnostic equipment. In addition, China reportedly also assisted Pakistan in the construction of its reprocessing facility at Chasma, which in combination with the Khushab facility would provide Pakistan with weapons-grade plutonium. It is widely known that China has provided extensive assistance to ostensibly civilian nuclear power programs, and the two countries signed a peaceful nuclear cooperation agreement in September 1986 to govern joint design, construction, and operation of uranium enrichment facilities and nuclear reactors. Blueprints for nuclear weapons designs and other papers turned over to the United States by Libya in November 2003 "yielded dramatic evidence of China's long-suspected role in transferring nuclear know-how to Pakistan in the early 1980s. . . . The Chinese designs were later resold to Libya by a Pakistani-led trading network" headed by the "father" of Pakistan's nuclear program, A. Q. Khan.[14] While some of Pakistan's nuclear facilities are under international safeguards, many are not, and outside analysts express concern that China's civil nuclear cooperation with Pakistan could provide a cover for more assistance on Pakistan's nuclear weapons program.

Another area of significant proliferation concern in Sino-Pakistan relations involved extensive ballistic-missile-related cooperation. Beginning in the mid-1980s, China held discussions with a number of countries—including Syria, Libya, Iran, and Pakistan—to sell its new, made-for-export, M-series ballistic missiles. Pakistan was apparently most interested in the shorter range M-11 variant, a land-mobile, solid-fueled missile with a range of about 300 kilometers (about 190 miles). With a potential payload capacity of approximately 500 kilograms, perhaps 800 kilograms, the missile is believed capable of carrying a basic single-warhead nuclear device. By 1991 China had transferred a training missile and launcher and by the end of 1992 had shipped a complement of thirty-four M-11 missiles. Moreover, in addition to the shipment of complete missile systems, from the mid-1990s onward, China engaged in extensive cooperation in support of Pakistan's indigenous missile development program. China's missile-related cooperation with Pakistan remains a concern and has resulted in numerous sanctions by the United States against China. In its September 2001 report covering global proliferation activities for the last half of 2000, the CIA stated:

> Chinese entities continued to provide significant assistance to Pakistan's ballistic missile program during the reporting period. With Chinese assistance, Pakistan is moving toward serial production of solid-propellant SRBMs [short-range ballistic missiles], such as the Shaheen-I and Haider-I. Pakistan flight-tested the Shaheen-I in 1999 and plans to flight-test the Haider-I in 2001. Successful development of the two-stage Shaheen-II MRBM [medium-range ballistic missile] will require continued Chinese assistance or assistance from other potential sources.[15]

The CIA's January 2002 report on proliferation further confirmed such findings, stating that "Chinese entities provided Pakistan with missile-related technical assistance" in early 2001 and repeating its concern with China's solid fuel assistance for Pakistan's Haider-I and Shaheen-I and -II ballistic missile programs. In 2004 the CIA stated that "Chinese entities continued to work with Pakistan . . . on ballistic missile-related projects" and "Chinese entity assistance has helped Pakistan move toward domestic serial production of solid-propellant SRBMs and has supported Pakistan's development of solid-propellant MRBMs."[16] As a result of these and other weapons and technology transfers, the United States frequently issued sanctions against the Chinese government as well as against Chinese companies and individuals (see appendix).

CHINA AND MISSILE DEFENSES

Chinese views toward missile defenses provide another good illustration of the country's past approach to nonproliferation and arms control issues. China stood out as an early and increasingly vocal opponent to the development and deployment of missile defenses. Beijing voiced its opposition to the Reagan-era Star Wars programs and was particularly strident in opposing the U.S. missile defense programs of the 1990s, especially toward the end of the decade as American missile defense plans made important advances. The Rumsfeld Commission Report, issued in July 1998, which warned of an increasing missile threat against the United States, was later bolstered by the surprise North Korean launch in August 1998 of a three-stage ballistic missile capable of reaching U.S. territory.[17] In early 1999 Secretary of Defense William Cohen announced that the United States would augment funding for missile defense research and testing, which was followed by the president's July 1999 decision to sign legislation requiring the United States to deploy a national missile defense as soon as technologically feasible. These developments, followed by the refusal of the U.S. Senate in October to ratify the Comprehensive Test Ban Treaty, crystallized Beijing's opposition to U.S. missile defense plans in the late 1990s.

During this period, Chinese objections to U.S. missile defense plans coalesced around four principal points. First, Chinese strategists voiced concern for what missile defense might mean for China's comprehensive security situation. The Chinese claimed that a U.S. move toward missile defense would upset the basic strategic balance that has kept the world free from major, widespread warfare among the major powers for the better part of a century. Relatedly, many Chinese analysts believed missile defenses would embolden the United States to act with less restraint and pursue unilateralist, hegemonist policies potentially detrimental to Chinese interests. One of China's principal arms control officials, Sha Zukang, was blunt in this view: the U.S. goal in missile defense is "to break the existing global strategic balance" and to "seek absolute security for itself and to realize its ambition for world domination."[18]

Second, China was opposed to missile defense on arms control and nonproliferation grounds. Chinese strategists argued that the 1972 Anti-Ballistic Missile (ABM) Treaty was the cornerstone of global nuclear stability and that U.S. efforts to modify or possibly abandon the treaty were provocative and destabilizing. In the view of many Chinese analysts, a post-ABM world would simply drive countries, including China, to develop and deploy more, not fewer, sophisticated missiles in order to counter missile defenses and ensure their legitimate national security interests.

Third, in a worst-case scenario for Beijing, whatever few missiles remained of its relatively small ICBM force after suffering a massive first strike attack would have an even more difficult time in retaliating against a system designed to intercept two dozen or more such targets. In the Chinese view, this would lay the country open to nuclear blackmail from the United States.

The fourth principal concern for China about missile defense is related to the third and has to do with Taiwan. Chinese strategists were concerned that, in a Taiwan contingency, a viable missile defense in the United States would embolden Washington to act with impunity (including issuing nuclear threats as during the Taiwan Crisis of 1958) because of China's inability to retaliate. These several concerns led China in the late 1990s and early 2000s to sponsor UN resolutions (along with Russia and Belarus) opposing missile defenses and supporting the ABM Treaty, to insist on the initiation of negotiations in the United Nations Commission on Disarmament on a treaty to prevent the militarization of space, and to step up its confrontational official rhetoric opposed to American missile defense plans.

The Changing Approach

In contrast to these past approaches, since the mid-to-late 1990s and into the 2000s, China's nonproliferation and arms control policies have begun to evolve in a more constructive and positive direction. In response to its changing security environment and building on the notions of a new security concept and China's peaceful rise, Beijing expanded its profile and participation in multilateral arms control and nonproliferation agreements, reached a series of important bilateral commitments with the United States to stem sensitive Chinese exports, established a formal set of national arms export control regulations and mechanisms, and reduced its arms and sensitive technology exports. Exports of concern from China to countries such as Iran and Pakistan significantly dropped off. In addition, since 2001 Beijing has curtailed its rhetoric opposing U.S. missile defenses and has sought a strategic nuclear dialogue with Washington.

This changing approach emerges from the three key factors motivating China's new security diplomacy more broadly. First, by taking a more constructive approach toward nonproliferation and arms control, Beijing looks to reduce tensions and instabilities in its external security environment, particularly around its periphery, so it can focus on pressing economic, political, and social reform challenges at home. Second, a more proactive and responsible approach toward nonproliferation and arms control helps Beijing project its influence in a more reassuring way toward its neighbors and key international partners. Third, China's changing approach to nonproliferation and arms control aims to quietly balance against American influence while defusing overt confrontation with Washington. China's more constructive approach has had a generally positive impact on global nonproliferation and arms control trends and presents both opportunities and challenges for strengthening the global nonproliferation and arms control agenda.

GLOBAL, REGIONAL, AND BILATERAL MEASURES

Beginning in the mid-1990s, China became especially active in joining and adhering to a range of global and regional nonproliferation and arms control mechanisms (see box 3-1).

Box 3-1. *China's Participation in Major Nonproliferation and Arms Control Regimes and Agreements*

1980

United Nations Conference on Disarmament (CD): China joined this group in 1980.

Partial Test Ban Treaty: China participates in the treaty de facto, since China's last atmospheric test was in October 1980

1984

International Atomic Energy Agency (IAEA): China joined in 1984. In May 1996 it pledged to the United States not to provide nuclear assistance to countries without safeguarded nuclear facilities.

Biological and Toxin Weapons Convention (BTWC): China acceded to the convention in 1984 and has been an active participant in negotiations to strengthen verification protocols from 1995 to the present.

1989

Convention on Physical Protection of Nuclear Material: China acceded to this convention in 1989.

1991

Permanent 5 Talks on Arms Control in the Middle East (ACME): China joined these talks in 1991, taking part in discussions among the permanent five members of the UN Security Council. It withdrew from the talks following the U.S. decision to sell advanced fighter aircraft to Taiwan in fall 1992.

1992

Nuclear Nonproliferation Treaty (NPT): China acceded to the treaty in 1992. In 1995 Beijing supported the indefinite extension of the treaty.

Missile Technology Control Regime (MTCR): In February 1992, in a letter to the United States, China agreed to abide by the original 1987 MTCR guidelines; in November 2000 it agreed not to assist any country in any way with ballistic missiles capable of delivering nuclear weapons and to strengthen its missile export controls; and in August 2002 it issued regulations and a control list closely consistent with MTCR. China was seeking membership as of late 2006.

(continued)

Box 3-1. *(continued)*

United Nations Register on Conventional Arms (UNROCA): China participated from 1992 through 1996. It suspended participation in 1997 in protest against U.S. inclusion of arms transfers to Taiwan. China did not vote on the resolution establishing UNROCA in 1991, but it voluntarily submitted basic reports to UNROCA during 1992–96.

Threshold Test Ban Treaty (TTBT): China participates in the treaty de facto, its last 660-kiloton test having been in May 1992.

1993

Chemical Weapons Convention (CWC): China acceded to the convention in 1993 and ratified it in April 1997.

1994

Fissile Material Cutoff Treaty (FMCT): China in 1994 agreed with the United States to seek "earliest possible achievement" of an FMCT; in 1997 it agreed with the United States to seek "early start of formal negotiations" for an FMCT; and in 2004 it stated that it "supports an early conclusion of the treaty through negotiations." No formal negotiations have begun.

1996

Comprehensive Test Ban Treaty (CTBT): China signed the treaty in 1996 but has not ratified it. China is a de facto participant in the regime, as it has not carried out a nuclear weapons test since July 1996.

In addition, Beijing also worked with the United States to encourage North Korea's commitment to a nuclear-weapons-free Korean peninsula, including hosting the six-party talks on Korean peninsula denuclearization and stability (see chapter 2). Beijing also strongly condemned the North Korean nuclear test of October 2006. China joined other major powers to oppose the nuclear tests by India and Pakistan in 1998 and was a principal drafter of the UN Security Council Resolution 1172 setting out a framework for the denuclearization of Indo-Pakistani rivalry. In recognizing the link between terrorism and the spread and potential use of weapons of mass

1997

Australia Group: China declined an invitation to join the group in 1997, although it "conducts dialogue" with the group.

Nuclear Suppliers Group (NSG): In September 1997 China issued nuclear export control regulations, the control list for which matches the NSG control list. China joined the group in 2004.

Zangger Committee: China joined the committee in 1997, following U.S.-China negotiations related to China-Iran nuclear cooperation.

Organization for the Prevention of Chemical Weapons (OPCW): China joined the organization in April 1997, as a founding member, upon entry into force of the Chemical Weapons Convention (CWC).

1998

Wassenaar Arrangement: China is not a member of the Wassenaar Arrangement, but in November 1998 it issued new export controls covering 182 dual-use technologies also controlled in the Wassenaar dual-use list. China has established a dialogue mechanism with the organization and seeks to become a member.

Source: Revised and updated from information compiled by the East Asia Nonproliferation Program, Center for Nonproliferation Studies, Monterey Institute of International Studies (www.nti.org/db/china/regimes.htm).

destruction, China joined the U.S.-sponsored Container Security Initiative (CSI) in July 2003 and has called for multilateral arms control discussions to address the threat of terrorism and weapons of mass destruction.[19] In joining the CSI, Beijing agreed to the posting and observation role of U.S. agents in Chinese ports, a step impinging on Chinese sovereignty that would have been almost impossible to contemplate just a few years ago. Although it has yet to formally join the initiative, China has also expressed an interest in learning more about the Proliferation Security Initiative, a more intrusive set of counterterrorism policies led by the United States.

Interestingly, China took on some of these commitments even though it was under no international obligation to do so. For example, Beijing's bilateral pledge with Washington in 1997 to cut off all new nuclear-related cooperation with Iran arguably contravened China's commitments under article 4 of the NPT, which calls for the fullest possible assistance, under verifiable safeguards, for the development of peaceful nuclear energy programs.[20] Similarly, Beijing's 1997 agreement to stop selling antiship cruise missiles to Iran is strictly a bilateral pledge to the United States, since no international arrangement prohibits the sale of such weapons (common examples of such exports worldwide include the U.S. Harpoon, the French Exocet, and the Russian Sunburn antiship cruise missiles).

DOMESTIC MEASURES

As part of its increasing global, regional, and bilateral commitments, Beijing from the mid-to-late 1990s began to take a number of important domestic steps to govern and limit the export of sensitive military-related products, chemicals, dual-use biological agents, missile-related items, and their related technologies. In some cases China took steps domestically to come within de facto adherence to certain nonuniversal regimes while not formally participating in them. For example, Beijing formally applied for admission to the MTCR in 2004 but has not been invited to join. Nevertheless, China has introduced export control laws roughly parallel to the strictures on missile-related exports within the MTCR. Similarly, in introducing new national nuclear export control guidelines in 1997, China included the same export control list as that employed by the Nuclear Suppliers Group (NSG). In another example of this approach, China claimed in June 1998 that its chemical export control list had added ten additional substances not controlled under the Chemical Weapons Convention protocols; these ten also appear among twenty such non-CWC chemicals monitored within the Australia Group, a group of mostly Western countries that seek to tighten and harmonize export controls on dual-use chemicals. China's expansion of its chemical control list was seen as a step toward coming into de facto adherence with the more demanding export controls of the Australia Group. Subsequently, China's October 2002 revisions to its chemical export controls brought it in line with the standards of the Australia Group, though China remained outside that organization.

Other important domestic measures taken by Beijing include statements of principle. These principles date back to the late 1980s and were prominently reissued in China's first white paper on arms control and disarmament in November 1995, in its first white paper on national defense in July

1998, and again in its November 2003 white paper on nonproliferation—documents that in themselves unilaterally signaled a more open and constructive approach to nonproliferation and arms control matters in Beijing.[21] In the July 1998 defense white paper, the Chinese government states that "China respects the right of every country to independent or collective self-defense and to acquisition of weapons for this purpose in accordance with the principles contained in the Charter of the United Nations." But the white paper adds, China is also "concerned about the adverse effects on world security and regional stability arising from excessive accumulations of weaponry." In balancing these principles, the Chinese white paper lays out three basic principles for the transfer of conventional weapons and technology: "The exports of weapons must help the recipient nation enhance its capability for legitimate self-defense; it must not impair peace, security, and stability of the relevant region and the world as a whole; and it must not be used to interfere in the recipient state's internal affairs."[22] These principles are open to broad interpretation and implementation, but they publicly lay out a highly authoritative set of standards by which Chinese arms control and nonproliferation commitments can be judged.

Beginning in the mid-to-late 1990s, the Chinese government also issued a number of regulations meant to govern China's exports of militarily relevant products and technologies.[23] Before this time, much of China's foreign trade, sensitive or otherwise, was regulated by centrally issued, often vague "decrees." For example, the Foreign Trade Law of May 12, 1994, and the Temporary Rules on the Management of Export Goods, dated January 1, 1993, recognized the need to restrict trade in certain items through the use of export licenses and permits on the basis of national security and international treaty obligations, but comprehensive control lists were not provided. However, by the mid-to-late 1990s, follow-on regulations, addressing specific types of export, went into greater detail as to licensing procedures, penalties, and control lists. China's recent efforts to strengthen its export control system, undertaken in late 2002, include catchall provisions to regulate exports of chemical-, biological-, and missile-related exports.

In the run up to China's ratification of the Chemical Weapons Convention in 1997, Beijing moved to set up regulations controlling chemical-related exports. China's 1995 regulations on controlled chemicals contained a list based on the CWC list of sensitive materials subject to export control scrutiny. The regulations categorized the controlled chemicals into four parts: those that can be used as chemical weapons; those that can serve as precursors in chemical weapons production; those that can serve as the primary raw materials in chemical weapons production; and discrete organic chemicals excluding explosives and hydrocarbons. Subsequent regulatory guidelines issued by the Chinese government in March and August 1997, in June 1998, and again in October 2002 further strengthened China's chemical export controls, by restricting the number of trading companies permitted to export dual-use chemicals and by requiring special permission and end-user certificates for controlled exports to countries that are not signatories to the CWC.

In October 2002, for the first time, China publicly issued regulations and a control list to govern exports of "dual-use biological agents and related equipment and technologies." The twenty-five-article set of regulations, effective December 1, 2002, stipulates a licensing procedure for exporters of dual-use biological agents, requirements for end-user certificates and declarations, the bureaucratic process by which export licenses for such items would be granted, and the fines and penalties for violators of the regulations. The accompanying control list is understood to parallel similar control lists within the international community, such as that employed by the Australia Group.

In September 1997, in the run-up to the first Clinton-Jiang presidential summit, China issued its first public export control regulations to govern the export of nuclear materials and technologies that could contribute to the development of nuclear weapons in the recipient country. A licensing and approval system is outlined in the regulations, and they prohibit assistance to unsafeguarded nuclear facilities abroad (China had made this pledge to the United States in May 1996; these regulations codified the bilateral pledge into law). In June 1998, China expanded its export controls over nuclear-related items by issuing regulations to cover nuclear dual-use items as well. (These new regulations also handed licensing authority over to the Ministry of Foreign Trade and Economic Cooperation; under the September 1997 regulations, licensing authority rested with the China Atomic Energy Agency, which, owing to its association with China's nuclear industry at the time, would have a potential conflict of interest in overseeing nuclear-related exports.)

China issued regulations on the export of conventional weapons in October 1997; the regulations became effective in January 1998 and were revised in October 2002. These regulations set out for the first time the detailed procedures by which conventional weapons could be exported, the government agencies responsible for overseeing these procedures, and the penalties for violating them. Only certain companies are approved to engage in conventional weapons transfers, strengthening the government's ability to oversee such exports. As is the case with regard to the Australia Group for chemical weapons and the Nuclear Suppliers Group for nuclear-related exports, China does not belong to any international grouping of like-minded countries seeking to limit conventional arms sales, such as the Wassenaar Arrangement. However, in November 1998 China issued a list of dual-use technologies that would be subject to tighter controls.[24]

China also issued export control regulations for missiles and missile-related technologies. After reaching an agreement with the United States in November 2000 to issue such regulations, the Chinese side eventually published a twenty-four-article set of missile export control regulations and a related control list in August 2002 (see more detailed discussion below on the U.S.-China discussions before the issuance of the regulations).[25] With some exceptions, the regulations and technologies in these documents hew closely to procedures and items found within the approach of the MTCR, both in terms of the Chinese "presumption of denial" approach and in terms of the specific items and technologies to be controlled.[26] The regulations outline the proper procedures to register as an exporter of missile-related technologies and to obtain export licenses for controlled items and technologies, require end-user certificates for recipients of controlled items, and set out penalties for violations. In issuing the regulations and the control list, the Chinese government made its most authoritative, public, and high-profile statement to date expressing concern for and opposition to missile proliferation. Article 3 of the regulations declares: "The State shall exercise strict control on the export of missiles and missile-related items and technologies so as to prevent the proliferation of missiles and other delivering systems listed in the control list that can be used to deliver weapons of mass destruction."[27] Nevertheless, a close analysis of the regulations reveals that while they cover nearly all the systems and technology exports that led to U.S. sanctions in the past, the regulations leave open the possibility of some exports of concern, which could create disputes in the future.[28]

DIMINISHING WEAPONS EXPORTS

The sheer volume of Chinese arms exports declined significantly over the course of the 1990s and into the 2000s. On the conventional weapons front, for example, China's share of the world market dropped precipitously from approximately 4.0 percent over the five-year-period 1992–96 to below 2.0 percent for the five-year-period 1995–99, dipping to as low as 1.0 percent for 2000. In 2001 China's share of conventional arms exports worldwide bumped up again, to 3.6 percent, for an average global share of only about 1.5 percent for the five-year-period 1997–2001; China ranked as the ninth largest conventional arms exporter for the period 1996–2001.[29] In 2002 and 2003 China again dipped to a smaller share of conventional arms exports to 1.06 percent and

1.17 percent, respectively.[30] China ranked as the eighth largest conventional arms exporter for the 2000–04 period, with a 1.7 percent global share. In addition, China's list of conventional weapons recipients likewise declined, as has the geographic scope of its arms exports. These trends can be attributed to market forces both inside and outside of China that have undercut China's weapons exports. Chinese nonproliferation commitments in the mid-to-late 1990s, consistent with its new security diplomacy, also dramatically dampened the supply of Chinese conventional weaponry.[31]

Some of the most important steps in this direction involved the reduction of weapons and sensitive technology exports to countries of concern, such as Iran and Pakistan, though proliferation-related cooperation continues between Chinese entities and partners in these countries. Chinese nuclear-related cooperation with Iran dates to the mid-1980s, before Beijing's February 1992 accession to the NPT. After Beijing joined the NPT, both China and Iran insisted that their nuclear cooperation was entirely consistent with the provisions of article 4 of the NPT, which allows for peaceful nuclear cooperation and that, in any event, Iranian nuclear facilities were under IAEA safeguards. Nevertheless, the United States has strongly pressured China to end its nuclear-related cooperation with Iran, an effort that led to the cancellation of a 20-megawatt research reactor deal in 1992 and the scrapping of a deal to transfer two Chinese Qinshan 300-megawatt civil nuclear power plants to Iran in September 1995.[32]

In negotiations before the U.S.-China presidential summit in October 1997, China made a number of important commitments regarding its nuclear cooperation with Iran. On the day of the formal meeting between the two presidents, China provided confidentially to the United States "authoritative, written communications," stating that it would provide no new nuclear assistance to Iran. Under this agreement, China would complete two existing projects that were not of proliferation concern to the United States: the construction of a zero-power research reactor that uses natural uranium and heavy water; and a zirconium-cladding production factory. Following completion of these projects, which was expected by late 1997 or early 1998, China was not to provide any new, follow-on assistance. In addition, the two sides agreed specifically that Beijing would not provide power reactors and UF6 conversion facilities, which were under discussion with Iran at that time.[33] National Security Adviser Sandy Berger stated after the summit: "We have received assurances from the Chinese that they will not engage in any new nuclear cooperation with Iran and that the existing cooperation—there are two projects in particular—will end. That is the assurance we have received."[34] Beyond assistance to Iran, Beijing also agreed to publicly issue nuclear export control regulations that were comprehensive and nationwide, that included dual-use items, and that were catchall; the regulations were issued in September 1997. In addition, in association with the summit, China joined the Zangger Committee in October 1997. Also in the run-up to the 1997 U.S.-China summit, China agreed to halt the future sales of antiship missiles to Iran.[35]

Since the mid-to-late 1990s, China has also reduced its weapons and sensitive technology exports to Pakistan. Following revelations in early 1996 that Chinese exporters supplied Pakistan's Kahuta nuclear research laboratory, an unsafeguarded facility, with some 5,000 ring magnets (important components for building the high-speed centrifuges necessary to enrich uranium for nuclear weapons use) and subsequent intense negotiations with Washington, Beijing publicly pledged in May 1996 it would no longer provide nuclear assistance to unsafeguarded nuclear facilities, such as those in Pakistan. Subsequent U.S. officials' statements have largely confirmed the belief that China is abiding by this pledge. Moreover, China's September 1997 public regulations on nuclear-related export controls state that exports to unsafeguarded nuclear facilities are prohibited. China appears to have tightened nuclear and other sensitive technology exports to Pakistan as Beijing came to more fully grasp the gravity of the situation unfolding in South Asia in the late 1990s. With its nuclear tests of May 1998, Pakistan openly realized its long-standing effort to become a nuclear weapons state. China reacted by joining the other permanent five members of the UN Security Council in condemning the Pakistan tests (and the previous tests by India). In addition, during the U.S.-China presidential summit of June 1998, the two sides produced a joint statement on South Asia that said they would "prevent the export of equipment, materials, or technology that could in any way assist programs in India and Pakistan for nuclear weapons."[36]

Similarly positive steps were also taken by Beijing in the late 1990s and early 2000s to stem the flow of missile-related technology to Pakistan, though cooperation in this area between the two countries probably continues. After many years of intense wrangling between the United States and China, dating back to the early 1990s, China steadily cut back on missile and missile technology exports to Pakistan and strengthened its missile nonproliferation policies in general, over several phases. First, in verbal assurances to Washington in November 1991, followed by private, written assurances in February 1992, Beijing pledged that it would abide by the basic guidelines and parameters of the MTCR. In a second phase (under pressure from the discovery by

U.S. intelligence of some thirty-four M-11 missiles shipped from China to Pakistan, additional sanctions, and continued negotiations), Beijing agreed in October 1994 not only to abide by the basic guidelines of the MTCR but also to apply the concept of "inherent capability" in limiting its missile exports. That is, even though China argued that the M-11's advertised range, at about 280 kilometers (about 174 miles), fell below the basic MTCR threshold, the missile was still "inherently capable" of longer ranges if its payload was reduced slightly. By accepting the notion of "inherent capability," Beijing appeared to agree to a halt in further M-11 shipments. Based on this understanding, in November 1994 the Clinton administration lifted its August 1993 sanctions against China, citing national security considerations. In June 1998, during the U.S.-China summit and shortly after Pakistan detonated several nuclear devices to become a de facto nuclear weapons state, China joined the United States to reaffirm its October 1994 pledge, stating that its policy was to "prevent the export of equipment, materials, or technology that could in any way assist programs in India or Pakistan for nuclear weapons or for ballistic missiles capable of delivering such weapons" and that, to that end, they would strengthen their "national export control systems."[37] This statement appeared to remove any remaining doubt about China's commitment to stop missile-related assistance.

However, with formal, public revelations that China was assisting Pakistan to develop and produce its own indigenous missiles and that Pakistan was in possession of complete Chinese M-11 missiles, new, tougher sanctions were threatened against China in September 1999. This led to a third phase of new commitments by China, issued on November 21, 2000. First, the Chinese side stated it "has no intention to assist, in any way, any country in the development of ballistic missiles that can be used to deliver nuclear weapons (that is, capable of delivering a payload of at least 500 kilograms to a distance of at least 300 kilometers [about 190 miles])." Second, China agreed that it would "further improve its export control system, including by publishing a comprehensive export control list of missile-related items, including dual-use items" and that it would issue such a control list and related regulations "at an early date." The statement added that with regard to these regulations, in the case of transfers to countries that were developing ballistic missiles capable of delivering nuclear weapons, China would exercise special scrutiny and caution, even for items not specifically contained on the control list.[38]

However, as the Bush administration took office in early 2001, concerns persisted that Chinese entities had not stopped their cooperation with Pakistan's ballistic missile program. As a result, on September 1, 2001, the Bush administration leveled new sanctions against Chinese entities for their MTCR category-2-related activities (the provision of technologies and subcomponents, rather than complete missile systems) in support of Pakistan's missile programs. The sanctions prevented the resumption of most commercial space-related cooperation between the United States and China, including satellite launches on Chinese rockets.[39] In response, in late August 2002, in the run-up to the October Crawford, Texas, summit between Presidents Jiang and Bush, the Chinese took a fourth important step by issuing the long-awaited set of missile export control regulations and a related control list.[40]

ARMS CONTROL, NUCLEAR WEAPONS, AND MISSILE DEFENSES

One of the most important arms control steps taken by China in the mid-1990s was to negotiate and sign the Comprehensive Test Ban Treaty; China was the second country to sign the treaty, following the United States.[41] Since the treaty was concluded in 1996, China, along with the other four CTBT signatory nuclear weapons states (France, Russia, the United Kingdom, and the United States), has abided by an informal moratorium on nuclear testing, even though the treaty has not entered into force.[42] Of the five major nuclear weapons states, China has the smallest strategic nuclear arsenal and the smallest testing program, so its willingness to sign on to and abide by the CTBT is significant.

In the late 1980s and early 1990s, China was reluctant to enter into negotiations over a test ban. Beijing abstained from a 1990 UN resolution calling for a test ban treaty, and in May 1992 it conducted its largest underground nuclear test to date. However, following its thirty-ninth nuclear test in October 1993, Beijing declared it was prepared to enter into CTBT negotiations and expressed its hope that the treaty could be concluded no later than 1996.[43] Formal negotiations began in the UN Conference on Disarmament in January 1994. The process was characterized by a number of Chinese attempts to link the treaty to other issues or to limit its effectiveness. For example, Chinese negotiators began by insisting that the CTBT be accompanied by a pledge by the other nuclear powers that they would not be the first to use nuclear weapons (a unilateral pledge that China had consistently stated from the beginning of its status as a nuclear power). China dropped this effort but later argued that "peaceful nuclear explosions" should be allowed under the treaty. This effort failed as well. Beijing had better luck in preventing the use of "national technical means"—that is, the use of individual nations' intelligence capabilities such as satellites or espionage—to verify compliance under the treaty; instead, an international monitoring system under the aegis of the treaty was set up. China also succeeded in making it more difficult for the treaty's executive council to launch an on-site inspection; under China's proposal, which became a part of the treaty, an on-site inspection is possible only when thirty of fifty-one executive council members (rather than a simple majority) vote in the affirmative to do so. China also continued its nuclear weapons testing program through to the very final stages of CTBT negotiations, the only nuclear weapons state to do so. Its last test was in July 1996.[44]

In the end, in September 1996, China signed on to the CTBT, agreeing to place a verifiable qualitative cap on its nuclear weapons modernization program, over the objections of its military and strategic scientist communities—and in spite of having tested far fewer times than other nuclear weapons powers. With 1,032 tests, the United States had conducted twenty-three times the number of Chinese tests. The Soviet Union had conducted 715 tests, and France 210 tests. The United Kingdom and China both had tested 45 times.[45] While Chinese leaders have declared their intention to ratify the treaty, it is unlikely they will do so until after the United States ratifies it.

In recent years, China has also taken a more proactive position in support of nuclear-weapons-free zones. It has signed and ratified the protocols for the Treaty of Tlatelolco (Latin America and Caribbean nuclear-weapons-free zone), the Treaty of Rarotonga (South Pacific nuclear-weapons-free zone), and the Treaty of Pelindaba (Africa nuclear-weapons-free zone). Closer to home, China has expressed its commitment to sign the protocols associated with the Treaty of Bangkok (Southeast Asia nuclear-weapons-free zone) and has been active in official discussions to establish a nuclear-weapons-free zone in Central Asia.

Within the UN Conference on Disarmament (CD), China has also taken a high-profile position on several global arms control measures, especially since the late 1990s. For example, China supported the establishment in 1998 of an ad hoc committee to negotiate a Fissile Material Cutoff Treaty (FMCT). While supporting this effort in principle, Beijing also argued that such negotiations should be carried out in parallel with negotiations in the CD aimed at a global treaty on "preventing an arms race in outer space." China's position was succinctly presented before the CD in a working paper issued in February 2000, in which the Chinese government claimed that "outer space belongs to all mankind" but that there are "attempts, programmes, and moves unilaterally to seek military and strategic superiority in or control over outer space." Such moves, the Chinese argued, "may lead to the weaponization of outer space in the near future or even to a multilateral arms race in outer space." As such, according to the working paper, the CD must "re-establish the Ad Hoc Committee . . . to negotiate and conclude an international legal instrument prohibiting the testing, deployment, and use of weapons, weapons systems, and components in outer space." Based on these views, the Chinese side argued that the "importance of nuclear disarmament and PAROS [preventing an arms race in outer space] is no less than that of FMCT" and that issues related to nuclear disarmament, such as FMCT and PAROS, "are interrelated and should be addressed as a whole. Singling out any one item while excluding the others is unjustified and unhelpful."[46]

While China has taken a more prominent role since the late 1990s within the CD to advocate more far-reaching arms control measures at the global level, the UN has been unable to proceed, largely owing to differences between Beijing and Washington. China long argued that negotiation on an FMCT should proceed in parallel with other negotiations related to PAROS, whereas the United States opposed negotiations on PAROS, preferring to proceed first with FMCT discussions. In 2003 the CD closed for the fifth year in a row without holding negotiations, despite a major concession from China, which dropped its insistence that any work program include the simultaneous drafting of a treaty on PAROS (both China and Russia still want less formal discussions on PAROS to proceed).[47] The CD negotiations remained stalled in 2005, in part due to the revision of the U.S. position on the FMCT. In 2004, following an internal policy review, the Bush administration announced that "it no longer viewed as 'effectively verifiable' a proposed fissile material cutoff treaty, which would prohibit the production of highly enriched uranium and plutonium for nuclear weapons purposes," arguing that a loophole allowing for the retention of existing fissile material stockpiles and continued production for civilian use would allow cheaters to violate the FMCT with little fear of being caught.[48] Washington has failed to convince other members to endorse its position, and because the CD can only operate on the basis of consensus, the body continues to be unable to agree on a new work agenda.

With regard to missile defenses, China's positions have likewise become somewhat more constructive and less confrontational, especially since 2001. When it became clear in late 2001 that the United States intended to withdraw from the ABM Treaty and to proceed apace with missile defense plans, Beijing's rhetoric on the issue subsided considerably. Since 2002 Beijing stopped sponsoring resolutions in the United Nations opposed to missile defense. Its white paper on nonproliferation in 2003 and its white paper on national defense in 2004 expressed some concern about missile defenses, repeating China's position on the need to conclude an international legal instrument to prevent the weaponization of outer space. The 2004 defense white paper even suggested that the Chinese air force would develop antimissile weapons of its own. China was open to the regular, senior-level efforts by the Bush administration to brief Beijing on the motivations and plans behind the U.S. missile defense program. In 2003 and 2004 China and the United States held three rounds, at the undersecretary level, of consultations on strategic security, multilateral arms control, and nonproliferation, where missile defense issues were discussed. In April 2006 Presidents Bush and Hu agreed to establish a strategic nuclear dialogue between the two countries. On the downside, however, it is widely believed that China is likely to expand its nuclear arsenal, both quantitatively and qualitatively, in no small measure out of concern over U.S. missile defense plans that may be capable of undermining China's nuclear deterrent.

Conclusions

Overall, however, since the mid-1990s, China has put forward a more constructive and positive set of nonproliferation and arms control policies and practices at global, regional, bilateral, and domestic levels, increasingly consistent with the interests of its neighbors, international partners, and international norms. This approach can be attributed in large measure to the fundamental goals of China's new security diplomacy: defusing tensions abroad, and especially on its periphery, in order to focus on the economic, social, and political challenges on its domestic agenda; reassuring regional neighbors and other international players about the peaceful and constructive nature of China's rise; and countering U.S. influence, in a relatively quiet and nonconfrontational way, to promote Chinese security interests.

For example, in implementing and enforcing its domestic export controls and nonproliferation pledges, Beijing seeks to more effectively police illicit activities within its own borders at a time of rapid economic transformation, decentralization, and marketization of business, trade, and industrial sectors at home. Moreover, by stemming the flow of potentially destabilizing weapons and technologies to troubled regions on China's doorstep—such as in Central, South, and Southwest Asia—Chinese policymakers can better focus on domestic sociopolitical and socioeconomic challenges if it is not dealing with instabilities on its periphery. The willingness of Chinese leaders to draft and implement these domestic statements and laws (most of which introduce a more cumbersome regulatory and bureaucratic process and limit exporters' activities) demonstrates at the very least a stronger recognition of the importance of nonproliferation and arms control norms and the critical role to be played by domestic mechanisms, such as export controls, in enforcing these norms. By giving the effect of national public law to many domestic nonproliferation and arms control efforts, the Chinese government acknowledged the need to expose its domestic industry more directly to the problems of proliferation as well as to the penalties they would face if they choose to violate export restrictions.

China's more constructive approach to nonproliferation and arms control also springs from a desire to reassure regional neighbors and other international players about the peaceful and constructive nature of China's rise. It is clear that China's accelerated participation in and adherence to agreements and norms on nonproliferation and arms control over the past two decades occurred in parallel with, and for the most part in support of, the country's larger effort of opening and reform. The grand national strategy of reform and opening comes close to holy writ among Chinese leaders, and any activities that justifiably contribute to this process—such as establishing friendlier, more constructive, and more cooperative relations with outside powers through arms control and nonproliferation cooperation—gain support and encouragement as long as they do not undermine China's overall security interests. By actively joining nonproliferation and arms control covenants, China can promote its image as a great power, burnish its credentials as a constructive international citizen, and reassure the international community of China's constructive intentions, all part and parcel of Beijing's long-term strategic aspirations.

For example, China's willingness to join and abide by certain international arms control and nonproliferation regimes—even when doing so would have a direct impact on limiting China's military modernization effort, such as the CTBT—was motivated in large measure by Beijing's desire to project a more benign and constructive international image, particularly in the developing world, and to reassure the international community about China's role as an emerging and responsible great power. It became clear to the Chinese CTBT negotiating team in Geneva that the conclusion of a strong and verifiable CTBT was overwhelmingly supported by the international community. Not only was such a treaty broadly supported in the developing world, where China wanted to be seen as a leader, but it was also strongly supported by all other nuclear weapons states, not to mention Beijing's most important counterparts, the United States, Russia, and Japan. Signing onto the CTBT was also seen as an important step to help bring some greater stability to U.S.-China relations following a rocky period between the two countries, especially escalating tensions in 1995–96 over Taiwan. Recognizing these trends, those in China concerned with China's image and key relationships won out in a fierce internal debate, and the country went on to support a robust CTBT treaty and verification infrastructure.

Similar concerns with China's image and with reassuring the international community can help explain the country's willingness to abandon opposition to so-called supply-side cartels and become an active member of such nonuniversal nonprolilferation regimes as the Zangger Committee and the Nuclear Suppliers Group; and to establish domestic export control regulations consistent with such other mechanisms as the Missile Technology Control Regime (MTCR), the Wassenaar Arrangement, and the Australia Group (while also seeking membership in the MTCR and Wassenaar Arrangement). In supporting the establishment of nuclear-weapons-free zones, China again burnished its image, especially in the developing world, as a responsible great power. China's expressed support for nuclear-weapons-free zones in its close neighborhood—such as in Southeast and Central Asia—is especially important in this regard.

The implementation and enforcement of domestic export control laws also send a signal to China's neighbors and the international community of China's willingness to take its obligations seriously and to be held publicly accountable by its critics abroad when the government fails to properly implement and enforce its own laws and regulations. This growing set of publicly declared statements, laws, and regulations offers the international community a yardstick by which to measure Chinese commitments and progress (or lack of it) regarding nonproliferation and arms control. For China's neighbors and other international players, this approach gives more concrete and reassuring effect to Beijing's claims to be a peacefully rising power.

Beijing's new security diplomacy seeks in part to quietly balance—but not openly confront—U.S. power, but to do so in ways that meet Chinese long-term interests. The best examples of this approach are found in the many occasions in which Beijing took on additional nonproliferation and arms control commitments in order to avoid an open and damaging confrontation with Washington—and instead to develop a more beneficial and stable bilateral relationship. Time and time again throughout the 1990s and into 2000s, Beijing steadily conceded ground to the United States on a range of nonproliferation questions, principally having to do with Pakistan and Iran. But in so doing, Beijing also signed on to more far-reaching nonproliferation and arms control commitments with global applications.[49]

But these steps were not for Washington's benefit alone or simply meant to avoid a clash with the United States. Beijing, too, steadily came to recognize the interests it has in stemming the proliferation of weapons and technology, especially to areas of potential instability around its periphery. Moreover, in finding common ground on nonproliferation and arms control issues with the United States, Beijing has expectations of possibly limiting U.S. power and promoting Chinese interests. As Chinese arms control and nonproliferation strategists became more familiar over time with the norms and procedures of international arms control efforts, the country's leadership appeared to recognize more clearly the value these processes might have for matters of Chinese national interest, especially to the degree such agreements would limit others' capabilities while having less effect on China. For example, by joining the Nuclear Nonproliferation Treaty as an acknowledged nuclear weapons power, China had nothing to lose regarding its own military capacity but could expect the regime to slow the emergence of new nuclear powers. By joining and supporting various nuclear-weapons-free treaties around the world, China loses little, as it does not deploy nuclear weapons abroad, but may gain by putting an onus on other countries to limit their nuclear weapons deployments by respecting such treaties. Even in cases in which China accepts verifiable limits on its own military capabilities—such as Beijing's agreement to sign on to the Chemical Weapons Convention and the Comprehensive Test Ban Treaty—it does so having reached the self-interested expectation that such restraints would apply to other powers as well.

In addition, by joining and promoting nonproliferation and arms control mechanisms, China will have a role in shaping the rules and outcomes of these mechanisms, especially in the formulating stages. Under certain circumstances, it may be possible to dilute the influence of other major powers, such as the United States, relative to China's and to achieve outcomes suited to Chinese interests. China's increased participation in nonproliferation and arms control agreements may also realize certain other, less tangible, benefits: access to better information and resources, social back patting, enhanced legitimacy, and bargaining and side payments. As Alastair Iain Johnston and Paul Evans note, "[Chinese] participation in international security institutions has bred further participation. . . . That participation, in conjunction with an evolving Chinese identity as a responsible great power, has generated image costs and benefits that appear to have positively influenced the quality (within limits) of Chinese participation."[50] In seeking these benefits, China in turn gains further incentives for even deeper participation in the regime, and the costs of dropping out from the regime, or opposing it, steadily rise.

To be sure, numerous concerns persist about China's approach to nonproliferation and arms control matters. As the U.S. Central Intelligence Agency wrote in 2004, "Over the past several years, Beijing improved its nonproliferation posture through commitments to multilateral nonproliferation regimes, promulgation of expanded export controls, and strengthened oversight mechanisms, but the proliferation behavior of Chinese companies remains of great concern."[51] In spite of encouraging progress in overhauling its export control regulations, Beijing still has considerable work to do to improve the system and prevent Chinese companies and individuals from proliferating proscribed weapons and technologies. U.S. intelligence reporting continues to cite Chinese entities as suppliers of sensitive nuclear-, chemical-, and ballistic-missile-related technologies and components to Iran, and nuclear- and ballistic-missile-related technologies and assistance to Pakistan.[52] The United States continues to issue sanctions against Chinese entities for their proliferation activities. On broader questions of nuclear weapons and arms control, Chinese strategists continue to harbor antagonistic views toward U.S. missile defense plans, and the country is engaged in a buildup of its nuclear and missile arsenal. Official policy in Beijing and Washington also strongly differs in many respects over how the global arms control agenda should proceed.

With these positive and negative developments in mind, the United States and the international community should recognize and better understand the significant strides China has taken to strengthen its commitment to nonproliferation and arms control: reduced arms and weapons technology exports; increased membership in and adherence to a broadening array of nonproliferation and arms control regimes; more binding bilateral commitments; a vastly improved domestic export control system; and more constructive dialogue with international partners on such questions as proliferation, nuclear weapons, and missile defenses. At the same time, Washington and other key partners need to monitor persistent concerns about China's political will and practical ability to further strengthen its nonproliferation policies. Beijing also has important differences with Washington and other major powers over certain key questions on the international arms control agenda.

Looking ahead, stemming the proliferation activities of such countries as Iran and North Korea will call for even greater involvement and cooperation from China. Understanding the nature and goals of China's new security diplomacy in these developments will leverage opportunities and moderate the challenges inherent in China's changing approach to nonproliferation and arms control.

4 | Sovereignty and Intervention

> The U.S.-led intervention [in Yugoslavia] involves the fundamental question of what kind of international order should be established and in what direction the twenty-first century should go.
>
> —Chinese President Jiang Zemin, June 1999

> China . . . has long pledged not to seek hegemony, not to join any military bloc, and not to pursue its own spheres of influence.
>
> Chinese Vice President Hu Jintao, April 2002

Chinese leaders and strategists staunchly defend a traditional understanding of sovereignty that justifies Beijing's absolute authority over China's expansive territory, strengthens regime legitimacy, deflects internal criticism of its domestic policies, counters the encroachment of foreign influence, and wards off outside involvement in such sovereignty claims as Taiwan and Tibet. When Chinese look beyond their borders, these strong views on sovereignty are reflected in the country's policies regarding foreign interventions abroad.

However, as part of China's new security diplomacy, Chinese views on sovereignty and intervention display signs of greater flexibility and pragmatism across a range of security-related questions, including such critical issues as peacekeeping and counterterrorism. To be sure, Chinese approaches remain largely wedded to traditional understandings of such questions. But in an age of increasing interdependence and globalization, Chinese views on sovereignty and intervention show some convergence with much of the international community, consistent with the view expressed by UN Secretary General Kofi

Statement of President Jiang Zemin is from Sa Benwang, "Impact of the Kosovo War on the International Situation," *International Strategic Studies* 4 (October 1999), p. 1. Statement from Vice President Hu Jintao is from "Hu Jintao Says China Opposes Strong Nations Bullying the Weak," *Agence France-Presse*, April 24, 2002.

Annan: "State sovereignty, in its most basic sense, is being redefined—not least by the forces of globalisation and international co-operation."[1]

Beijing's more flexible approach to sovereignty and intervention is driven by the fundamental goals of its new security diplomacy: alleviate external tensions in order to address challenges on its domestic front, assure neighbors about a growing China's peaceful intentions, and find ways to balance, but not confront, the United States to achieve Chinese interests more effectively. While not as advanced or proactive as China's policies toward regional security mechanisms or nonproliferation, Beijing's changing approach to sovereignty and intervention merits closer scrutiny and raises interesting new opportunities and challenges for the international community.[2]

China's Traditional Approach

Generally speaking, Chinese policy strongly defends the sovereign territorial rights of other nations and consistently insists on adherence to sovereignty principles as stipulated in the United Nations Charter and other international declarations safeguarding traditional state sovereignty, such as the Five Principles of Peaceful Coexistence. According to a Western analyst in the early 1990s, "the tyranny of sovereignty looms . . . large in Chinese thinking and behavior, inhibiting a more positive and co-operative engagement in the creation of a more just and peaceful world order."[3]

HISTORY AS A GUIDE

Chinese leaders of the past several centuries have displayed a general reluctance to intervene beyond a geographically limited area adjacent or close to China's strategic core region, or heartland, and an adamant opposition to encroachments upon the territorial and political integrity of Chinese sovereignty. These views, which continue to shape thinking about sovereignty and intervention today, derive from three key historical lessons.

First, Chinese leaders have historically had to combat the challenge of managing large and often far-flung territories with large populations. On the one hand, the large endowment of territory and population helped China over past millennia to maintain enormous political, cultural, and military sway over most of the eastern and southeastern portions of the Asian continent. On the other hand, however, China's geographic expanse and sovereignty over ethnic peoples at its periphery has over the centuries made it perpetually vulnerable to foreign incursion, both overland across the open plains of the north and northeast and, particularly since the late eighteenth century, from its lengthy eastern seaboard. Under these historical conditions, Chinese leaders continually focused on protecting Chinese sovereignty and territorial integrity from intervention and encroachment. Today, China has the world's largest population (at approximately 1.3 billion), a geographic expanse slightly larger than the United States, the world's longest land borders (extending some 22,150 kilometers, or about 14,000 miles), direct land frontiers with fourteen states, and close maritime proximity with several others.[4] Concerns with sovereignty, territorial integrity, and defending the Chinese mainland from foreign influence and intrusion never seem far from the surface of official thinking.

Second, the dissolution of sovereign dynastic control over China was not only a challenge from abroad but also, more often than not, arose from internally generated domestic threats. Hence a critical part of maintaining sovereignty concerned quelling potential domestic challenges and ensuring domestic tranquility in addition to keeping foreign forces at bay. The relative success or failure in dealing with this combined internal-external conundrum is linked throughout Chinese history to the rise and fall of dynasties. The potential challenges arising at home underscored for Chinese leaders the need to protect Chinese sovereignty from unwelcome foreign influences— and continue to shape Chinese leaders' concerns with outside influences, "spiritual pollution," and "peaceful evolution."[5]

Third, Chinese history has judged the morality, legitimacy, and survival of its dynastic rulers in part by their ability to exercise sovereignty over a stable and prosperous China, free from foreign coercion and encroachment. This historical linkage between successful governance and legitimacy is most closely associated with the so-called mandate of heaven, by which dynastic emperors gained their sovereign legitimacy to rule. This mandate in practice derived from the ruler's ability to foster well-being for the domestic body politic, prevent domestic disorder and the rise of internal rivals to power, and, particularly over the past 500 to 800 years, defend the Chinese heartland from foreign, non-Han Chinese incursion and attack. "Just" rulers possessing the proper legitimacy were at once able to advance internal cohesion and domestic tranquility, deter unwelcome external influence, and generate foreign deference and respect. To do so within the traditional Confucian ethic can only legitimately occur through the exercise of benevolent governance (*wangdao*). Achieving these aims through needless coercion, despotic rule, or hegemony (*badao*) was considered illegitimate and ultimately would result in failure and the loss of power. Thus, the use of force for just reasons, such as preserving domestic tranquility or maintaining the public good, is an acceptable extension of *wangdao*, while war and intervention merely for territorial, economic, or strategic aggrandizement is unjust and reflects *badao*, or hegemonic intent. Guided by this understanding, China's traditional strategic culture justifies military expansion when it is a necessary step for domestic tranquility and maintenance of legitimate sovereignty rather than overt territorial or material gain.[6] Those rulers who, through the exercise of *wangdao*, maintain domestic stability and prosperity while also achieving peace and respect abroad earn the mantle of sovereign legitimacy. Failure to do so spells a loss of legitimacy, fall from power, and disgrace.

This interpretation of history's lessons regarding sovereignty and intervention weighs heavily in the minds of Chinese leaders and reinforces their desire to ensure domestic sovereign control, keep foreign influences at bay, guard the prerogatives of state sovereignty on the international scene, maintain a basic defense of Chinese territorial integrity, and ultimately ensure regime survival.

CONTEMPORARY EXPERIENCE AS A GUIDE

China's self-perception as a weak and aggrieved nation leads it to cling to a narrow definition of sovereign prerogatives and to resist an expanding international norm of acceptable interventionism. Indeed, China's calamitous contemporary experience as a new entrant in the Western-dominated international system serves to sustain China's historical positions regarding sovereignty and interventionism. In the Chinese view, the period from the mid-nineteenth to the mid-twentieth century brought China enormous suffering and a "century of shame" at the hands of foreigners: extraterritoriality, invasion, and all-out warfare. Weakened by outsiders, China's domestic situation turned chaotic: throughout this period the Chinese proved themselves entirely capable of turning on themselves, with scores of millions of Chinese killed in the domestic struggles of the Taiping Rebellion (1850–64), periods of warlordism throughout much of the Republican period (1912–49), and the Chinese Civil War (1927–49).

The ascent of the Chinese Communists to power in Beijing in 1949 did not bring an end to this dynamic, as heated and bloody confrontations with foreign powers continued around China's periphery. The country fell prey to major domestic upheavals, in which tens of millions perished: the Great Leap Forward (1958–60), the massive famines of the early 1960s, and the Cultural Revolution (1966–76). Hence, in the contemporary period, mainland China did not emerge from national chaos as a confident, viable nation-state in the

Westphalian sense until well into the second half of the twentieth century (and was not fully accepted by the international community as a member of the United Nations until 1971). In this sense, China entered the international system like much of the developing world did in the latter half of the twentieth century: as a result of ousting imperial powers; undergoing intense ideological struggle, revolution, and civil war; juggling cold war loyalties; and forging a difficult domestic consensus around stability and development. As Samuel Kim has argued, contemporary Chinese views of sovereignty developed during the period of turbulence in the late Qing dynasty of the nineteenth century and became identified with state building, a project greatly aided by China's adopting a sovereign-centered approach to international relations. In turn, this modern effort combines with traditional Chinese conceptions of a Sinocentric world order to define current notions of national sovereignty.[7]

Beginning most prominently with the Five Principles of Peaceful Coexistence expressed at the Bandung Conference of 1955, the modern-day People's Republic held closely to a strict definition of sovereignty. Indeed, all of the Five Principles of Peaceful Coexistence, which continue to form an important pillar in Chinese official views on the conduct of international affairs, incorporate and support the primacy of sovereignty:

—Mutual respect for territorial integrity and sovereignty
—Mutual nonaggression
—Noninterference in each other's internal affairs
—Equality and mutual benefit
—Peaceful coexistence.

Nearly fifty years after the Bandung Conference, in the late 1990s, the resilience of these ideas was made clear when they were repackaged and reissued under the rubric of the new security concept.[8] China's second defense white paper, issued in October 2000, reiterated this theme with even stronger language. The document notes, for instance, that "hegemonism and power politics still exist and are developing further in the international political, economic, and security spheres. Certain big powers are pursuing neointerventionism, neogunboat policy, and neoeconomic colonialism, which are seriously damaging the sovereignty, independence, and developmental interests of many countries and threatening world peace and security."[9] The white paper reemphasized the need for a new security concept, the core of which should be "mutual trust, mutual benefit, equality, and cooperation," buzzwords referencing the Five Principles of Peaceful Coexistence. It further states that China "resolutely opposes hegemonism and power politics and combats the policies of war, aggression, and expansion. China also objects to any country imposing in any form its own political system and ideology on other countries."[10]

Looking beyond such high-level official statements, other Chinese writings of the 1990s also offer explicit theoretical conceptions of sovereignty consistent with an absolute position:

> According to the standards of international relations, the meaning of national sovereignty is undoubtedly of the greatest importance for the entity of the nation-state. The crucial principle is that the national authorities that rule over the people within a specific area are the ultimate authority for dealing with all domestic and foreign affairs faced by the nation-state. These authorities alone enjoy these rights and responsibilities, to the exclusion of any other actor. Within their territorial area, they can freely and independently stipulate their national system and form of government, their internal organization, foreign policy, and the form of legally sanctioned use of force [*hefa shiyong baoli de shouduan*].[11]

According to another prominent international relations analyst, each country has an "endowed" right to national survival and national economic development. However, in seeking these interests, a state cannot endanger other states' sovereignty through interventionism. To do so would be "power politics" or "hegemonism." While each state has its own "spheres of sovereignty" in which its interests should be respected, exceeding these spheres is "not legitimate." The appropriateness of one country's "proper sphere" should be determined by international society, broadly conceived, while the forced expansion of one country's morals or ideals should be opposed by international society.[12]

Even the terminology illustrates the differences of opinion over questions of sovereignty and the use of force. Chinese analysts seek to distinguish between a "world order" (*shijie zhixu*) (a set of worldwide regulations that might threaten sovereignty) and the concept preferred by the Chinese, "international order" (*guoji zhixu*) (certain statist norms designed to ease transactions between states).[13] After use of the term "new world order" (*xin shijie zhixu*) by U.S. President George H. W. Bush in the early 1990s, Chinese analysts have tended to view this concept as an indication of Washington's desire to maintain its global dominance in the post–cold war era. As one writer put it: "The developed countries, including the United States, do not want to sacrifice their sovereignty, no matter how they talk about the 'global village' or about how the United Nations has already become a 'world government'; is this not just a bold attempt to force small and mid-sized states to return anew to the era of colonialism?"[14] Another contemporary Chinese analyst put it even more strongly in 1999: "Interventionism is a very offensive, aggressive, and highly risky foreign policy of a country that is related to hegemonism. The implementation of such a policy is the root of turbulence in the world and modern warfare."[15]

Contemporary Chinese authors have even turned the Western notion of humanitarian intervention on its head by suggesting that the best way for a country to defend its citizens' human rights is to resist foreign intervention: "Sovereignty is important to protect the collective human rights of a nation's people from being harmed by foreign powers."[16] The former Chinese president Jiang Zemin underscored this position in a speech before the United Nations in 2000, arguing, "So long as there are boundaries between states and people live in their respective countries, to maintain national independence and safeguard sovereignty will remain the supreme interests of each government and people. Without sovereignty, there will be no human rights to speak of."[17]

As in the past, contemporary Chinese concerns about sovereignty and intervention boil down to practical interpretations of national interests, domestic legitimacy, and regime survival. Yan Xuetong noted, for example, that the "political liberalism instigated by certain Western countries in China is harmful to China's political stability."[18] Another Chinese scholar was more explicit about this linkage, arguing that national sovereignty and territorial integrity form the "crux" of China's ideologically related security interests, because "the primary manifestation of these security interests is in maintaining the leadership of the Communist Party, in preserving Socialism as the fundamental social system in China, and in maintaining domestic political stability." He urged on his fellow citizens the need to resist cultural "Westernization."[19] As Samuel Kim argued, Chinese leaders resist incursions into state sovereignty because they "threaten to take away the party-State's last remaining source of ... legitimacy grounded in the national ... mission of restoring China's great power status in the world."[20]

Finally, in reviewing contemporary Chinese approaches to questions of sovereignty and intervention, it is also worth considering China's evolving understanding of national self-determination and separatist movements abroad. The Chinese Communists from their earliest days in the 1920s built much of their legitimacy on the notion that theirs was an internal "people's" movement of national self-determination and state building in the face of transgressions perpetrated by imperialist powers. This line remained critical to maintaining Chinese Communist legitimacy well after the formal founding of the People's Republic in 1949 and helped justify the continued rooting out of bad elements at home and the resistance to imperialist hostility abroad. During this period of Chinese domestic political development, Beijing was highly supportive of what they defined as antiimperialist and anticolonial movements of national self-determination, movements that challenged the sovereignty over vast swaths of territory held mostly as colonial dominions by Western powers.[21] In short, supporting movements of national self-determination abroad were at the time a way for Chinese leaders to strengthen their own legitimacy at home.

But these positions on national self-determination and separatist movements changed over the latter years of the twentieth century. For example, noting a worldwide trend of "radical nationalism" in the early post–cold war period, one leading Chinese analyst expressed concern for its potential impact on China's restive Tibetan and Muslim populations in China's far southwest and west.[22] In recent years, Chinese analysts and officials tended to dismiss the importance of nonstate or substate actors on the international scene, concerned that their growing acceptance internationally has implications for Chinese sovereignty.[23] Of course, China's opposition to "splittism" is most firmly established in its policies toward Taiwan, which Beijing (and most of the rest of the world, officially speaking) accepts as part of "one China." With its own domestic situation in mind, China is far less likely to support movements toward self-determination today than in the early years of the People's Republic.

How does China justify this apparent shift in its view of sovereignty, intervention, and self-determination? Drawing heavily from China's historical experience, Chinese authors typically note the changing structure of the international system, with particular reference to a distinction between past "anti-imperialist" movements (which were acceptable) and current "state-dividing" movements (which are not). Chinese analysts argue that in the 1950s and 1960s, China stood with the United Nations and overall world opinion in supporting the decolonialization movement that swept the globe and sanctioned the transfer of national self-determination to local peoples. However, with the completion of the anticolonial enterprise and the legitimate establishment of a sovereign state, further separatist movements within that state cannot be justified. In the view of many Chinese scholars, such movements may be "imperialist" or "hegemonic" themselves, to the degree they are supported by outside powers seeking to extend their influence under the guise of human rights and democratization. Rather, "the right of national self-determination is not applicable for just any part of an independent state or for just any minority race within a multiethnic state." According to this view, in today's world, intervention in support of these activities is dangerous as it "provokes, creates, and sharpens national contradictions . . . supporting dismembering sovereign states and destroying other countries' territorial sovereignty."[24] In short, self-determination, democratization, and other forms of political separatism today—either within China or abroad—often generate serious concerns for Chinese leaders and strategists.

In the 1990s Chinese foreign policy practice reflected these broader and strongly held ideas about sovereignty and interventionism. For example, even in cases in which UN authorization was present, Beijing expressed concerns over the use of force and the expansion of that mandate. In the case of the Somalia intervention in 1993, the principal concern for Chinese analysts was not dealing with local warlords who sought to disrupt the UN mandate but rather with how UN forces were given excessive leeway on the use of force in the absence of a political settlement on the ground. In this view, UN forces too easily became a party to the dispute, breaking an essential precondition to remain neutral.[25] In Bosnia-Herzegovina, NATO's use of force in the early 1990s to try to make peace was seen as particularly destructive by some analysts in Beijing. Chinese analysts argued that showing patience with the arms embargo combined with mediation efforts offered "the only possible way to peacefully resolve the dispute."[26] Even in Cambodia in the early 1990s, when China made a large contribution of troops to an operation generally viewed as one of the UN's success stories, some Chinese analysts were concerned that the global body overstepped its limits in imposing order.[27] Of course, China strongly opposed the interventions that did not have a United Nations mandate, as was the case, for example, for the U.S.-led NATO action against Yugoslavia in 1999 and for U.S. unilateral strikes against sites in Sudan and Afghanistan in 1998. China opposed—though in a low-profile way compared to other countries such as France, Russia, and Germany—U.S.- and U.K.-led efforts to launch the war against Iraq in early 2003 as well as Washington and London's attempt to gain a more explicit UN Security Council resolution to endorse such action.

China's actions during the Kosovo crisis of 1998–99 are especially instructive in understanding Beijing's past and current approach to questions of sovereignty and intervention. As the crisis unfolded in 1998, China's initial priority was to resist UN involvement in what Beijing termed a domestic dispute, despite obvious regional security and humanitarian implications. In explaining China's decision to abstain on a vote supporting the arms embargo on Serbia, Ambassador Shen Guofang argued that it was "inappropriate to bring into the Council the differences between the Organization for Security and Cooperation in Europe (OSCE) and FRY (Federal Republic of Yugoslavia)," particularly since the situation did not threaten international peace and security and since it involved complicated "ethnic issues."[28]

With the advent of war in March 1999, and particularly with the accidental bombing of the Chinese embassy in Belgrade by a U.S. warplane in May, Chinese opposition rose to angry vehemence. The authoritative "Observer" and "Commentator" columns in *Renmin Ribao* [People's Daily] furiously denounced the bombing as a "barbarian crime" [*yeman zuixing*] and likened the United States to Nazi Germany in its efforts to become "Lord of the Earth."[29] Accompanied by widespread and at times violent public protests at the U.S. embassy and consulates in China, subsequent front-page columns decried the U.S. "global strategy for world hegemony" and called the air campaign "an aggressive war" that was "groundless in morality or law."[30]

The Changing Approach

In spite of these long-standing—and often heated—views regarding sovereignty and interventionism, Chinese positions on these issues are clearly changing. From the initial opening to the outside world of the People's Republic in the 1970s, and increasingly since the 1990s, China has steadily acquiesced in accepting the slow erosion of strict sovereign prerogatives both for itself and for other nation-states. As David Zweig argued, "the domestic hunger in China for global linkages . . . brought down institutional impediments to transnational relations and weakened the state's control over its citizens, resources, and sovereignty."[31] As China pursues its new security diplomacy, seeks to play a larger role on the international stage, and assumes more in the way of great power status, its leaders recognize it must increasingly accept encroachments upon sovereignty—whether on China or on other countries—when necessary to more effectively achieve China's interests. Increasingly, as China's new security diplomacy pragmatically engages the outside world and seeks a role as a responsible great power, Chinese policies about sovereignty and interventionism are likewise changing and becoming more flexible.

For example, some prominent analysts in China argued in the mid-1990s that a single, inflexible, and exclusive definition of "sovereignty" should not stand in the way of achieving China's overriding, supreme national interests.

One exemplar of this group argued that "sovereignty is not synonymous with national interests anymore; rather, it should be subject to overall national interests, not protected at all costs."[32] Other analysts recognized that advancing the overall goal of enhancing China's comprehensive national power requires at least some level of cooperation with international society.[33] Another Chinese analyst recognized that "absolute sovereignty" is actually an unsustainable concept and pondered whether China could simply stand back if another Hitler rose up, or large-scale atrocities against ethnic Chinese in Indonesia occurred. Considering a hypothetical Indonesia scenario, he argued, "if these were on an even greater scale or lasted for a longer time, or if they were explicitly supported by the government, or if the government's goal was to expel ethnic Chinese, leading to a massive influx of immigrants to China . . . China would probably call for the international society to intervene."[34] In the words of other analysts, "the struggle to protect our sovereignty has not stopped" with the end of the cold war, but the challenges have become more complex and subtle. As a result, in this view, "China should be pragmatic in responding to a perceived threat, with a mix of elasticity and hardness in response."[35] Even on the question of preventive diplomacy, some authors recognized that, in seeking balance between the interests of international society and those of nation-states, "certainly any international organization will create certain restraints upon the sovereign rights of its member states" and that China needed to put a greater effort into "crisis management" in the East Asia region (though China must apply this effort cautiously and be vigilant not to cross the divide into "illegal interference").[36]

China's greater willingness to accept constraints on national sovereignty has been most far-reaching in the economic realm, where, in order to reap the benefits of globalization, comparative advantage, and market share, Chinese officials, elites, and common citizens embraced the outside world, in spite of difficult challenges and commitments imposed upon China's domestic economic decisionmaking. By entering the World Trade Organization in 2001, for example, China must submit to the decisions of an outside legal authority adjudicating trade disputes. This marked a significant change in Beijing's understanding of sovereignty.

Despite lingering concerns, Chinese officials and analysts clearly recognize the beneficial trade-off in relinquishing some sovereign economic authority to realize a stronger China over the long term.[37] For example, Yan argued in the early 1990s that "China participates in international and regional economic cooperation in order to minimize economic damages caused by economic pressure and sanctions imposed by some foreign powers."[38] He later argued in favor of even more economic integration for China, saying, "As China's level of needs for Western markets and high technology rises, the ability of Western countries to use economic measures to interfere in China's internal affairs does grow, this is incontestable fact. However, economic dependence goes both ways, this is called 'interdependence.'" As a result, "on the issue of [most favored nation trading status for China], the United States government has no choice but to manage the issue prudently." Therefore, he wrote, "increasing our level of interdependence with Western economies can cause them to not casually interfere in China's internal politics due to their consideration of their own economic interests."[39] Another analyst on the question of economic sovereignty put it succinctly when he wrote that China must "create conditions that will hasten the benefits and avoid the pain." According to this approach, this is done "partially through limited entrance into the global economy and through enhancing China's national strength via economic growth, so that it can resist foreign domination."[40]

Another illustration of China's ability to be flexible when it suits its interests involves the "one China, two systems" concept as applied to Hong Kong. The return to Chinese sovereignty of Hong Kong was a highly sensitive issue, laden with historical baggage from the "century of shame." Nevertheless, the Chinese proved pragmatic in providing the "special administrative region" of Hong Kong with a significant degree of political, economic, and social autonomy and self-governance, within well-defined—but for Beijing uncommonly broad—parameters.

Taylor Fravel has also shown that on other issues of high historical significance and sensitivity—the settlement of disputed border and territorial claims with neighbors—China has likewise demonstrated greater flexibility and pragmatism in recent years. According to his extensive study on this question, Fravel points out that China "has also frequently used cooperative means to manage its territorial conflicts, revealing a pattern of behavior far more complex than many portray." Of its twenty-three territorial disputes with other governments, China has settled seventeen since 1949. Moreover, "it has offered substantial compromises in most of these settlements, usually receiving less than 50 percent of the contested land." Fravel concluded that "for China, resolved territorial disputes are a powerful indicator of peaceful relations and another reflection of China's status-quo orientation in most of its territorial conflicts."[41]

These subtle changes in Chinese positions regarding sovereignty and intervention are part and parcel of China's new security diplomacy and are motivated by its broader goals. First, in pursuing a more proactive and flexible approach to issues of sovereignty and intervention, Chinese leaders focus primarily on domestic socioeconomic and sociopolitical problems by lessening potential security tensions abroad. Second, China's changing approach to these issues helps Beijing present a more benign and responsible face to its neighbors while reassuring them about China's growing power and influence. Third, becoming more active and responsible on questions of sovereignty and interventionism provides China the opportunity to counter or constrain (but not confront) U.S. influence, so that China can pursue its security interests more effectively.

PEACEKEEPING

China's more open and active policies in support of international intervention and peacekeeping in recent years offer interesting examples of the new security diplomacy at work.[42] In the early 1990s, as UN peacekeeping activities dramatically expanded, Chinese strategists expressed concern that the world body might become a supranational government (*chao guojia de zhengfu*) and insisted that it remain a state-based organization aimed primarily at reducing transaction costs, enhancing cooperation, and defending the interests of sovereign states.[43] Chinese concerns about the future of UN peacekeeping and other multilateral uses of force by the international community became especially pronounced by the mid-to-late 1990s. Beijing saw problems as the lines between peacekeeping and peacemaking became fuzzier, as expansion was accompanied by civilian missions concerned with human rights, refugees, and inspections, and as these missions had less-than-complete support from host nations (such as in Iraq in the mid-1990s). By the mid-to-late 1990s, China expressed growing concern with an increasing global trend to support the concepts of limited sovereignty and humanitarian intervention.

Chinese analysts in the early to mid-1990s also feared that the United Nations was becoming an instrument of "hegemonism and power politics" and a thin veil behind which "certain powers," such as the United States, could justify pursuit of their own interests to the detriment of others. As the United Nations expanded its missions, Chinese analysts recognized that only the United States and its NATO allies possessed sufficient resources to send out properly trained troops with the necessary speed. Thus, these states would come to dominate UN forces and, therefore, decisions on peacekeeping.[44] This presented a problem for China: as one Chinese analyst put it as early as 1994, "If the United Nations becomes a tool for a select few countries to protect their own interests, it cannot receive broad support." Another later warned that "the United Nations should remain in the service of a large number of states, rather than a 'dependency' of the United States."[45] Beijing was most deeply shaken by the U.S.-led NATO intervention against Yugoslavia in 1999, which circumvented the United Nations all together.

In response, official Chinese publications outlined several principles that must be respected in order to gain Chinese support for initiating a UN peacekeeping operation.[46] First, "UN peacekeeping operations must strictly adhere to the purposes and principles of the UN Charter, especially the principles of respect for state sovereignty and noninterference in other countries' internal affairs." Second, "no UN peacekeeping operations should be launched without the prior consent of the countries concerned." Notably, the focus on "countries" implies that peacekeeping should be concerned with interstate conflict; in the case of intrastate conflict, the term "countries" suggests no need to consider the views of opposition forces. Third, "all UN peacekeeping forces should strictly observe neutrality and nonuse of force except for self-defense." Fourth, decisions to send peacekeepers should be based on "practicability and capability," and "no peacekeeping operation should be launched when conditions are not ripe." Finally, UN peacekeepers "should not become a party to a conflict." Other Chinese analysts placed even stiffer conditions on the use of force by the international community, arguing that UN intervention should take place only when the conflict in question truly threatens regional or global peace and that such cases should be interstate (not domestic) disputes.[47] Other scholars wrote that UN action should not become a matter of "peace creation" or "peacemaking," should strictly abide by international law, should avoid acts of "military intervention," and should have a "political settlement" in place on the ground before the deployment of peacekeepers.[48]

However, in parallel with the emergence of China's new security diplomacy of the late 1990s and early 2000s, China began to show a far more active and flexible approach toward UN peacekeeping operations. The most obvious feature of this new approach is a far more active level of direct Chinese participation. Before the late 1990s, China's single largest contribution to UN peacekeeping operations was the provision of 800 engineering troops (in two separate batches of 400 each) accompanied by 47 military observers to the UN mission in Cambodia (UNTAC) from 1992 to 1994. However, since 1999 China's contribution to UN peacekeeping operations has dramatically expanded in number, scope, and type, growing from approximately 50 persons in 1998 to more than 1,600 troops, civilian police, and military observers in mid-2006.[49] By 2006 China had jumped from the middle rankings of UN peacekeeping contributors in the late 1990s (China was typically the forty-fifth largest contributor of eighty-five or ninety total contributors) to the twelfth largest contributor, providing more civilian police, military observers, and troops to UN peacekeeping operations than any of the other permanent five members of the UN Security Council—and more than any NATO country. As of mid-2006, China was participating in ten of nineteen ongoing UN peacekeeping operations and contributing to six of the seven operations in Africa. Its contribution in 2004 of 597 peacekeepers to the UN Observation Mission in Liberia (UNOMIL) was the largest single contribution of personnel China ever made to a UN peacekeeping mission; it was made up of a transportation company, sappers, a hospital team, military observers, and civilian police. As of 2006, of the sixty-one UN peacekeeping operations past and present, China took part in twenty-four of them between 1989 and 2006, contributing approximately 2,500 personnel.[50] Nine Chinese peacekeepers have died while serving the United Nations.[51]

Since the late 1990s China has also diversified its contribution to UN peacekeeping operations. Before that time, the bulk of Chinese peacekeepers were military observers, who join other forces serving the United Nations to monitor truces, patrol disputed border areas, and act as part of an international buffer zone between past or potential adversaries, such as on the Iraq-Kuwait border and in the Golan Heights. However, in 2000 China took a new step by dispatching civilian police for the first time to a UN operation, deploying them as part of the Transitional Administration in East Timor (UNTAET) and (as of May 2002) the Mission of Support in East Timor (UNMISET). China also sent civilian police to the Mission in Bosnia-Herzegovina (UNMIBH) in early 2001 and dispatched civilian police to the newly established Interim Administration Mission in Kosovo (UNMIK) in 2004. In November 2004, 95 members of a 125-member contingent of Chinese riot police left Beijing to join the UN Stabilization Mission in Haiti. It marked the first time China dispatched riot police to participate in peacekeeping operations.[52] In November 2001 China began sending troops again as part of UN peacekeeping missions and has since rapidly expanded its contributions.

The following list shows Chinese contributions to UN peacekeeping activities in the month of September 2006:[53]

—MINURSO: 15 military observers (total, 15)
—MINUSTAH: 130 civilian police (total, 130)
—MONUC: 218 troops, 14 military observers (total, 232)
—UNMEE: 7 military observers (total, 7)
—UNMIK: 1 military observer (total, 1)

—UNMIL: 565 troops, 5 military observers, 23 civilian police (total, 593)

—UNMIS: 443 troops, 15 military observers, 15 civilian police (total, 473)

—UNOCI: 7 military observers (total, 7)

—UNTSO: 3 military observers (total, 3)

For the month of September 2006, China contributed 1,413 troops, 67 military observeers, and 168 civilian police.

Past studies emphasized China's reluctance to support nontraditional UN interventions, including interventions falling within chapter 7 of the United Nations Charter, which authorizes "all necessary means" and the use of force under national, rather than UN, command.[54] Yet in the case of East Timor, China played a supportive role in shaping the UN response to the growing postelection violence in East Timor. On September 15, 1999, the Security Council, with China voting in favor, authorized the establishment of a multi-national force, the Australia-led International Force in East Timor (INTER-FET), to restore peace and security in East Timor, to protect and support UN Mission in East Timor (UNAMET), and to facilitate humanitarian assistance operations. The resolution authorized the multinational, non-UN force "to take all necessary measures to fulfill this mandate."[55] The next day, Beijing committed to sending civilian police to the UN mission being formed to take up peacekeeping duties in East Timor.[56] One month later, in the Security Council, China supported the establishment of the UN Transitional Admin-istration in East Timor (UNTAET), which was explicitly created under the authority of chapter 7 of the UN Charter.[57] The resolution authorized UNTAET to use "all necessary measures" in the completion of its mandate.

Similarly, China supported UN resolutions sanctioning U.S.-led use of force against Afghanistan in the wake of the September 11, 2001, terrorist attacks against the United States.[58] The Chinese government in late 2001 also expressed an interest in contributing to a UN peacekeeping force in Afghanistan, should one be mandated: "On the question of the dispatch of UN peacekeeping troops to Afghanistan, China respects the accord reached by the parties concerned on this question under the lead of the United Nations. We believe that the peacekeeping troops should have the authoriza-tion of the Security Council. . . . China is willing to make its contributions toward peacekeeping actions in Afghanistan."[59] In July 2002 the Chinese ambassador to Afghanistan proposed that twenty officers of the Afghan mil-itary receive training in China. The Chinese ambassador to the United Nations reaffirmed China's cooperation with Germany to provide training to the Afghan police force and to provide Afghanistan with 20,000 police uni-forms and pairs of boots and 50,000 sets of military uniforms, boots, and other clothing.[60] Beijing also contributed a civilian police officer to the United Nations Assistance Mission in Afghanistan (UNAMA) during parts of 2005 and 2006. Since the inception of the International Security Assistance Force in Afghanistan, China has consistently voted in favor of extending United Nations approval of the force and authorizing it to use "all necessary measures" to fulfill its mandate.[61] China was similarly supportive of UN authorization to use "all necessary measures" to implement the chapter 7 mission of the multinational Stabilization Force (SFOR) in Bosnia-Herzegovina, dating back to its support for the establishment of SFOR in December 1996.[62]

In other key steps, China also took part in the unanimous vote on Security Council Resolution 1441 in November 2002, which found Iraq in "material breach" of its disarmament obligations, recalled past resolutions that authorized certain member states to use "all necessary means" to enforce previous resolutions concerning Iraqi compliance aimed at "restoring international peace and security in that area," and reminded Iraq it would face " serious consequences as a result of its continued violations of its obligations."[63]

China's more supportive position regarding UN and other international peacekeeping and interventions includes its commitments to the UN Standby Arrangements System. In May 1997 China expressed its willingness to participate in the Standby Arrangements System, whereby UN members commit to have specific "rapid response" resources—including troops, civilian personnel, equipment, and services—on standby and ready for speedy deployment. By 2002 China formally made a Level 1 commitment to the system, providing a basic list of capabilities that would make up its contribution; China is one of about eighty UN member states to make such a commitment. According to the Chinese defense white paper of 2002, this Level 1 commitment meant that China was "ready to provide the UN peacekeeping operations with engineering, medical, transportation, and other logistical support teams at appropriate times" and was "able to provide these operations with 1 UN standard engineering battalion, 1 U.N. standard medical team, and 2 UN standard transportation companies."[64]

By the early 2000s the Chinese leadership signed onto a joint statement by the permanent five members of the Security Council that emphasized strengthening the world role in "conflict prevention and settlement." The relevant portion of the September 2000 statement, signed by Jiang Zemin and the other four leaders, reads:

Strengthening Peacekeeping. The nature and number of international conflicts demanding UN involvement has shifted fundamentally over the past decade, a change that has yet to be reflected in structural reforms to equip the UN to fulfill the array of mandates it now faces. We pledge to move expeditiously to endow the UN with resources, both operational and financial, commensurate to the tasks it faces in its peacekeeping activities worldwide. Enhancing the United Nations peacekeeping capacity should strengthen the UN's central role in conflict prevention and settlement.[65]

In June 2001 Beijing joined all other members of the Security Council in approving a sweeping resolution aimed at enhancing the effectiveness of UN peacekeeping activities. The resolution encouraged greater cooperation between the Security Council and troop-contributing countries, greater multinational peacekeeping cooperation (including the establishment of regional peacekeeping centers), improved ongoing evaluation and assessments of UN missions, and enhanced information and analysis on peacekeeping to guide UN decisions.[66]

Beijing has also proven more flexible and supportive of UN peacekeeping missions even where the Taiwan question becomes involved. In the past, China used its Security Council veto over peacekeeping activities to protest states' establishment of diplomatic ties with Taiwan. For example, after Haiti invited Taiwan's vice president to its presidential inauguration in 1996, China held up a subsequent peacekeeping operation to Haiti for several weeks. After Guatemala recognized Taiwan in 1997, China vetoed a proposed UN peacekeeping mission to the area, although it subsequently reversed its vote. During the Kosovo crisis, in January 1999, Macedonia established diplomatic relations with Taiwan. China subsequently vetoed a proposed resolution to extend the UN force (UNPREDEP) then safeguarding Macedonia's borders.[67] However, in 2004, in a striking reversal of past practice, China chose to dispatch a large contingent of civilian police officers to the UN Stabilization Mission in Haiti (MINUSTAH), even though Haiti has official diplomatic relations with Taiwan.[68]

Some of the clearest indicators of an expanded Chinese interest in participating in peacekeeping activities are strengthened bureaucratic mechanisms to facilitate the effort, including the establishment and expansion of training programs for peacekeepers in China. Two principal groups within the Chinese military are tasked with overseeing peacekeeping issues. The first group consists of officers based at the Office of Peacekeeping (Weihe Bangongshi), under the General Staff Headquarters of the People's Liberation Army (PLA). It has a range of responsibilities, including selecting peacekeepers, monitoring peacekeeping developments, and communicating with relevant branches and offices both inside and outside China. These tasks are augmented by the work of the second group, consisting of Chinese military officers serving with the Chinese mission at the United Nations in New York. These officers play an important role both in representing Chinese military-related policies in the United Nations and in providing information and expertise on peacekeeping for top decisionmakers back in Beijing. Both groups of officers claim to play a limited lobbying role in urging their superiors within the PLA to give more serious and sustained consideration to China's peacekeeping role.[69]

The Office of Peacekeeping also helps administer, staff, and support the PLA's peacekeeping training program, based at the military's International Relations Academy in Nanjing, a facility closely associated with China's *er bu,* or defense intelligence and defense attaché system. From 1989 through 2002, about ten or twelve ninety-day training programs were run—or about one a year. With the augmentation of China's contribution to UN forces, the pace of training has increased. According to official Chinese information provided to the United Nations, officers for UN peacekeeping missions are chosen on the basis of their "physical fitness and knowledge of English" and must have had at least six years of military service.[70] Classes are held on topics such as peacekeeping principles and the UN Charter; there are classes on writing reports, organizing patrols, and conducting medical and communications procedures; also offered is training such as driving and language study.[71]

The Public Security Bureau, China's national police force (PSB, or Gong'an Bu), initially participated in its own training program for UN missions at the PLA facility in Nanjing. The PLA helped run the first round of these classes, probably in late 1999, but the PSB began holding the program independently in 2000, establishing the China Civilian Peacekeeping Police Training Center in the city of Langfang, about fifty-five kilometers (thirty-four miles) outside Beijing. During a visit to the facility by the UN undersecretary general for peacekeeping in 2002, it was announced the center would be the largest UN police training facility in Asia, with new grounds of about 13.5 hectares and floor space of some 17,000 square meters, to be completed in 2003 at a cost of RMB160 million (about US$19.35 million). The enlarged center will be able to train up to 250 officers at one time.[72] The training center is administered by the Chinese People's Armed Police Force Academy under the command of the PSB. Trainees, who are currently serving as Chinese police officers, undergo a two-month course intended to meet UN standards on such duties as conducting investigations and arrests, enforcing laws, and training local police. The trainees gain a basic knowledge about the United Nations and UN peacekeeping operations, learn of the mission and mission area, study English, and hone such necessary skills as map reading, driving, handling of weapons, radio communication, first aid and health precautions, and public safety measures.[73]

To be sure, China's willingness to engage even more proactively in peacekeeping activities will be hindered by certain obstacles in the years ahead. Beijing will likely continue to insist that interventions take place only when two core requirements are met: host nation acquiescence and Security Council approval. China will also continue to carefully gauge its strategic and political interests in making decisions regarding the dispatch of international intervention forces, under a UN flag or otherwise.

Practical matters of political, military, and bureaucratic will and capacity will also be a factor slowing Chinese responsiveness in peacekeeping affairs. To begin with, and not unlike apprehensions in other nations, one key PLA concern is the "body bag syndrome": the political implications of casualties incurred, especially among single-child, only-son families.[74] Simple logistics also stand in the way. China has not yet provided a "planning data sheet" to the UN Standby Arrangements System (also known as a Level 2 commitment); the data sheet provides, among other items, a detailed list of major equipment, unit organization, level of self-sufficiency, and movement data to the United Nations Department of Peacekeeping Operations. Nor has China provided the United Nations with a formal memorandum of understanding, which would further solidify its commitment to the standby arrangements system (considered a Level 3 commitment).[75] The basic standby arrangements have a "preferred" response time of 7 days for individual personnel, 15 days for initial units, and 30 days for additional units and elements. In addition, the standby arrangements guidelines suggest that rapidly deployed forces should be "self-sufficient" logistically: "recommended stockage level is 180 days for spare parts and 60 days for all other items. Also recommended is a minimum stockage level of 30 days . . . to ensure uninterrupted capability."[76] Chinese officers explain that China has difficulty in deploying the requisite air- or sea-lift capacity and logistics train to efficiently transport and sustain a significantly large number of troops and associated materiel over transcontinental and transoceanic distances.

In addition to such logistical issues, the PLA has problems retaining enough qualified officers with the necessary language skills. After undergoing peacekeeping training, many officers spread out to military schools as instructors, to border regions, and to China's embassies and missions abroad.

Those who are promoted are often difficult to recall or to retain on permanent alert, as the UN standby arrangements would require. The pool created by this training program is thus drying up.[77] The sclerotic pace of the bureaucratic process may also impede Chinese participation. In the case of East Timor, for example, although both the Office of Peacekeeping and PLA officers based at the United Nations supported sending military observers, by the time the central authorities in Beijing issued their approval, all the UN military observer slots for that mission had been filled.[78]

COUNTERTERRORISM

China's approach to counterterrorism efforts has moved over time from support in the 1970s for groups associated with insurgency and terrorist activities to carrying out counterterrorism activities at home and abroad by the late 1990s and into the 2000s.[79] In recent years, although China has not been the target of major international terrorist acts, Chinese citizens have been victims, including three who died in the September 11, 2001, attack on the World Trade Center (see box 4-1). Beijing claims that it faces a domestic terrorist challenge with links to international terrorist organizations including al-Qaeda. According to Chinese officials, Osama bin Laden "has been an active sponsor of separatists in Xinjiang and ran training camps for them in Afghanistan." Between 1992 and 2001, "about 100 'terrorists' trained by bin Laden returned to Xinjiang to carry out attacks . . . [claiming] the lives of 162 people . . . another 440 were wounded."[80] Following the war in Afghanistan in 2001, 22 Chinese Uighurs were captured fighting for the Taliban and were detained at Guantanamo Bay, Cuba.[81] According to the U.S. State Department, the East Turkestan Islamic Movement (ETIM), a group identified by both Washington and Beijing as a terrorist organization, has "received training and financial assistance from al-Qa'ida." In addition, two ETIM members were deported from Kyrgyzstan to China in May 2002 for allegedly plotting to attack the U.S. embassy in Bishkek as well as other U.S. interests abroad.[82]

Over the years from 1949 to the early 1990s, China provided military assistance to no fewer than twenty-nine armed liberation movements worldwide (not to mention more than forty countries).[83] In the 1960s and early 1970s these recipients included the Indonesian Communist Party in their fight against Suharto; other Communist movements, such as the Pathet Lao and the White Flag Communists, seeking the overthrow of "revisionist" regimes in Southeast Asia; and a number of independence and guerilla movements in Africa, including COREMO (Comité Revolucionário de Moçambique),

Box 4-1. *Chinese Victims of International Terrorism on and since September 11, 2001*

September 11, 2001	New York	Attack on World Trade Center	3 dead
April 12, 2002	Israel	Suicide bombing	2 dead
June 29, 2002	Kyrgyzstan	Assassination of Chinese officials	2 dead
July 17, 2002	Israel	Suicide bombing	2 dead
January 5, 2003	Israel	Suicide bombing	1 dead
February 6, 2003	Laos	Attack on bus	1 dead
March 20, 2003	Sri Lanka	Attack on fishing boat	15 dead
March 27, 2003	Kyrgyzstan	Attack on bus	19 dead
April 12, 2004	Iraq	Attack on workers	7 kidnapped
May 3, 2004	Pakistan	Car bombing	3 dead
June 11, 2004	Afghanistan	Attack on workers	11 dead, 4 injured
October 9, 2004	Pakistan	Attack on engineers	2 kidnapped
January 18, 2005	Iraq	Attack on workers	8 kidnapped

Source: Revised and updated from David M. Lampton and Richard Daniel Ewing, *The U.S.-China Relationship Facing International Security Crises: Three Case Studies in Post-9/11 Bilateral Relations* (Washington: Nixon Center, January 29, 2004). See www.nixoncenter.org/publications/monographs/USChinaRelations2003.pdf.

FRELIMO (Frente de Liberataçao de Moçambique), FNLA (Frente Nacional de Libertaçao de Angola), UNITA (Uniao Nacional para a Indepéndencia Total de Angola), Pan-Africa Congress of South Africa, ZANU (Zimbabwe African National Union), FLN (Front de Libération National, Algeria), and anti-Western rebels in the Congo, Malawi, Niger, and the Central African Republic.[84] Support was also extended to groups such as the PLO and the Popular Front for the Liberation of the Occupied Arab Gulf (later the Popular Front for the Liberation of Oman), which not only shared China's anti-imperialist ideology but also employed the Chinese Communist Party's early guerilla tactics to achieve their aims.[85] Between 1965 and 1969, shipments of

Chinese weapons valued at some US$5 million were sent to the Palestinians free of charge.[86]

During this period, three far-left factions emerged within the PLO: the Popular Front for the Liberation of Palestine (PFLP); the Democratic Front for the Liberation of Palestine (DFLP); and the Popular Front for the Liberation of Palestine–General Command (PFLP-GC), which pioneered many of the terrorist strategies in use today. During the 1970s, as these factions carried out deadly attacks, China "offered material assistance" to the PLO and invited it to open an office in Beijing.[87] In 1969 PLO leader Yasser Arafat expressed his appreciation for China's support: "The Chinese people's support for the revolutionary cause of Palestine, which is being occupied and plundered, forms an important pillar of the Palestine revolution. It is no secret if I say that Fatah, initiator of the Palestine revolution, received aid first from Peking."[88] Such actions began to sow discord between China and many developing world countries and, in some cases, led to the breaking off of bilateral relations. For example, the new Indonesian government under Suharto charged China with complicity in the 1965 coup attempt in Jakarta, and several African nations accused China of subversion during the tumultuous early years of the Cultural Revolution (1966–69).

By the early 1970s, as China emerged from the worst period of the Cultural Revolution, it also began a reevaluation of its support for insurgencies and terrorist actions. In 1971 the People's Republic of China was granted China's seat at the United Nations, and throughout the 1970s China was recognized diplomatically by an increasing number of states. China's perception that the Soviet Union was now a greater threat than the United States led to gradual rapprochement with Washington, to China's greater integration in the international community, and to its diminishing support for insurgent and terrorist groups around the world. In 1978 China welcomed the peace talks between Israel and Egypt and began to shift its position on the Arab-Israeli conflict, declaring for the first time in 1980 that "every country in the Middle East should enjoy the right to exist and be independent."[89] The gradual warming of ties with Israel culminated in the formal establishment of diplomatic relations in 1992.

However, while China's direct links with groups associated with terrorist activities appeared to have waned by the 1980s, serious concerns have continued, particularly in Washington, about Beijing's support for certain states, many of which are on the U.S. list of states that support terrorism. Beijing's support included close military-technical ties and arms exports to Pakistan; the export of missiles and missile-related technology to Pakistan, Iran, North

Korea, Syria, and Libya; the export of nuclear-related materials to North Korea and Iran and assistance to Pakistan in the early development of its nuclear weapons program; and sensitive chemical exports to Iran. China was also cited for providing advanced communications equipment to the Taliban during its reign in Afghanistan.[90] By and large, however, these concerns have diminished over time as Beijing has introduced stricter export control measures and come into greater compliance with international nonproliferation rules and norms.

As the Chinese leadership demonstrated a greater concern for terrorist activities abroad, so too it increased its vigilance and response to what it saw as a terrorist challenge within its own borders, particularly from ethnic minority Uighurs in China's far western province of Xinjiang.[91] Differences between Chinese rulers and Uighurs date back more than a century. Under the Treaty of St. Petersburg signed in 1881, China and Imperial Russia split the Uighur homeland of Turkestan between them, though China did not exercise complete control over this vast region, especially during the upheavals of dynastic collapse, civil war, and foreign invasion, which plagued China in the first half of the twentieth century. A brief period of independence (1945–49) for what was known as East Turkestan ended when the new Chinese Communist leaders sent troops into the area and established the Xinjiang Uighur Autonomous Region. The PLA faced as fierce a resistance as had their Qing dynasty predecessors, and during the 1950s thousands of Uighurs were executed for advocating "separatism." The Cultural Revolution was a particularly difficult time for the Uighurs, as they saw their mosques destroyed, imams jailed, and the native language banned from schools. It is estimated that 500,000 Uighurs fled to the Soviet Union during this period.[92] Tensions have also been exacerbated by the official encouragement of Han migration to Xinjiang: the Han population increased from an estimated 6–7 percent in the 1940s to an estimated 40–45 percent in 2000.[93]

Simmering tensions over Beijing's rule exploded in the 1990s, when an uprising broke out in Baren, near Kashgar, during which a reported 3,000 Uighurs were killed. While reports vary on what sparked the incident—some say opposition to the arrest of a popular mullah and others say police response to Uighur attacks on local government offices—the Chinese government's swift and harsh crackdown only hardened opposition among certain Uighur groups. The collapse of the Soviet Union in 1991 and the establishment of independent states in the former Soviet Central Asian republics were further sources of inspiration for some separatist-minded Uighurs and other ethnic groups in China's far northwest. During this period in the early to mid-1990s, disparate separatist organizations emerged—some of which advocated violent methods to achieve their aims. In 1995 PRC security forces reportedly uncovered a stash of 4,000 sticks of dynamite, 600 guns, and 3,000 kilograms of explosives in Xinjiang. In 1996 a high-ranking member of the Xinjiang People's Political Consultative Conference was assassinated and a number of railroad lines bombed.[94] On the day of Deng Xiaoping's funeral in 1997, nine people were killed when bombs exploded on three buses in Xinjiang's capital, Urumqi. Two weeks later, a bomb exploded in Beijing, wounding nine people; this was later blamed on Xinjiang "splittists."[95]

Whether the independence movement in Xinjiang should be viewed as a legitimate struggle for Uighur human rights or not is open to debate. However, it is clear that by the 1990s China had already identified some of these groups as "terrorist" organizations. Although still using the terms "splittist" and "separatist" to condemn activities in Xinjiang, by the mid-1990s Chinese media were describing events in Xinjiang as "terrorist activities," and predictably, the Chinese government clamped down on these groups in its 1996 "Strike Hard" campaign.[96] In a departure from past practice, however, Beijing authorities—which had suppressed media reports on separatist activities in Xinjiang for years—not only admitted that they had a problem but also began to see the genesis and development of these groups as linked to events beyond China's borders, the solution of which required a multinational regional response.

In part as a response to these developments, in April 1996 China, Russia, Tajikistan, Kazakhstan, and Kyrgyzstan formed the Shanghai Five, with the goal of establishing a regional security mechanism through which to resolve border issues and beef up border security. The fall of Afghanistan to the Taliban in September 1996 sent shock waves through regional governments and further focused the attention of the Shanghai Five on the potential challenges of more radicalized Islam in the region. In June 2001 the group admitted Uzbekistan and established a permanent regional security mechanism, the Shanghai Cooperation Organization (SCO). Under the SCO charter, members committed themselves to combat the "three evil forces: terrorism, separatism, and extremism."

Three months later, China's top leader, Jiang Zemin, watched along with the rest of the world the tragic events of September 11, 2001, and immediately called an emergency meeting of the Communist Party's political bureau standing committee. On September 12 Jiang telephoned President Bush to express his condolences and to offer China's cooperation in the fight against terrorism, one of the first world leaders to do so. On September 21, 2001, Foreign Minister Tang Jiaxuan told U.S.-China Business Council members that September 11 "shows that international terrorism has become a serious threat to world peace and stability," adding that "international cooperation is both necessary and pressing. . . . China stands ready to enhance dialogue and cooperation."[97] Commenting on China's response at the Asia-Pacific Economic Cooperation (APEC) conference in Shanghai on October 19, 2001, President Bush said, "China responded immediately to the attacks of September 11th. There was no hesitation, there was no doubt that they would stand with the United States. . . . There is a firm commitment by this government to cooperate in intelligence matters, to help interdict financing of terrorist organizations."[98]

Despite differences between the United States and China over how the fight against terrorism should be prosecuted, China by and large supported the U.S.-led war on terrorism, and this cooperation became an important factor in improving U.S.-China relations. Significantly, Beijing's support extended to the authorization of interventions to roll back and combat terrorist activities. For example, in September 2001 China voted in favor of UN Security Council resolution 1368, authorizing the international use of force against Afghanistan and the Taliban, and UN Security Council resolution 1373, aimed at stemming terrorist financing. China also joined the international Financial Action Task Force (FATF) as an observer, in January 2005. The FATF was established by the G-7 summit in Paris in 1989, in response to growing concerns over money laundering. Following September 11, 2001, however, the group expanded its focus to coordinate international efforts to combat terrorist financing.

China also played a supportive role in the U.S.-led war against the Taliban and al-Qaeda in Afghanistan and in the postwar reconstruction of Afghanistan. China closed its border with Afghanistan to stem the exodus of Taliban and al-Qaeda supporters and also permitted U.S. warships to stop in Hong Kong on the way to Afghanistan. More important, China launched a diplomatic offensive in late 2001 to persuade Pakistani President Pervez Musharraf to cooperate with Washington. In January 2002 China pledged US$150 million to the postwar reconstruction effort in Afghanistan and exempted the new government of President Karzai from repaying previously owed debts. In addition to its pledge to provide Afghanistan with uniforms and boots for its police force and army, it also pledged office supplies for 80,000 civil servants of the new interim administration.[99] In 2003 and 2004 China followed up with assistance worth US$47 million and US$15 million, respectively, including support for Afghan elections, local police training, and regional drug control cooperation.[100]

Beijing even began to accept greater U.S.-China cooperation on sensitive counterterrorism and security issues, including greater activities by U.S. law enforcement, intelligence, and other security representatives on Chinese soil. In December 2001 the U.S.-China interagency counterterrorism working group was established, comprising representatives from law enforcement, intelligence, military, diplomatic, and financial agencies. In May 2002 biannual meetings began between U.S. officials and their Chinese counterparts on preventing and combating terrorist financing. During a visit to Beijing in October 2002 U.S. Attorney General John Ashcroft announced the opening of the first Federal Bureau of Investigation (FBI) liaison office in Beijing. The office handles counterterrorism, international crime, and other issues. In another bilateral measure, on December 12, 2002, the U.S. Trade and Development Agency announced a US$272,660 grant agreement with Chinese civil aviation officials to assist in working toward aviation security in Southwest China. In December 2002 Assistant Secretary of State James Kelly also confirmed that the two sides were sharing intelligence "to an unprecedented extent."[101] In addition, in July 2003 China joined the U.S. Container Security Initiative (CSI). The CSI is designed to increase the screening of cargo entering the United States and included plans for U.S. customs officials to be stationed in the world's twenty busiest ports, of which China controls three: Hong Kong, Shanghai, and Shenzhen. Through these and other activities, China was also able to gain Washington's support on a matter of Chinese domestic concern. In August 2002 the United States announced that it considered the East Turkestan Islamic Movement (ETIM) based in Xinjiang "a terrorist organization" and that the State Department had determined the group "has committed, or poses a significant risk of committing, acts of terrorism that threaten the security of U.S. nationals or the national security, foreign policy, or economy of the United States." On September 11, 2002, the United Nations also announced that, at the request of both the United States and China, it was placing ETIM on the UN list of terrorist organizations.[102]

China has also supported other international and multilateral counterterrorism activities. For example, China has acceded to ten of the twelve international conventions against terrorism and has signed one of the remaining two.[103] China has also carried out a number of important steps in support of counterterrorism by partnering with neighboring countries and regional security organizations, especially in Central Asia. Particularly notable are the joint military counterterrorism exercises carried out by Chinese and Kyrgyz forces in October 2002 and the "command post" exercises among China, Kazakhstan, Kyrgyzstan, Russia, and Tajikistan in August 2003. China and

Russia held joint military exercises in 2005, ostensibly under the banner of counterterrorism, and the SCO announced in 2006 that armed forces from all six member states would conduct joint counterterrorism exercises in Russia in 2007. The SCO opened its Tashkent-based Regional Antiterror Structure in June 2004. As the only antiterrorist center in Central Asia, its goal is to coordinate the member states' counterterrorism activities, monitor terrorist activities in the region, recommend counterterrorist activities for the member states, and exchange information with other international organizations.

China had already begun to foster closer relations with ASEAN in the 1990s, emphasizing cooperation on "nontraditional" and transnational security issues, including countering terrorism. The two sides have also entered into a number of security cooperation agreements that aim to address terrorist challenges, including the 2002 Joint Declaration of ASEAN and China on Cooperation in the Field of Nontraditional Security Issues, in which counterterrorism is highlighted as a priority for ASEAN-China security cooperation. In 2004 the two sides signed a memorandum of understanding to implement the 2002 Joint Declaration. The memorandum states that the parties will develop practical measures in accordance with their national laws and regulations to enhance the capacity of each country and the region as a whole to deal with nontraditional security issues such as terrorism, arms smuggling, and money laundering. The parties also agreed to enhance cooperation in the exchange of intelligence and law enforcement. China will host workshops and training courses to upgrade the capacity of all parties to combat nontraditional security threats.[104] In November 2004, at the first ASEAN Regional Forum Security Policy Conference held in Beijing, participating officials from the Asia-Pacific region observed an antihijacking drill conducted by Chinese Special Forces.

Beijing has also used its intensified relationship with other regional partners, such as APEC and the European Union, to express its support for counterterrorism on terms more consistent with the UN Charter and other international conventions. For example, at the Shanghai APEC summit in October 2001, Chinese leader Jiang Zemin accepted U.S. President George W. Bush's recommendation that the leaders' meeting focus primarily on counterterrorism rather than on broad economic issues. China is a member of APEC's Counterterrorism Task Force, which was set up by senior officials in February 2003 to coordinate and implement the Leaders' Statement on Fighting Terrorism and Promoting Growth. In that statement, APEC leaders agreed to dismantle transnational terrorist groups that threaten their economies, to eliminate the threat posed by weapons of mass destruction, and to confront other direct threats to the security of the region. In August 2003 China and other APEC members submitted their Counterterrorism Action Plan, detailing a checklist of measures that each had undertaken to combat terrorism, including maritime, aviation, customs, immigration, and financial measures.[105] At the 2004 APEC summit meeting in Chile, Chinese foreign minister Li Zhaoxing stated that "as a firm supporter and participant of the antiterrorism combat, the Chinese government will continue to support APEC's constructive role in the antiterrorism field"[106]

At the China-EU summit in September 2006, the joint statement declared the following on the counterterrorism issue:

> The two sides reaffirmed their commitment to the fight against terrorism and reiterated that antiterrorism action must accord with the purpose and principles of the United Nations Charter and the norms of relevant International Law and fully respect human rights. The two sides underlined the leading role of the United Nations with respect to counter-terrorism and the importance of the universal implementation of all UN Security Council resolutions, UN conventions and protocols related to counter-terrorism. Both sides remain committed to achieving consensus on the UN Comprehensive Convention on International Terrorism and call upon the UN General Assembly to adopt the counter-terrorism strategy without delay, as mandated by the World Summit.[107]

Conclusions

China's changing approach to questions of sovereignty and intervention—especially including its changing views toward peacekeeping and counterterrorism—has led to a broadening set of new and, for China, unprecedented activities on its security agenda. These attitudes and activities are shaped by the three goals of China's new security diplomacy. First, China's changing approach to sovereignty and intervention helps Beijing to defuse tensions abroad so as to focus on domestic social, political, and economic challenges. Second, Beijing's more flexible approach to issues of sovereignty and intervention seeks to reassure regional neighbors and others about the peaceful and constructive nature of China's rise. Third, China hopes this approach to sovereignty and intervention can help counter, co-opt, or circumvent—while avoiding confrontation with—U.S. influence in order to achieve Chinese security interests more on Chinese terms.

China's domestic concerns with ethnic unrest and separatism, especially in Xinjiang in the 1990s, helped lead Beijing to adopt a more flexible policy toward sovereignty and intervention, especially as it concerns counterterrorism. Beijing was particularly concerned about the domestic implications of Islamic radicalism emerging in Afghanistan as well as ethnic separatism in other parts of Central and South Asia, fearing its spread into China. It is clear that even before the events of September 11, 2001, and the advent of the U.S.-led war on terrorism, China already considered itself a victim of domestic terrorism, understood the transnational nature of the problem and its connection to external Islamic groups, and introduced measures through regional efforts to combat the problem. In supporting the U.S.-led war on terrorism, voting in the UN Security Council in favor of international use of force against the Taliban in Afghanistan, and committing political and financial resources to establish the SCO, Beijing softened past positions on sovereignty in order to gain greater international and regional support for its efforts to quell potential unrest and terrorism along its long Central Asian borders. In part through these policies and others, Beijing has secured U.S. endorsement for listing a Uighur group, the ETIM, on both U.S. and UN terrorist lists. In addition, by partnering with Central Asian neighbors and gaining their support for combating the "three evils" (terrorism, separatism, and religious extremism), Beijing can expect their acknowledgement of Chinese domestic security concerns over separatism and territorial integrity, cooperation to subdue cross-border challenges to domestic security, and cooperation in pacifying potentially volatile border areas through improved state-to-state political and economic relations.

Research by Taylor Fravel amply demonstrates the link between Beijing's desire to address domestic tensions and its greater willingness to settle territorial sovereignty and border disputes with its neighbors, often on less advantageous territorial terms for China. On the basis of his study, he writes, "In territorial disputes, leaders are more likely to compromise when confronting internal threats to regime security, including rebellions and legitimacy crises. . . . Embattled leaders are willing to cooperate with other states in exchange for assistance in countering their domestic sources of insecurity."[108] This is clearly the case when examining Beijing's approach to suppressing Uighur uprisings in China's northwest Xinjiang Province in the mid-to-late 1990s. Faced with these challenges, China not only moved to pool diplomatic and financial resources to establish the SCO but also pressed ahead in bilateral negotiations with Kazakhstan, Kyrgyzstan, and Tajikistan to settle long-standing territorial sovereignty disputes. In each case, China sought to address domestic security concerns in part by compromising in the settlement of sovereignty disputes with these neighbors.[109]

More broadly, it appears that Beijing has come to recognize the need to stabilize "failed states" in its region in order to prevent spillover effects within China's borders. As part of this approach, Chinese leaders and analysts have come to balance long-held views on sovereignty and nonintervention against great power concerns with regional peace and security. Beijing has increasingly recognized the value of regional stability for its own national interests and to see U.N. peacekeeping as a mechanism that can help secure those interests (in contrast to past studies outlining Chinese reservations over the role that UN peacekeeping activities can play).[110] If an intervention is perceived as likely to "advance the condition of peace and stability," according to one Chinese analyst, it is thus "a just war."[111] Interviews with Beijing-based strategists and former UN peacekeeping participants highlight the importance of achieving stability and avoiding problems posed by failed states as decisive factors in Chinese thinking regarding intervention and peacekeeping.[112] This view is particularly strong when potential instability and failed states arise in China's neighborhood, such as in Cambodia, East Timor, and Afghanistan, and may be applicable to potential scenarios in the future involving North Korea.

China also exhibited a greater flexibility and proactiveness on sovereignty and intervention issues as a means to reassure its neighbors and other international counterparts about the peaceful and constructive nature of China's rise. China's willingness to settle its border disputes peacefully, and on terms more advantageous to its neighbors, is a clear example of how China's more flexible and pragmatic approach to sovereignty aims to bolster confidence about China's regional intentions. In his keynote speech at the opening of the ASEAN summit in November 2002, Vietnamese Prime Minister Phan Van Khai "spoke highly of China's efforts and initiatives aimed at creating a peaceful and stable environment for joint development" and "hailed" the signing of a statement on the code of conduct in the South China Sea between China and ASEAN "as an important measure to help maintain regional peace, stability, and security as well as a new expression of the good and reliable neighborliness between ASEAN and China."[113] Following Premier Wen Jiabao's highly successful visit to India in April 2005, during which the two Asian giants announced a new strategic partnership—including work on a roadmap aimed at resolving the long-standing sovereignty and border dispute that was the cause of their 1962 war—India's foreign secretary, Shyam

Saran, told reporters: "We do not look upon each other as adversaries but we look upon each other as partners."[114]

Beijing's more open approach to sovereignty and intervention likewise seeks to reassure its neighbors and the international community more broadly. For example, through its significantly expanded contribution to UN peacekeeping activities, Beijing claims its growing weight and influence in international affairs is accompanied by an increasingly responsible approach to global and regional stability. Making a more active contribution to peacekeeping burnishes China's international image and provides evidence of Beijing's intention to be a responsible great power and pursue a path of peaceful development. A Chinese vice minister of public security put it this way: "China's active involvement in peacekeeping missions of the United Nations, especially in Haiti, which has not set up a diplomatic relationship with China, fully exhibits a peace-loving and responsible image of the country."[115]

Finally, China's new security diplomacy and its approach toward sovereignty and intervention also aims to quietly balance the United States and shape China's regional security environment in ways more consistent with Chinese interests. At times, this entails China's greater support for interventionism, as when China joined the international community to support the U.S.-led intervention against Afghanistan in 2001 and cooperated on counterterrorism activities with the United States and other international partners. In other cases, China did not overtly oppose certain interventions, such as the U.S. invasion of Iraq in 2003.

However, China's more flexible approach to questions of sovereignty and intervention will continue to have important limitations. Beijing has tended to resist stepped-up and more robust involvement of the international community, including military action, to address concerns in countries such as Sudan and Iran. Overall, Beijing seeks a greater, consensus-based role for international and regional mechanisms, as opposed to ceding to the unilateral actions of the United States or other major powers. For example, Beijing is interested in seeing the United Nations and the UN Security Council (where China has a permanent seat and veto power) continue to play a central role in defining the international response to regional security crises. Beijing's experience with the Kosovo intervention in 1999—in which the United States and the North Atlantic Treaty Organization took matters into their own hands, circumventing the United Nations over China's strenuous objections—is especially instructive and marked an important turning point in Chinese views toward interventionism. In the face of a more unilateralist

America, and in order to retain some influence for itself and the United Nations on issues of international security, China had to rethink its approach to questions of sovereignty and intervention. The Kosovo experience reinforced a desire in Beijing to be more engaged in the United Nations so as to help shape the norms and responses regarding intervention by the international community. Evidence of its new and more flexible approach was seen almost immediately in China's response to the East Timor crisis in 1999, in which China accepted a humanitarian justification for using force, authorized chapter 7 action by a non-UN force as well as a UN force, and contributed a sizable civilian police contingent for the first time. More recently, Beijing played an important but behind-the-scene role in placing political and economic pressure on North Korea and Sudan. In the former case, such pressure was intended to bring North Korea back to the six-party talks. In the latter, Beijing sought and gained Sudan's acceptance of a larger United Nations role in support of African Union peacekeepers operating in Sudan.

The United States and the international community as a whole need to take greater note of how and whether China's policies and practice on questions of sovereignty and intervention signal a more flexible and pragmatic approach. Such assessments by the international community need to be tempered with a sober understanding of China's hard-headed views on certain sovereignty questions, such as Taiwan. Moreover, China's lingering, traditional concerns about sovereignty and intervention—especially with regard to what it perceives as excessive American unilateralism and hegemony—may often constrain an even more supportive Chinese position vis-à-vis interventionism by the international community. However, overall, China's new security diplomacy has led to a more pragmatic and constructive approach to these issues than in the past, and that inclination will likely continue, though certainly not always smoothly. While not as advanced or proactive as China's policies toward regional security mechanisms or nonproliferation, Beijing's changing approach to sovereignty and intervention merits closer scrutiny and raises interesting challenges and opportunities for the international community, for regional security, and for U.S. interests.

5

Challenges for U.S. Policy

In short, when handling Sino-US relations, we must see both the favorable and the difficult aspects. At times when Sino-US relations improve and develop, we must keep clear heads and think of danger in times of peace. At a time when Sino-US relations encounter difficulties and setbacks, we must deal with things in a composed fashion and keep firm confidence in victory. . . . We should struggle by our wits and boldness, not with rage, and should not strive for temporary joy or temporary superiority.

—China's Vice Premier Qian Qichen, September 2002

Our strategy seeks to encourage China to make the right strategic choices for its people while we hedge against other possibilities.

—National Security Strategy of the United States, March 2006

The preceding chapters demonstrate that by and large China has increasingly carried out global and regional security policies convergent with international norms, regional expectations, and U.S. interests and aimed at improving its image and position in world affairs. However, potentially serious challenges and uncertainties lie ahead over the medium to longer term. Having made gains in security and diplomatic terms through the exercise of its new security diplomacy—and with the likelihood that further gains lie ahead—Beijing will find itself in an increasingly better position to achieve more self-interested goals on its own terms and in its own favor. These might include resolving its disputes with Taiwan on its own terms; controlling outcomes for the nuclear standoff on the Korean peninsula; challenging Japan for regional leadership; deflecting international pressures on regimes such as Burma, Iran, and Sudan; and extending its military power in the region.

Quote by Vice Premier Qian Qichen taken from his speech "The International Situation and Sino-US Relations since the 11 September Incident," appearing in *Waijiao Xueyuan Xuebao* [*Foreign Affairs College Journal*], no. 3, September 25, 2002, pp. 1–6, and translated in Foreign Broadcast Information Service, *Daily Report: China,* CPP20021015000192. The National Security Strategy of the United States of America can be accessed at www.whitehouse.gov/nsc/nss/2006/nss2006.pdf.

Given long-standing security interests of the United States, especially in the Asia-Pacific region, these potential challenges are of particular concern. In the framework of this book, these concerns arise in three broad areas. First, regarding China's evolving approach to alliances and regional security mechanisms, the United States should keep a watchful eye on China-Taiwan relations, China-Japan relations, the North Korea nuclear standoff, alternative structures to the U.S. alliance system (especially in Asia), and China's partnerships with U.S. friends and allies. Second, regarding China's new security diplomacy and its approach to arms control and nonproliferation, U.S. policymakers will need to deflect challenges arising out of specific and persistent Chinese proliferation activities and out of differences on how the global arms control agenda should proceed. Third, regarding Beijing's policies on questions of sovereignty and intervention, the United States should expect continuing challenges from China in its approach to objectionable and threatening regimes and in gaining greater Chinese cooperation in carrying out counterterrorism and humanitarian intervention measures worldwide.

Alliances and Regional Security Mechanisms

As explained in chapter 2, formal alliances play no role in China's current security strategy, and China has had ill-fated experiences in the past with alliances and other security coalitions, both as a participant in alliances and as a target of them. As part of its new security diplomacy, however, Beijing has embraced participation in a range of security-related mechanisms such as bilateral partnerships and confidence-building measures, the Shanghai Cooperation Organization (SCO), the Association of Southeast Asian Nations Regional Forum (ARF), and various multilateral approaches.

However, many Chinese strategists remain wary of U.S.-led security mechanisms and alliances, as they could embolden what China sees as American unilateralism and hegemony, could raise regional tensions, and could be directed against China either as part of a general containment strategy or, more particularly, during a conflict over Taiwan. While official Chinese statements about the U.S. alliance system have moderated somewhat in recent years, many questions remain about China's medium- and long-term views about the role and value of U.S. alliances, especially those in Asia. Official Chinese statements in recent years "do not oppose" American alliances, but at the same time, in the view of many Chinese, U.S. alliances remain "historical remnants" that will fade with time; they must be directed at a certain "enemy," hence may be intended to "contain" or (with regard to Taiwan) "split" China; and they represent American hegemonic efforts, which run counter to the general trend of the post–cold war era toward cooperative security and a more multipolar world. Many key strategic thinkers in China find the post–September 11, 2001, environment all the more worrisome for Chinese security precisely because it has helped reinvigorate existing U.S. alliances and created new opportunities and justifications for the United States to bolster military relations with new states, many of them on China's doorstep, such as Afghanistan, Pakistan, India, Mongolia, Kazakhstan, and Kyrgyzstan.

Five challenging areas stand out for the United States in how China's new security diplomacy approaches alliances and regional security mechanisms: China-Taiwan-U.S. relations; China-Japan-U.S. relations; differences over the resolution of the North Korea nuclear standoff; the emergence of alternatives to the U.S. alliance system, especially in Asia; and China's partnerships with U.S. allies.

CHINA-TAIWAN-U.S. RELATIONS

Beijing's relations with Taiwan, like those with Japan, have often proven an exception to the country's new security diplomacy. Indeed, no issue so challenges the application of China's new security diplomacy, or so undermines attempts to convince the international community of China's peaceful rise, than Beijing's policies toward Taiwan. Events in 2005, such as the passage of Anti-Secession Law in China, have some observers asking, "Have old problems trumped new thinking?" and commenting that "on diplomatic policies . . . Beijing has appeared bullying, emotional, and ineffective. These outcomes do not match the Chinese Communist Party's self-styled image as a peaceful, responsible, and constructive rising power."[1] China's approach to Taiwan has obvious challenging implications not only for China's new security diplomacy but also for U.S.-China relations, for Beijing's views of American alliances and other security relationships in the region, and for the way China chooses to take part in regional security mechanisms and confidence-building measures.

Taiwan's population is less than 2 percent of China's, and the island itself is less than 0.5 percent of Chinese territory. Yet the differences across the Taiwan Strait, the Chinese approach to Taiwan, and the U.S. and U.S.-allied involvement in the Taiwan issue stand out as major potential trouble spots for peace and stability in the region. At the heart of the Chinese position toward Taiwan is its "one China" principle and its notion of "one country, two systems." For the vast majority of mainland Chinese and all of the Chinese leadership, the issue of sovereignty over Taiwan is not really a question at all and is certainly not open to negotiation; the only outcome for China is reunification, and by force, if necessary.[2]

From the Chinese perspective, its sovereign claim to Taiwan is rooted in history, legal interpretations, subtle diplomatic language, and, perhaps most important, raw emotion. The Taiwan issue deeply resonates with China's humiliation at the hands of foreign powers during the period the Chinese call the *bainian guochi*, or the "century of national humiliation" (especially with regard to Japan and Japan's occupation of Taiwan between 1895 and 1945). The blame for Taiwan's continued separation from China is often laid at the feet of malign foreign intent, with obvious implications for the role of the United States and the U.S.-Japan alliance in defending Taiwan against China. Moreover, China's claims to sovereignty over Taiwan are also linked to questions of national stability, regime survival, and legitimacy for the rulers in Beijing. Although the issue is rarely mentioned in public documents, open-source analyses by Chinese scholars as well as discussions with Chinese policymakers and leaders make clear their view of what the "loss" of Taiwan could mean to China: the chaotic breakup of China and the downfall of the Chinese Communist Party. Having installed themselves in power in 1949 in part on their claim of ousting foreign influence and bringing the motherland together, the Chinese leadership is especially sensitive to what they see as their uncompleted mission of fully unifying the country by bringing Taiwan back into the fold. Indeed, the Chinese Communist Party leadership has so unwaveringly insisted on the recovery of Taiwan under the one-China principle and the one country, two systems formula, they leave themselves almost no room to fail.

China's threatening missile tests into the waters around Taiwan in 1995–96, its continuing missile buildup opposite Taiwan, and its military modernization focused on a Taiwan contingency all demonstrate the seriousness with which Beijing takes the Taiwan question. The passage of the Anti-Secession Law by the National People's Congress (NPC) in early 2005 provides another good example of how insistent the Chinese leadership intends to be on this issue. At a time when cross-strait relations were at their most stable in years, the NPC sent a very negative message by passing a law that states, in part:

In the event that the "Taiwan independence" secessionist forces should act under any name or by any means to cause the fact of Taiwan's secession from China, or that major incidents entailing Taiwan's secession from China should occur, or that possibilities for a peaceful reunification should be completely exhausted, the state shall employ nonpeaceful means and other necessary measures to protect China's sovereignty and territorial integrity.[3]

In spite of this position, there has been some encouraging news out of Beijing regarding its Taiwan policy. By the early to mid-1980s and continuing into the 1990s, China's approach toward Taiwan exhibited some signs of flexibility and pragmatism. Over this period, China welcomed Taiwan investment on the mainland, the primacy of "peaceful reunification" was emphasized, and Beijing began calling for *san tong*, the "three links" of direct cross-strait postal service, trade, and communications, and *si lu*, or the "four exchanges": academic, cultural, economic, and athletic interactions. Chinese President Jiang Zemin's "eight-point proposal" of January 1995 claimed that China would not challenge "nongovernmental economic and cultural ties by Taiwan with other countries" nor Taiwan's membership as an economic entity in certain international organizations. While not renouncing the use of force, if necessary, to achieve reunification, Jiang emphasized that peaceful reunification should be the goal, "since Chinese should not fight fellow Chinese."[4]

There have even been some indications that China is prepared to offer a more flexible definition of the idea of one China and of the concept of one country, two systems, which have been perennial sticking points between the two sides. Beijing usually employs the formula: "there is one China, and Taiwan is a part of it," implying Taiwan's subordinate status. However, in remarks made in August 2000 by Vice Premier Qian Qichen, China's foreign policy eminence grise, this formula changed. Qian said, "With regard to cross-strait relations, the one China principle we stand for is that there is only one China in the world; the mainland and Taiwan all belong to one China; and China's sovereignty and territorial integrity are indivisible."[5] This subtle change suggested that the mainland and Taiwan could both be treated as parts of China, without stating which is a subordinate part of the other. Critics argued that this more accommodating definition of the mainland-Taiwan relationship only appeared in discussions Qian had with foreigners and did not have high-profile authority. The language disappeared from official Chinese statements as tensions mounted between Beijing and the leader of Taiwan, President Chen Shui-bian, in the early 2000s.

What flexibility there is in Beijing's approach reflects a necessary and pragmatic reaction to evolving realities on Taiwan. Beginning in the mid-1980s under President Chiang Ching-kuo, and continuing when Lee Teng-hui took the presidential office in 1988, the Taiwan government started down the path of greater social and political liberalization and multiparty democratization, formally abandoned its claim to sovereignty over the mainland, and under the presidency of Lee Teng-hui initiated the widely popular effort of "Taiwanization," to establish a distinct Taiwan political identity, distinct from Communist China on the mainland. Under Lee Teng-hui, certain quarters of Taiwan politics also came to more eagerly embrace the idea of de facto independence from the mainland, as embodied by Lee's call in July 1999 that the two sides conduct their bilateral affairs on the basis of "special state-to-state relations." The full blossoming of Taiwan democracy and the Taiwanization of the island's politics came together with the closely fought presidential election and the victory of Democratic Progressive Party candidate Chen Shui-bian in March 2000. This marked not only the first democratic alternation of party power in Chinese history but also the ascendance to the Taiwan presidency of a career-long advocate of Taiwan independence. Overall, China's strategy has remained unchanged and has even hardened somewhat: strict adherence to the one-China principle, continued diminishment of Taiwan's diplomatic presence abroad, and a strengthened capability to use force if necessary. But tactics have changed: courting opposition politicians on Taiwan, providing incentives to bolster Taiwan business interest in the mainland, and allowing greater academic, cultural, and person-to-person exchanges.

Through this process, cross-strait interaction and exchange has reached an unprecedented intensity, in spite of periodic setbacks. For example, in January 2005 the two sides agreed to allow direct charter flights between the countries during the Chinese New Year, the first since 1949. A succession of landmark visits by Taiwan politicians began in the spring of 2005: Kuomintang (KMT) Vice Chairman Chiang Pinkung in March, KMT Chairman Lien Chan and People First Party Chairman James Soong in April, and New Party Chairman Yok Muming in July. These visits, which included meetings with senior Chinese officials, including Prime Minister Wen Jiabao and President Hu Jintao, signaled a new turn in cross-strait relations, though with these moves Beijing purposefully kept Chen Shui-bian, the elected leader of Taiwan, isolated.

Economic integration across the Taiwan Strait continued to deepen. Even before the Taiwan government lifted its ban on direct investment on the mainland in 2001, businesses circumvented official policy and poured an estimated US$60 billion to US$100 billion into China, a total growing by US$5 billion to US$10 billion a year. In the first nine months of 2004, investment increased by 47 percent over 2003. The mainland is Taiwan's largest trading partner as well as its number-one export market. Total cross-strait trade in 2004 reached US$61.6 billion, a 33 percent increase over 2003. There are an estimated 750,000 to 1 million Taiwanese businessmen and their families now living on the mainland. China is also becoming increasingly dependent on Taiwanese investment, expertise, and trade to maintain its economic growth and stem unemployment. According to one estimate, in 2003, 40 percent of mainland exports came from Taiwan-invested firms, and Taiwan business made up 65 percent of the investment in China's expanding high-tech sector; Taiwan's imports from China, mainly light-industrial products and steel, reached US$18.8 billion in 2004.[6]

In spite of some encouraging signs in cross-strait relations, the strategic situation there remains uncertain and potentially volatile. The close interest the United States has in the peaceful resolution of the China-Taiwan dispute means that Beijing and Washington face off directly—and could directly clash militarily—on such issues as China's forceful assertion of sovereignty over Taiwan, American intervention on the Taiwan side, and the comparative willingness of the two sides to use force in seeing their interests served in the Taiwan Strait. Indeed, Beijing interprets many of the most contentious issues between the United States and China through the lens of the Taiwan issue. In addition, the framework for handling the Taiwan question between Washington and Beijing, first constructed as the two sides sought a compatible rapprochement in the early and mid-1970s, has come under new pressures unforeseen at the time, particularly with political changes on Taiwan since the late 1980s and early 1990s.

The fact that under almost any scenario for U.S. intervention in the Taiwan Strait, Washington would need to rely on support from its allies, especially Japan, presents further challenges to U.S. and Chinese approaches toward the proper role of alliances and regional security mechanisms. To the degree that regional alliances—such as those between the United States and Japan and the United States and Australia—are structured and strengthened, both militarily and politically, to intervene in the Taiwan Strait or to otherwise prevent the reunification of Taiwan with China, Chinese appreciation for U.S.-led alliances and other security relationships in the region diminishes. On the other hand, China's participation in regional security mechanisms and other security-related confidence-building measures is predicated on the parties' agreement that the Taiwan question not form part of their discussions; in many cases, such as within the Shanghai Cooperation Organization, Beijing demands that the parties frequently reiterate the one-China principle as part of their official communiqués.

CHINA-JAPAN-U.S. RELATIONS

As with Taiwan, China's strained relations with Japan contrast sharply with its diplomatic successes elsewhere, especially when compared to vastly improved relations with such former foes as India, Russia, and Vietnam. Instead, China's bilateral relations with Japan are characterized by emotionally raw historical memories coupled with the contemporary emergence of strategic competition for economic resources and regional primacy.[7] As Japan is a close and powerful regional neighbor with a range of contending interests with China, Chinese officials and strategists naturally view the U.S.-Japan alliance with concern and suspicion. This is particularly true regarding the role the alliance would play in defending Taiwan against Chinese coercion or attack. More deeply, because of Japan's record of aggression against China over the first half of the twentieth century, Chinese strategists harbor a special loathing and deep misgiving for Japanese military activities in general, and within the U.S.-Japan alliance in particular.[8]

Again, the Taiwan issue is not deep below the surface. One of the most humiliating experiences during China's "century of shame" was its first war with Japan during that period (1894–95): Japan crushed the Chinese fleet and land armies and took possession of Taiwan and the Pescadores, which they held for the next sixty years. As such, China's general concerns with the U.S. alliance-based regional security system are all the more troubling to Beijing in the case of Japan. Of particular concern in the post–cold war era is what Beijing views as fundamental shifts in the thinking of the U.S.-Japan alliance. In this view, with the demise of the Soviet Union, the raison d'être of the alliance has shifted from containing the Soviets to containing China, and the alliance has moved from an essentially defensive to an essentially offensive organization. The expansion of Japan's regional security role (especially in the post–September 11, 2001, period) and Japan's increasing conservative nationalism (symbolized by the visits by the Japanese prime minister to the Yasukuni Shrine) generate especially strong concerns in China.

Chinese official anxiety about the U.S.-Japan alliance has increased considerably since the mid-1990s and has particularly intensified since 2001. China's concerns toward Japan and the U.S.-Japan alliance increased with developments in 1995–96, such as Chinese missile firings against Taiwan and especially the April 1996 U.S.-Japan decision to revise the alliance defense guidelines. These new guidelines emerged from the Clinton-Hashimoto summit of April 1996, when the two sides agreed to initiate a review of the 1978

Guidelines for Japan-U.S. Defense Cooperation and to focus on the need to "promote bilateral policy coordination, including studies on bilateral cooperation in dealing with situations that may emerge in the areas surrounding Japan and that will have an important influence on the peace and security of Japan."[9]

For China, the most controversial aspect of the guidelines was their consideration of "situations in areas surrounding Japan," as this phrase envisioned a potentially more robust Japanese military response in situations beyond the basic defense of the Japanese home islands, especially regarding Taiwan. More broadly, Chinese views of the U.S.-Japan alliance and the revised defense guidelines rejected the argument that the alliance was necessary to handle loosely defined threats to regional security. Chinese analysts not only believed that such regional threats in East Asia were abating or did not exist but also understood such language as a thinly veiled reference to containing China. Chinese strategists were particularly concerned that a new purpose of the alliance would be to deal with Chinese threats to Taiwan, including armed intervention and direct military conflict with China. As Chinese leaders became more impatient about reunifying Taiwan and China, so too the realization grew that U.S. defense commitments to Taiwan relied very heavily on operations and logistics support based in Japan. Chinese analysts understood that the combination of enhanced alliance responsibility for Tokyo and the U.S. policy of "strategic ambiguity" toward Taiwan increased the chances that Japan would be involved in a Taiwan contingency.[10] Finally, the new defense guidelines confirmed even more strongly for Chinese observers their view that Japan was intent on returning to its militaristic past.

Thus, Chinese analysts believed that, rather than having the alliance work to constrain Japanese militarism, the United States was actually empowering Japanese militarism. With the issuance of the Armitage Report in the fall of 2000, which strongly advocated a far more robust U.S.-Japan alliance, and the ascent to political power of many of its adherents in the first administration of George W. Bush, Chinese concerns deepened.[11] In the immediate aftermath of September 11, 2001, Chinese concerns about increasing Japanese military power were comparatively muted but have intensified with time. Without a difficult constitutional debate about its use of military assets, Japan acted swiftly in October and November 2001 to dispatch a Japanese naval force to the Indian Ocean in support of the U.S.-led counterterrorism war in Afghanistan. This was the most dramatic expansion of Japan's security role since World War II and signaled an important step in strengthening the U.S.-Japan alliance.

Additional irritants emerged regarding regional security, further testing relations and reminding all sides of how the U.S.-Japan alliance is enmeshed in China-Japan disputes. Following an incursion by a Chinese submarine into the waters off Okinawa in November 2004, Japan unveiled new defense policy guidelines in December 2004, allowing a greater role for its armed forces in international military operations, while reaffirming its pacifist constitution and naming China as a possible military threat for the first time.[12] In response, China expressed "deep concern over the major readjustments of Japan's military and security strategy and the possible impacts arising thereof."[13] Subsequently, China expressed "grave concern" over the U.S.-Japan joint statement issued in February 2005, which declared Taiwan as a common security issue.[14] A Chinese Foreign Ministry spokesman called the U.S.-Japan security alliance "a bilateral scheme spawned during the cold war period," which "should not function beyond the bilateral framework," adding that "the Chinese government and Chinese people firmly oppose the U.S.-Japan statement on the Taiwan issue, which concerns China's sovereignty, territorial integrity, and national security."[15]

At a high political level, China-Japan relations suffered as well. The last state visit by a Chinese leader to Japan was the disastrous trip by Jiang Zemin in 1998, and Koizumi Junichiro spent only one day in China in 2001. When Koizumi became the first Japanese leader since 1985 to resume visits to the controversial Yasukuni Shrine—in which fourteen convicted Japanese war criminals are memorialized among Japan's war dead—it touched off a firestorm of protests from China and other countries in the region. The row over Japan's colonial legacy boiled over at the beginning of April 2005, when anti-Japanese riots broke out in several major Chinese cities, including Beijing, Shanghai, Guangzhou, and Shenzhen, protesting Japan's new history textbooks. In Beijing, 10,000 protestors marched through the streets and threw stones at the Japanese embassy; in other cities, Japanese businesses were attacked and a boycott called on Japanese goods.[16] An online petition against Japan's bid for a permanent seat on the UN Security Council garnered more than 22 million Chinese signatures.[17] At the time, Chinese officials deemed the relationship at its lowest point since the establishment of diplomatic relations in 1972.[18]

The painful history between the two nations continues to touch off sensitivities among the Chinese public that are increasingly in conflict with growing impatience over the subject among the Japanese public, leading to rising nationalism on both sides, which neither government can afford to ignore but which undermines bilateral relations. The visit to China of newly elected Japanese Prime Minister Shinzo Abe in October 2006 set an initally more positive tone for the relationship, but Beijing will continue to eye Japan and the U.S.-Japan alliance warily.

DIFFERENCES OVER NORTH KOREA

The United States and China have broad common interests in the Korean peninsula. Both wish to see a denuclearized and stable Korean peninsula at peace with its neighbors and not a source for broader regional tensions. Both the United States and China wish to see this outcome realized through diplomatic and peaceable means. However, the two sides differ over how to prioritize those ends and how they will be achieved.[19]

To begin, China seeks stability first and foremost on the Korean peninsula, especially in the near to medium term, even if it means tolerating the Pyongyang regime. North Korea's proximity to China—sharing a 1,400-kilometer (about 900-mile) border—unavoidably makes Beijing lean toward a go-slow, diplomatic approach that abjures disruptiveness. If and as instabilities arise in North Korea—whether from famine, political turmoil, or war—China can expect an influx of even more economic and political refugees. An estimated 300,000 North Koreans illegally live in China, mostly in China's economically distressed northeast. More refugees would increase pressures on the area's economic and political capacities and could even stir nationalist passions among China's ethnic Korean population along the Jilin Province–North Korea border.

Beijing's strong preference for stability supports its second priority: China wishes to see the evolution of political and economic outcomes on the peninsula favor Chinese interests. To put it in other terms, Beijing would prefer over time the emergence of a friendly, reunified peninsula that falls within China's geostrategic orbit. This helps explain Beijing's carefully crafted two-Korea policy, which since the early 1990s has allowed Beijing to develop relations with both Koreas. This approach also means that China would oppose solutions it sees as unilaterally imposed by the United States, such as the use of force or other coercion, which could result in outcomes favoring American, rather than Chinese, interests. Beijing would also want to avoid a rapid political and economic collapse in Pyongyang, not only for the potential refugee problem described above but also because such a scenario would probably entail a major U.S. political and military influence, if not presence, in North Korea for humanitarian, stabilization, and reconstruction purposes.

Such a scenario would add to the likelihood that political and economic outcomes on the peninsula would favor American over Chinese interests.

The third, and narrower, priority for Beijing concerns the realization of a nonnuclear Korean peninsula. Even before North Korea's nuclear test in 2006, Beijing understood that a nuclear-armed North Korea would create regional security problems, which would have a negative impact on China's security interests. Beijing is concerned with the possibility of North Korean nuclear weapons use and the possible transfer of North Korean nuclear materials and know-how to terrorists. However, unlike Washington, China does not sense a direct threat either from North Korean nuclear weapons themselves or from substate actors utilizing North Korean nuclear materials in terrorist acts against China. Rather, Beijing's concerns have to do with the broader ripple effects those weapons might have on regional security and Chinese regional interests. Hence Chinese negotiators continue to press for diplomatic solutions to forestall what Beijing would see as disastrous responses from others, such as an American military strike, a more military-oriented Japan, and steadily strengthening U.S.-Japan alliance ties. Japan's moves to develop and deploy missile defenses in cooperation with the United States—in part a response to the North Korean threat—are not viewed favorably in Beijing, especially to the extent those systems strengthen Japanese and U.S.-Japan allied postures during a Taiwan-related confrontation with China. In the wake of North Korea's nuclear test, Beijing was reluctant to support hard-hitting sanctions but in the end came to support United Nations Security Council resolution 1718 and a set of limited economic sanctions. Beijing also reportedly undertook certain unilateral actions of its own, such as curtailing food and energy shipments to North Korea and restricting financial transactions with North Korea.

Looking ahead further, the United States and China may differ on longer-range goals on the Korean peninsula. For example, with regard to developing a sustainable regional security approach toward North Korea, China's overarching goals are to constrain the role of American bilateral alliances in the resolution of Washington-Pyongyang tensions, to draw the United States toward a more accommodating stance vis-à-vis North Korea, and to urge either a direct U.S.–North Korea bilateral negotiation or a bilateral negotiation within a broad, multilateral framework in which China would have a key role in shaping outcomes. Washington has expressed some interest in a permanent multilateral framework for Northeast Asian security but will likely continue to look to its bilateral security alliances, especially with Japan and South Korea, to ensure stability on the Korean peninsula.

ALTERNATIVES TO U.S. ALLIANCES

A part of China's new security diplomacy has been to foster the development of region-based mechanisms and confidence-building measures. These groupings are interesting for the role Beijing has played in their formation and continued development, in the notable lack of U.S. participation in some of the groups, and the way they appear to present an alternative to the traditional U.S.-led alliance structure for regional security in Asia. The Shanghai Cooperation Organization and the East Asia Summit are leading examples of China's new security diplomacy in this regard, presenting potential challenges to U.S. interests in the region.

From its beginning as the Shanghai Five, and since its founding in 2001, the SCO has issued veiled criticism of U.S. security policies and practices. For example, the Shanghai Five Dushanbe statement in 2000 censured the U.S.-led NATO intervention in Yugoslavia while also criticizing what it termed "bloc-based, closed" regional missile defense systems, which would "undermine stability and peace . . . and lead to an escalated arms race in the Asia-Pacific." The statement also opposed the inclusion of Taiwan in any U.S.-led regional missile defense system.[20] In opposing outside interference in the region's political affairs, the Chinese media added that the document asserts the right of "every state . . . to choose its own political system, economic model, and path of social development, affirming that the five countries will support each other to safeguard their state sovereignty, independence, territorial integrity, and social stability."[21]

The founding document of the organization gave a high profile to the stated principles of China's new security diplomacy and provided an alternative security approach for the region: "The Shanghai Cooperation Organization firmly adhere[s] to the goals and principles of the Charter of the United Nations, the principles of mutual respect of independence, sovereignty and territorial integrity, equality, and mutual benefit, the solution of all issues through mutual consultations, noninterference in internal affairs, nonuse of military force or threat of force, [and] renunciation of unilateral military superiority in contiguous areas." In 2002, consistent with official Chinese positions, the SCO urged that counterterrorist activities be conducted in accordance with the United Nations Charter and other international norms and not adopt "double standards."[22]

Most controversially, as part of its annual leadership statement, the SCO in July 2005 called upon the coalition carrying out antiterrorist activities in Afghanistan to provide a timeline for their eventual withdrawal from bases in

Central Asia. The statement read, in part: "Considering the completion of the active military stage of antiterrorist operation in Afghanistan, the member states of the Shanghai Cooperation Organisation consider it necessary that respective members of the antiterrorist coalition set a final timeline for their temporary use of the above-mentioned objects of infrastructure and stay of their military contingents on the territories of the SCO member states."[23]

While not specifically naming the United States and its allies, the statement reflects a concern by China and others in the region about the long-term intentions of Washington and its allies in Central Asia and about America's security role in the region overall. SCO member state Uzbekistan was more forthright and in July 2005 ordered the United States to withdraw its forces from Uzbekistan within six months, which was accomplished by the end of November that year. In late November 2005 Uzbekistan prohibited European members of NATO from using Uzbek bases or airspace for coalition operations in Afghanistan, effective January 1, 2006.[24] At the annual leadership summit of the SCO in 2006, Iran was invited to participate as an observer at the same time that the international community—especially the United States and the EU-3 grouping of Germany, France, and the United Kingdom—were attempting to bring greater pressures on Teheran to halt its nuclear ambitions. It is difficult to assess the precise role China had in these decisions, but as a leading member of the SCO, China was certainly in a strong position to shape, if not actually to promote, them. There is little doubt Beijing was partially behind the call for U.S. and allied withdrawal from Central Asia, and Beijing undermined U.S. interests by supporting the invitation to the Iranian president to attend the SCO summit.

Similarly, there are concerns that Beijing had a role in seeing to the exclusion of the United States from the first East Asia Summit (EAS), which took place in December 2005. Participation in the EAS required joining the ASEAN Treaty of Amity and Cooperation in Southeast Asia, a step the United States has thus far not taken. According to a Department of State official, while the United States and ASEAN have "discussed the Treaty of Amity and Cooperation in the past, the United States has no current plans to sign the agreement" owing to "concerns about the text, including the rights of non-ASEAN members."[25] While this criterion for membership was publicly put forward by ASEAN states, it was widely reported that China had a quiet but influential role behind the decision not to include the United States, as part of a strategic plan to limit U.S. influence in the region. The *Wall Street Journal* opined, "Beijing's effort to exclude the U.S. is a raw show of China's new political muscle. Over time, a body without U.S. participation will tend to define itself in opposition to American purposes." Warning that the EAS is likely a precursor to the formation of an "East Asian Community" that will discuss political and military as well as economic issues, the *Journal* said that the EAS "offers Beijing an opportunity to fashion and dominate a new regional power axis, as opposed to the trans-Pacific organizations in which America plays an important role."[26]

On the other hand, it was also argued that focusing on China's role overlooks that fact that "Asia's lack of enthusiasm to include the U.S. in the [EAS]" should not come as a surprise, as "many Southeast Asian governments are frustrated by Washington's myopic focus on the 'war on terrorism' in the region, to the exclusion of regional concerns."[27] Malaysian officials have also been critical of Washington's reluctance to sign the Treaty of Amity and Cooperation in Southeast Asia, saying that "no country in the world that does not wish any harm to the countries of the region should have any difficulty in acceding to the treaty."[28] It should also be noted that even some treaty signatories, including Russia, Pakistan, and Mongolia, were not invited to join the initial EAS meeting as full members.

Chinese officials have been at pains to soothe American fears. In numerous public statements, China has stated that it is "always willing to be an advocate, supporter, and participant in the EAC [East Asia Community], while ASEAN countries should play a role of 'driver' for the EAC construction."[29] Cui Tiankai, Foreign Ministry Asian affairs chief, told reporters: "Why would China want to drive the U.S. out of Asia while we ourselves are opening our doors even wider for the American presence.... We recognize the U.S. long history and interests here. There is no intention to drive out the U.S."[30] Nevertheless, in spite of these points, as well as the inclusion of U.S. allies Japan, South Korea, and Australia in the EAS, concerns in Washington continue about the role of China in promoting regional cooperation and security dialogues in the absence of the United States. Depending on the course the EAS takes, such developments can be the source of additional tensions between the United States and China in the years ahead.

CHINA AND U.S. ALLIES

Strategic relations between China and European partners—both with the European Union and with individual member states—have become increasingly regularized, institutionalized, and mutually beneficial, encompassing a broadening range of political, economic, military, scientific, technological, educational, and cultural ties. Deepening security ties between Chinese and European partners will possibly encompass convergent views on the appropriate structure of the international security system as well as cooperation in a range of militarily relevant activities, from dual-use technology development, to military exercises, to military applications of the Galileo satellite navigation system.

Closer Europe-China relations already affect American interests: Europe-China ties are clearly moving in the direction of deeper, more constructive, and more positive political and security relations, which tend to see far greater opportunities than threats in one another. Indeed, the EU as well as many individual European countries have established strategic partnerships with China characterized by regular, senior-level contacts, including security and defense consultations and a range of concrete, cooperative programs across public and private sectors. The EU and China hold an annual summit, the ninth of which took place in September 2006. Both China and the EU issued major policy documents in October 2003, which outlined their relationship and aimed for a continued strongly positive strategic relationship overall.

A similar case might be made for how China's new security diplomacy has helped foster closer relations with other U.S. allies, such as Australia and South Korea. Statements by Australian Prime Minister John Howard and Foreign Minister Alexander Downer suggest that China has strengthened relations with Australia relative to U.S.-Australia relations. Foreign Minister Downer, during his August 2004 visit to China, was asked whether the pursuit of a strategic partnership between Australia and China would contradict Australian commitments to its alliance with the United States, especially in the context of a conflict in the Taiwan Strait, in which Washington might seek Canberra's military help. Downer questioned whether the U.S.-Australian alliance treaty, the ANZUS pact, would require Australia to join the United States to intervene in the case of a conflict across the Taiwan Strait. He added:

> The ANZUS Treaty is invoked in the event of one of our two countries, Australia or the United States, being attacked. So some other military activity elsewhere in the world . . . does not automatically invoke the ANZUS Treaty. . . . [W]hat we are seeing through what Premier Wen said to me about building a strategic relationship between Australia and China is a significant development, . . . China has seen Australia in years gone by as an important economic partner and a less important political and strategic partner, and I think now there is a recognition by Chinese leadership [of] the significant role that Australia plays in the

region, for all sorts of reasons, value for both of us, not just for one of us, but for both of us, to work much more closely together on political and security issues in the region . . . . But I think we are seeing the evolution of a much stronger and much fuller relationship which encompasses many challenges of the Asia Pacific region of the political and security nature, not just of an economic nature. And this is, as I say, evolutionary, but it's something that I think is profoundly important in Australian foreign policy over the medium term.[31]

During Prime Minister Howard's summit meeting with President Bush in Washington a year later, the two leaders were asked to comment on their respective approaches to China. President Bush stressed the "complexity" and difficulties in U.S. relations with China, from economic questions to democratic values, while Prime Minister Howard focused on Australian interests in a positive relationship with China, saying "we are unashamed in developing our relations with China, and I am well pleased with the way the economic relationship has developed. And I'll continue to do everything I can in the interests of Australia to ensure that it develops further."[32] Citing Prime Minister Howard's comments, Hugh White, a leading Australian strategic policy analyst, argued that "Australia, by its support for China's growing regional influence, is promoting a profound transformation in the strategic architecture of Asia, with immense implications for Australia's future security, including our alliance with the U.S." He concluded that "Australia's interests would be best served if the U.S. would allow China a somewhat bigger regional role, in return for China allowing Japan a larger say in regional affairs" and that Washington and Canberra need to begin a more serious dialogue on the future of U.S.-China-Australia relations in the Asia-Pacific region.[33]

It is also clear that Australians in general have had an increasingly favorable view toward China in recent years, especially with regard to economic relations—and in ways that compare quite favorably to attitudes toward the United States. A poll taken by the Sydney-based Lowy Institute in February 2005 found that, in identifying the greatest potential threats to Australia on the international scene, 32 percent and 25 percent of Australians were "very worried" or "fairly worried," respectively (or 57 percent of those polled), about U.S. foreign policy, while only 16 percent were "very worried" and 19 percent were "fairly worried" about China's growing power. By contrast, Islamic fundamentalism was also identified by 57 percent of those polled as being either very worrisome or fairly worrisome. When asked if Australia's commitment to the ANZUS pact should mean following the United States into war with China over Taiwan, 79 percent of respondents answered no. On trade issues, the Lowy poll found that 34 percent support the free trade agreement with the United States, while 51 percent believed it would be a good idea to pursue such an agreement with China. When asked to rate countries or groups based on either positive or negative feelings toward them, China received a positive rating from 69 percent of the respondents; the United States garnered a positive rating from 58 percent. In addition to China, others ranking above the United States were New Zealand, the United Kingdom, Europe, Japan, Singapore, France, the United Nations, Malaysia, and Papua New Guinea.[34] A polling study by the Chicago Council on Global Affairs in 2006 found that Australians gave China a 61-point mean favorability rating (of 100) while giving the United States a 62-point rating. When asked how much they trust the United States and China to "act responsibly in the world," 39 percent of Australian respondents said "not at all" or "not very much" about the United States; 38 percent had the same opinions about China.[35]

Similarly, China appears to be making favorable inroads into South Korean opinion relative to the United States, both at the official level and with the broader public. A part of this stems from deeper cultural ties between China and South Korea, but it also derives from long-standing nationalist tensions in South Korea over the U.S. presence in the country. Since the early 1990s and the opening of diplomatic relations between Beijing and Seoul, China has also carried out a successful "two-Korea policy" to maintain good relations with both North and South Korea. In recent years, and especially with the ascent to power of South Korean Presidents Kim Dae-jung and Roh Moo-hyun, who have favored a more accommodationist and engaged approach toward North Korea, Seoul and Beijing have opened up even greater common ground. Political tensions between the Bush administration and incumbent Korean presidents, as well as a number of negative incidents in South Korea involving American soldiers, have not helped matters and have left greater openings for China to build a generally positive profile in South Korea. China and South Korea are also forging common ground in their opposition to an expanded Japanese security presence in East Asia, which stirs anti-Japanese emotions in the two countries that were once victims of Japanese military occupation and atrocities during the first half of the twentieth century.

Some of these shifts are seen in a range of public opinion data and analyses taken in South Korea in recent years. For example, the Pew Global Attitudes Project recorded a growing anti-American sentiment in South Korea over 2002–03, as the percentage of respondents registering an unfavorable view of the United States grew from 44 to 50 percent. In the same survey, three-quarters of the South Koreans polled felt that South Korean interests are not taken into account when Washington makes international decisions. These trends were especially pronounced among younger persons in South Korea. In the Pew Global Attitudes Project poll in 2003, the share of younger persons (aged eighteen through twenty-nine) who expressed an unfavorable view of the United States had grown by 20 percent between 2002 and 2003 (from 51 to 71 percent). In answer to a poll question asked by the *Chosun Ilbo* in August 2002, "Which country would you side with if war broke out between North Korea and the United States?" about 66 percent of respondents aged sixteen to twenty-five sided with North Korea, while about 28 percent said the United States. In a *Chosun Ilbo* poll taken in August 2005, when young persons (aged sixteen to twenty-five) were asked to give countries a favorable rating, some 63 percent expressed a favorable opinion toward North Korea, while about 51 percent expressed a favorable opinion toward the United States.[36]

As South Korean negative views toward the United States increased, South Korean opinions regarding China moved in the opposite direction. Drawing from a range of opinion poll data between 1988 and 2001, a Rand Corporation study issued in 2004 found that "where more South Koreans held more favorable attitudes toward the U.S. than toward China from 1988 to 1994, net favorable assessment toward China has since caught up with—and on a number of occasions even surpassed—that for the U.S. Indeed, in July 2001, 73 percent of those polled had favorable attitudes toward China, whereas only 66 percent held favorable views of the U.S." The Rand study continued, "China's growing economic importance to South Korea and its increasingly important role in influencing North Korean behavior could well portend more favorable attitudes toward China, possibly even at the expense of attitudes toward the U.S." The study also cites work by William Watts, who surveyed South Korean opinion leaders between the ages of thirty and forty-nine in 2002. Slightly more than half of these individuals felt that relations with China would be more important to South Korea than ties to the United States in ten years' time.[37] South Koreans polled by the Chicago Council on Global Affairs survey in 2006 gave China a mean favorability rating of 57 (of 100), while giving the United States a 58-point rating. When asked how much they trust the United States and China to "act responsibly in the world," 53 percent of South Korean respondents said "not at all" or "not very much" about the United States; 61 percent had these opinions about China.[38]

In some cases, Beijing has misstepped. It appears Beijing has deliberately sought to take advantage of weakened U.S.-Europe relations to promote more pro-China positions within EU policy circles and in individual member states, a move that has been resisted in Europe given fundamentally shared interests across the Atlantic.[39] China's passage of the Anti-Secession Law targeting Taiwan in March 2005 led to predictably negative reactions in both the United States and Europe. It also helped dampen European attitudes toward China and was a major factor in the EU decision to postpone lifting the arms embargo on China. China has also blundered in its relations with South Korea. For example, the dispute that arose during the summer of 2004 between the two sides over historical claims to the Goguryeo Kingdom enflamed nationalist passions in both countries and soured South Korean attitudes toward China. Australian officials were annoyed and unnerved by the warning issued by He Yafei, director general of the North America and Oceania Department of the Chinese Foreign Ministry:

> We all know Taiwan is part of China and we do not want to see in any way the Taiwan issue become one of the elements that will be taken up by bilateral military alliances, be it Australia-US or Japan-US. . . . If there were any move by Australia and the US in terms of that alliance [ANZUS] that is detrimental to peace and stability in Asia, then [Australia] needs to be careful.[40]

Nevertheless, China's increased political, economic, and security-related ties with U.S. allies has engendered a new dynamic in these relationships, one that is more favorable to China and certain Chinese interests than in the past. These developments could have a negative impact on U.S. alliance relationships and on U.S. regional security interests more generally.

Nonprolilferation and Arms Control

Chapter 3 notes that differences over nonproliferation and arms control have persisted as some of the most contentious issues on the U.S.-China bilateral agenda for nearly twenty years. Moreover, owing to the cross-cutting nature of nonproliferation and arms control issues, they are not easily isolated from the other problematic areas in U.S.-China relations, such as arms sales to Taiwan, China's missile buildup opposite Taiwan, the U.S. deployment of ballistic missile defenses, the U.S.-China nuclear weapons dynamic, and the proliferation of weapons of mass destruction (WMD) in the Korean peninsula, the Persian Gulf, South Asia, and Southwest Asia. Washington's long-standing concern with China's proliferation activities gained additional salience in recent years with the possibility that countries pursuing WMD might transfer such capabilities to terrorists to use against the United States. To provide concrete examples of these problems, chapter 3 examines China's military-technical relationship with Iran and with Pakistan, China's approach to nuclear weapons and missile defenses, and the ongoing arms control stalemate between the United States and China in the UN Conference on Disarmament.

As the U.S. Central Intelligence Agency wrote in 2004, "Over the past several years, Beijing improved its nonproliferation posture through commitments to multilateral nonproliferation regimes, promulgation of expanded export controls, and strengthened oversight mechanisms, but the proliferation behavior of Chinese companies remains of great concern."[41] U.S. intelligence reporting continues to cite Chinese entities as suppliers of sensitive nuclear-, chemical-, and ballistic-missile-related technologies and components to Iran, and nuclear- and ballistic-missile-related technologies and assistance to Pakistan. The United States continues to issue sanctions against Chinese entities for their proliferation activities with such countries as Iran and Pakistan. On broader questions of nuclear weapons and arms control, Chinese strategists continue to harbor antagonistic views toward U.S. missile defense plans, and the country is engaged in a buildup of its nuclear and missile arsenal. Official policy in Beijing and Washington also strongly differs in many respects over how the global arms control agenda should proceed.

In short, while China has come a long way since the late 1980s in adopting norms and practices more consistent with the international community's approach to nonproliferation, many outstanding questions remain about China's basic political commitment and procedural approach to nonproliferation, not to mention its practical ability to fulfill its nonproliferation pledges. On the broader international arms control agenda, while Washington and Beijing forged an impressive set of accomplishments in the mid-to-late 1990s, the two sides more recently have drifted apart, especially on the question of nuclear disarmament and the use of weapons in outer space. As a result of such differences, nonproliferation and arms control issues will remain challenging in the U.S.-China bilateral agenda, and Beijing's policies may complicate and thwart U.S. interests on these issues.

U.S.-CHINA BILATERAL CONCERNS

Many of the most positive developments in China's approach to arms control and nonproliferation resulted from bilateral understandings, pledges, and agreements reached with the United States.[42] However, as the United

States seeks to strengthen these agreements, questions about Chinese commitments will arise in five key areas. And as China continues to gain greater influence and power through its new security diplomacy, these problem areas could become more challenging for U.S. interests.

First, in Beijing's view, some commitments on arms control and nonproliferation sought by the United States often go beyond what is customary practice within the broader international community. For example, Beijing was not a strong supporter of American military action against Iraq in 2003, undertaken ostensibly to roll back Iraq's WMD ambitions. Beijing, along with many other countries, preferred to see the process of WMD inspections and enforcement proceed through the United Nations. Similarly, Beijing would likely be reluctant to support proposals to take forceful action outside of the United Nations or some other broad-based international consensus to deal with WMD concerns in Iran and North Korea. On the other hand, Beijing finds certain U.S. policies hypocritical, such as its turning a blind eye to Israeli WMD possession and striking nuclear cooperation deals with India in apparent contravention of American commitments to the Nuclear Nonproliferation Treaty. It is likely that these and other similar Chinese concerns will arise in the future to challenge U.S. policies and preferences.

Second, for many observers in China, the immediate benefits of such bilateral commitments to Washington support U.S. interests but not China's. U.S. diplomats, in negotiating these pledges with China, make the case that such steps help meet Chinese interests by ensuring stability in the Persian Gulf, countering threats to oil supplies passing through the Strait of Hormuz, and stopping the spread of nuclear weapons and ballistic missiles in Iran, North Korea, Pakistan. However, Chinese strategists sense no immediate military threat from these neighbors (certainly not to the degree felt in the United States), and in fact arms transfers and technical assistance to these countries may even promote Chinese strategic, political, and economic interests (just as such exports do for other powers). A good example of this concerns American interest in halting North Korean nuclear ambitions. While U.S. leaders and policy analysts have pointed to a nuclear-armed North Korea as a major threat and a key motivation for the pursuit of missile defenses, Beijing exhibits little concern about a North Korean nuclear threat directed at China. A similar difference in perception seems to be in place with regard to the threat posed by a nuclear-armed Iran. Such differing viewpoints have obvious implications for the urgency with which China will want to address these proliferation problems, and they pose challenges to the achievement of U.S. nonproliferation goals.

A third reason for Chinese circumspection in its nonproliferation agenda with the United States relates to Beijing's sense that it is often singled out for pressure from the United States. Chinese analysts point out that although Washington actively sought to curtail and terminate Sino-Iranian civil nuclear cooperation and to discourage conventional arms transfers to Teheran, it has done little to prevent Russian civil nuclear cooperation with Iran or to halt Moscow's conventional arms sales to that nation. In particular, the Chinese take issue with what they view as coercive tactics on the part of the United States, such as the threat and imposition of sanctions, as a means to gain Chinese cooperation on certain arms control and nonproliferation concerns. Beijing often points to the fact that the United States is easily the largest arms exporter in the world, accounting for more than half of global arms sales every year. In addition, Chinese officials and analysts question why a more positive and appreciative message does not come out of Washington, even though Chinese arms exports and proliferation activities have been drastically reduced when compared to a decade ago.

Fourth, as a result of these first three points, China often approaches its bilateral pledges with the United States on a quid pro quo basis. That is, because Beijing often questions the normative, strategic, and practical interests to be served by such agreements, it seeks something valuable in return from Washington as part of the bargain. Beijing has tried unsuccessfully to exercise this kind of linkage as a means to extract concessions from the United States regarding its arms exports to Taiwan. According to this Chinese line of argument, if Beijing agrees to curtail weapons transfers to areas of strategic concern to the United States, then so too should Washington limit arms exports to areas of strategic concern to China, such as Taiwan. Such linkage has never been explicitly accepted by the United States, though interviews with Chinese arms control and nonproliferation officials show that the Chinese attach such conditions to many of their arms control and nonproliferation commitments with the United States. In another example of quids and quos, the two sides struggled to reach a common understanding of the November 2000 bilateral agreement on China's missile exports. The United States sought the complete halt of all Chinese missile-related exports and the issuance of public missile export control regulations. In return, the Chinese expected a resumption of American satellite exports for launch aboard Chinese rockets and the lifting of sanctions against Chinese entities for alleged missile-related proliferation. China has moved ahead with its side of the agreement, but the United States has not as yet allowed for the resumption of U.S. satellite exports to China.

In addition, and more broadly, the Chinese side clearly expects that improved relations with the United States would result from its agreements to undertake certain arms control and nonproliferation steps. This was most apparent during the period of U.S.-China summits in 1997–98. Just before the Clinton-Jiang summit of October 1997, China agreed to a range of nonproliferation and arms control commitments with the United States, including cutting off all new nuclear cooperation with Iran, halting the transfer of antiship cruise missiles to Iran, introducing more explicit nuclear export control regulations, and joining the Zangger Committee. Some of these measures were intended in part to allow for the long-delayed U.S.-China Peaceful Nuclear Cooperation Agreement to go forward, but they also were important in supporting the two sides' declared intention at the summit to "build toward a constructive, strategic partnership in the twenty-first century." Similarly, during the June 1998 summit in Beijing, gaining China's acceptance to further restrain its ballistic-missile-related exports to South Asia rested in part on China's expectations for continued positive trends in the overall U.S.-China relationship. The upshot of this approach, however, is that Beijing understands such bilateral quid pro quo agreements to be contingent on what it views as continued American commitments to the arrangement (whether or not the American side shares the same understandings).

As a result of these factors, the two sides often come away from such agreements with quite different official understandings of what was achieved. U.S. negotiators tend to stress the ironclad nature of a new commitment from Beijing, without discussing the quids and quos that went into the agreement. Chinese officials, on the other hand, especially in private conversations, emphasize the contingent nature of the agreements and play up the "concessions" they claim to have gained from the American side while downplaying the precise nature of their side of the bargain. In many cases, while China may abide by the letter of certain commitments, it violates the spirit by changing the nature of its military-technical cooperation with countries of concern: shifting from the transfer of complete weapon platforms, for example, to the murkier realm of technology transfer, subcomponents, technical assistance, and research and development support. But most important, China's approach to such bilateral commitments means that Chinese commitment to these agreements may be fragile, tenuous, conditional, and contingent upon the degree to which the United States, in China's view, holds up its side of the bargain.

Fifth, questions arise over whether China has the necessary will and practical export control skills and capacities to enforce its own principles and regulations. Across the Chinese bureaucracy, a "nonproliferation culture" remains in its earliest stages. Some also question whether Beijing's domestic measures amount only to paper agreements, which Chinese authorities will enforce on a selected basis. And even if China fully enforces its export controls, problems may still arise if Chinese regulators do not see the same proliferation risk in exports they license as their counterparts in other countries might.

GLOBAL ARMS CONTROL

Beyond these questions in the bilateral U.S.-China nonproliferation agenda, a stronger and more influential China may also present challenges to the United States on broader international arms control concerns. As chapter 3 describes, following a period of considerable convergence in the early to mid-1990s, the two sides are now on opposites sides of the current stalemate in the UN Conference on Disarmament (CD), complicating progress on discussions to limit or ban biological weapons, halt the production of fissile material, and slow the deployment of space-related systems such as antimissile and antisatellite weapons. Since the late 1990s, the CD has languished without a new program of work. Indeed, the CD has taken up no new arms control negotiations since 1995, when an ad hoc group authorized by the CD started to develop a verification protocol for the Biological and Toxin Weapons Convention. This process collapsed six years later with the U.S. decision in July 2001 to reject the draft verification protocol as it stood.

The principal area of disagreement between the United States and China in the CD concerns the weaponization of outer space. Beijing supports the initiation of formal negotiations on PAROS, the acronym for "preventing an arms race in outer space." In a working paper presented to the CD in February 2000, the Chinese delegation claimed there are "attempts, programmes, and moves unilaterally to seek military and strategic superiority in or control over outer space." Such moves, the Chinese argued, "may lead to the weaponization of outer space in the near future or even to a multilateral arms race in outer space." As such, according to the working paper, the CD must "re-establish the Ad Hoc Committee . . . to negotiate and conclude an international legal instrument prohibiting the testing, deployment, and use of weapons, weapons systems, and components in outer space."[43] In June 2002 China, along with cosponsors Belarus, Indonesia, Russia, Vietnam, and Zimbabwe, submitted a draft, "Legal Agreement on the Prevention of the Deployment of Weapons in Outer Space," to the CD, but no formal negotiations have begun on this document.[44]

While Beijing has considerably toned down its opposition to U.S. missile defense plans, it still harbors deep concerns about the deployment and intentions of these weapons. Chinese concerns will likely center on two principal areas. First, the Chinese will not support and will try to undermine the deployment of missile defenses by the United States that are integrated with the forces of U.S. allies and friends around China's periphery, such as Japan, South Korea, and Taiwan. Beijing would not only see such steps as "aimed" at China but would be especially concerned with how such moves would strengthen existing military relationships, particularly U.S.-Taiwan and U.S.-Taiwan-Japan ties. China will be particularly active diplomatically in preventing the deployment of advanced U.S. missile defenses in South Korea and Taiwan; it has already had a measure of success in this effort.

Second, with the abandonment of the Anti-Ballistic Missile (ABM) Treaty, and gaining little traction in its effort to ban space-based weapons, Beijing has few options in response to missile defenses, which may undercut China's conventional and nuclear missile buildup. As such, China appears determined to field a missile force that will be both technologically and numerically capable of defeating state-of-the-art missile defenses. Beijing has greatly expanded its short-range missile production and deployments, especially opposite Taiwan, and has forged ahead in its strategic missile modernization program by improving the force both qualitatively (mobility, accuracy, survivability) and quantitatively. It is true that Beijing would likely take these steps, albeit on a more modest scale, even in the absence of missile defenses. But in any event these moves by Beijing do not serve U.S. interests and complicate Washington's approach to arms control and regional security questions.

It is also true that American interests might be challenged in cases in which China closely adheres to international nonproliferation and arms control agreements. China can attempt to quietly constrain U.S. influence and promote Chinese interests more effectively by joining and promoting nonproliferation and arms control mechanisms so as to have a role in shaping their rules and outcomes, especially in the formulating stage of a new regime or agreement. It may be possible to dilute the influence of other major powers, such as the United States, relative to China's and to achieve outcomes suited to Chinese interests. For example, as Chinese arms control and nonproliferation strategists became more familiar with the norms and procedures of international nonproliferation and arms control efforts, the country's leadership appeared to recognize more clearly the value these processes might have for matters of Chinese national interest, especially to the degree such agreements would limit others' capabilities while having less effect on

China. By joining the Nuclear Nonproliferation Treaty as an acknowledged nuclear weapons power, China had nothing to lose regarding its own military capacity but could expect the regime to slow the emergence of new nuclear powers. By joining and supporting various nuclear-weapons-free-zone treaties, China loses little (as it does not deploy nuclear weapons abroad) but may gain by improving its image, while putting an onus on other countries to limit their nuclear weapon deployments by respecting such treaties. This was clearly the case when China expressed its willingness to ratify the protocols for the Treaty of Bangkok (Southeast Asia nuclear-weapons-free zone) and promoted the idea of a Central Asia nuclear-weapons-free zone, both steps that the United States has so far not been inclined to take. Even when China accepts verifiable limits on its own military capabilities (such as Beijing's agreement to sign on to the Chemical Weapons Convention and the Comprehensive Test Ban Treaty), it does so with the self-interested expectation that such restraints apply to other powers as well.

Sovereignty and Intervention

Chapter 4 argues that traditional influences on Chinese thinking—including the constraints of Chinese geodemography, the dual nature of sovereignty in Chinese strategic thinking, the historical linkage in China between sovereignty and regime legitimacy and survival, and China's contemporary historical experience with the Western-dominated international system—combine in ways that often place China at odds with the United States on questions of sovereignty and intervention. Chinese leaders today maintain a comparatively narrow definition of sovereignty, a general reluctance to intervene beyond a geographically limited area adjacent or close to China's strategic periphery, and an adamant opposition to encroachments upon the territorial and political integrity of Chinese sovereignty. These views extend to others' interventions against sovereign countries, such as those by the United States or U.S.-led coalitions, especially when undertaken outside of the UN Security Council framework.

The differences between the United States and China are rooted in the contrasting history and national experience of the two countries and their respective strengths and interests. China typically exhibits strong support for traditional definitions of state sovereignty, especially with regard to security matters, and only cautiously validates some forms of intervention. Such validation, even then, is offered only in the presence of strong international support, usually in the form of a UN mandate, where Beijing can have its voice heard as an equal party. Politicians and strategists in the United States, on the other hand, see in the process of globalization and new transnational challenges the fading of traditionally defined state borders, the rise of substate threats such as terrorism, and the need for innovative and robust responses—including various forms of military intervention. As a result of these contrasting visions, one can expect the United States and China to frequently disagree on questions of sovereignty and intervention. As China leverages its new security diplomacy more effectively in the years ahead, these differences will be a bone of contention in U.S.-China relations and a challenge to U.S. interests in many cases around the globe. At least two key areas stand out: differing approaches to objectionable and threatening regimes and gaining greater Chinese cooperation to counter terrorism worldwide.

OBJECTIONABLE AND THREATENING REGIMES

For a variety of reasons, China has managed to establish cooperative and in some cases close relations with regimes that Washington deems objectionable at best and threatening at worst. These include Burma (Myanmar), Iran, North Korea, Sudan, and Zimbabwe. Of the world's major powers, China is Burma's closest partner, with a range of economic, political, and military ties. China shares a 2,185-kilometer (about 1,400-mile) border with Burma, across which passes approximately US$1 billion in legitimate trade but also much illicit trade as well: contraband and trafficking in people and, especially, drugs. China is a critical supplier of Burma's military equipment, including tanks, armored personnel carriers, small naval vessels, and jet aircraft; Beijing has also provided assistance in upgrading military facilities and training.

Beijing's principal economic interests lie in importing resources from Burma, including timber and wood products, precious stones, and natural gas. As of 2005, Chinese companies had invested some US$191 million in twenty-five projects in Burma.[45] China is also providing financial and technical support for building a new international convention center and hydroelectric power plants. Black market activities and illicit trade between China and Burma further extends their economic exchange.

In addition, Beijing has consistently defended the regime in Rangoon (Yangon) against international criticism in the United Nations as well as within the Association of Southeast Asian Nations (ASEAN) and has never condemned Burma's harsh political repression, calling only for continued stability and eventual "political reconciliation" in the country. Meanwhile, the United States has stiff economic sanctions on Burma in response to its human rights record and repression of democratic progress; the sanctions include a ban on Burmese exports to the United States and a ban on U.S. financial services to Burma.

China-Iran relations pose another potential problem for U.S.-China relations. The United States has distanced itself economically and politically from Iran since 1979 and the establishment of the Islamic Republic; China on the other hand has maintained close ties to Iran since 1971 and has expanded its trade, diplomatic, and military ties with Teheran. China is a major exporter of heavy machinery, light industrial goods, and textiles to Iran. Iran is one of China's largest foreign suppliers of oil, and Beijing has agreed to a thirty-year deal reportedly worth some US$70 billion, which will include China's purchase of 250 million tons of liquefied natural gas from Iran, development of Iranian oil fields, and the import of 150,000 barrels of oil a day. Chinese companies are active in Iran, constructing dams, power plants, shipbuilding facilities, electrical grids, and steel and cement plants and improving Iran's oil and gas production and export facilities.[46] With economic sanctions and trade restrictions placed on Iran by many Western powers, China sees an excellent economic opportunity to step into the vacuum. In addition, some Chinese defense producers continue to provide military systems and technology to Iran.

Beijing has staunchly supported diplomatic solutions to the ongoing impasse over Iran's nuclear programs, opposing military or sanctions-based approaches, especially sanctions by the UN Security Council. Instead, China strongly favors continued dialogue between Iran and the "five plus one group" (the five permanent members of the Security Council—the United States, Russia, China, France, and the United Kingdom—plus Germany) and between Iran and the International Atomic Energy Agency.

As described above, China–North Korea relations reflect a complex mix of geostrategic, security, and political considerations in Beijing. With its supplies of energy and food in particular, China is North Korea's principal economic partner and lifeline. Of the world's major powers, China maintains the closest political and diplomatic relations with Pyongyang, including party-to-party ties. In agreeing to host the six-party talks for resolving the North Korean nuclear problem and other disputes on the Korean peninsula, Beijing has kept the standoff within diplomatic channels and avoided more coercive or interventionist actions by either the United Nations or the United States. Even after Pyongyang's nuclear test in 2006, Beijing continued to oppose tough sanctions that might induce political change or social turmoil in North Korea.

In Sudan, Chinese companies have become deeply enmeshed in that country's oil production and export facilities, including large ownership shares in Sudanese oil companies and fields and the construction of related facilities such as pipelines and refineries. In addition, Chinese companies have helped Sudan develop its electrical power generation capacity through construction of power plants and dams. Reports suggest that Chinese military equipment and vehicles are used by Sudanese security forces. These relationships continue in spite of international condemnation of the Sudanese government for allowing genocide to unfold in Darfur, for overseeing massive and purposeful dislocation of people, and for human rights abuses.[47] China has avoided taking sides in Sudan's twenty-two-year civil war and has sought to deflect UN and other international action in response to the deteriorating conditions in the Darfur region. China abstained (along with Russia and Algeria) from the March 2005 UN Security Council resolution 1591, which imposes an arms embargo on Sudan and places travel and financial restrictions on Sudanese leaders; it also abstained from less onerous UN Security Council resolutions seeking to address the atrocities in Darfur. In addition, China abstained (as did the United States, Brazil, and Algeria) from the March 2005 UN Security Council vote to send persons connected to Darfur atrocities to the International Criminal Court. Given its interests in Sudan's oil deposits and exports, Beijing has signaled its opposition to international efforts to impose an embargo on Sudanese oil exports.[48]

China and Zimbabwe celebrated twenty-five years of diplomatic relations in 2005. The celebration included the seventh visit to China by Zimbabwe President Robert Mugabe, who was feted with a week-long state visit and meetings with China's top leaders and even the bestowal of an honorary professorship from the China Foreign Affairs University. China's ties to Mugabe date back to the 1970s and his pro-independence struggles, ties that the two countries repeatedly extol in their official communications. For decades, China has provided significant economic assistance to Zimbabwe, including the construction of stadiums, hospitals, university dormitories, and factories, as well as loans and other financial and technical assistance. From an economic standpoint, China is primarily interested in access to Zimbabwe's minerals and precious metals, including platinum. As Mugabe's international status has steadily worsened, owing to his repressive political and economic policies, China now stands as Zimbabwe's only major supporter. Beijing exports military equipment to Zimbabwe, including fighter jets, tanks, armored personnel carriers, artillery, and light weapons.[49] In contrast, the

United States maintains a number of travel, financial, and military trade restrictions on relations with Zimbabwe owing to the country's poor human rights record.[50]

Straightforward economic interests partially explain Beijing's relations with these regimes and its reluctance to interfere in their internal affairs. Chinese companies have established lucrative relationships with counterparts in Myanmar (logging and extractive industries), Zimbabwe (mining and agriculture), Iran, and Sudan. More broadly, these economic and political relationships help meet China's burgeoning demand for resources to support its economic growth, its improving prosperity, and its political stability. With such close neighbors as Burma and North Korea, strategic and security-related factors also help explain China's more supportive ties. In all cases, it may also be that Beijing seeks to promote its model of political authoritarianism combined with economic growth. Beijing also has good economic, political, or security relations with a host of other countries—Cuba, Kazakhstan, Tajikistan, Uzbekistan, and Venezuela—which significantly contrast with U.S. relations with those countries. Given China's views on sovereignty and intervention, Beijing will be reluctant to support international or unilateral American actions targeting these countries. Beijing's reluctance in turn will likely create problems for U.S.-China relations in the years ahead.

COUNTERTERRORISM

Beijing will likewise be slow to support a more aggressive and interventionist policy on the part of the United States to counter terrorism around the world.[51] This is especially true if Beijing perceives the United States as taking a unilateralist approach. Beijing's lack of support will increase if it believes that U.S. counterterrorism activities merely cloak a larger geostrategic agenda, especially around China's periphery.

China has stressed the importance of giving the United Nations a leading role in the global counterterrorism effort, in part as a way to constrain the actions of the United States. Shortly after the terrorist attacks against the United States in September 2001, China's permanent representative to the United Nations argued that the "United Nations, which is the important forum for States to cooperate with each other in combating terrorism, should play a leading role in the international effort to this end."[52] This concern will likely persist in Beijing. Following the U.S. invasion and occupation of Iraq in 2003, a leading Chinese military expert wrote:

The fight against terrorism requires conclusive evidence, clear targets, and conformity with the purpose and principles of the UN Charter and the universally acknowledged norms of international law. In this regard, the leading role of the UN and its Security Council should be brought into full play.... Terrorism should not be confused with a specific nation or religion, nor should dual standards be adopted in the fight against terrorism.[53]

China has also used the Asia-Pacific Economic Cooperation (APEC) forum to underscore its view that the United Nations (and not any single nation, such as the United States) needs to play the central role in global counterterrorism efforts. At the 2004 APEC summit in Chile, Chinese President Hu Jintao stated:

The elimination of terrorism has become a world issue that is putting our wisdom, courage, and resolve to the test. In countering the threats and activities of transnational terrorist groups, actions by individual countries tend to be ineffective, and international cooperation alone is the most effective means. China supports the international community in taking resolute collective action against terrorism in all its forms and manifestations within the framework of the United Nations and under the guidance of the UN Charter and relevant norms of international law.[54]

An international symposium convened in 2004 by the China Institute for International Strategic Studies (CIISS), the research institute for China's defense intelligence community, issued similar recommendations. The conference report underscored the Chinese position that leadership in combating the global war on terror ought to rest firmly with the United Nations and not with any single nation. The report argued that every country should enhance its own counterterrorism capacity and that international cooperation in the exchange of intelligence, the designation of terrorist organizations, and the improvement of extradition arrangements should be strengthened. The report further recommended that regional organizations should be involved in counterterrorism efforts and that a comprehensive treaty on international counterterrorism, reflective of an international consensus, should be enacted. The report concluded by recommending greater funding for the UN counterterrorism commission, so it could operate as a "counterterrorism functionary agency."[55]

Similarly, the host of that conference, PLA deputy chief of the General Staff and head of defense intelligence, General Xiong Guangkai, outlined the Chinese government's stance on the major issues of counterterrorism. Among his principal points, Xiong argued that an "international mechanism for fighting terrorism [must] be established as quickly as possible and give full play to the leading role of the UN and the Security Council in fighting terrorism" and that "no country in the world can undertake the task of fighting international terrorism all by itself."[56] It is clear that Beijing will resist U.S. unilateralist approaches to counterterrorism, a difference that will undoubtedly challenge U.S.-China relations.

Conclusions

As the preceding pages demonstrate, China's new security diplomacy across a range of issues—including China's approach to alliances and regional security mechanisms, nonproliferation and arms control, and sovereignty and intervention—presents a number of potentially difficult challenges to the international community, to regional security, and to U.S. interests. However, as explained in the next chapter, China's new security diplomacy presents many opportunities as well. Chapter 6 turns to these opportunities and argues that they cannot be overlooked and that they demand an equal if not greater amount of policy attention and action in the years ahead.

6

Opportunities for U.S. Policy

Qiu tong cun yi [Seek common ground while reserving differences].
—Chinese proverb

Without always pursuing the same policies, [the United States and China]
can still pursue the same policy goals with complementary approaches.
—U.S. Deputy Secretary of State Robert Zoellick, December 2005

This chapter turns to the many, often overlooked, opportunities presented to the international community and particularly to U.S. interests by
China's evolving security diplomacy. It is important to identify positive
aspects of China's new security diplomacy, determine those aspects that give
China a greater stake in global and regional stability, and defuse the potential
for confrontation between the United States and China so as to foster the
emergence of a more open, constructive, and responsible China. By and large,
China's new security diplomacy signals increasing convergence with these
goals, and Washington should more actively leverage these opportunities.
Recognizing the seriousness of the potential challenges outlined in chapter 5,
the United States can recalibrate its China policy to account for these challenges. Equally important, these challenges should not constrain U.S. policymakers from acting upon the emergent opportunities for U.S. interests that
arise from China's new security diplomacy.

Opportunities for the United States fall in three broad categories. First,
regarding regional security mechanisms, opportunities arise for U.S.-China
policy to intensify bilateral discussions on mutual regional security concerns,
to maintain and expand military-to-military relations, to deepen interaction
within regional security organizations, to strengthen coordination with

U.S. Deputy Secretary of State Robert Zoellick's quotation comes from "Deputy Secretary
Zoellick Statement on Conclusion of the Second U.S.-China Senior Dialogue," Office of the
Spokesman, United States Department of State, December 8, 2005.

regional allies, and to realize a long-term, nonmilitary resolution to differences between China and Taiwan. Second, regarding China's approach to issues of nonproliferation and arms control, Washington should increase pressure to resolve persistent proliferation cases, bolster China's domestic monitoring and arms export control capacity, establish a stable, long-term framework for bilateral strategic nuclear relations, improve cooperation on global arms control issues, and recognize and expand upon past nonproliferation successes with China. Finally, U.S. policy should leverage China's changing approach to questions of sovereignty and intervention by intensifying U.S.-China dialogue regarding objectionable and threatening regimes, by reaching common ground in defining and addressing new transnational threats, and by encouraging greater Chinese support and participation in peacekeeping and nation building.

Alliances and Regional Security Mechanisms

Chapter 2 details how Beijing has turned to regional security mechanisms—such as the ASEAN Regional Forum (ARF) and the Shanghai Cooperation Organization (SCO) and its support of a diplomatic resolution to tensions on the Korean peninsula—to deal with practical security problems, to alleviate tensions with regional neighbors, and to put forward a Chinese vision of cooperative security diplomacy. In response, Washington should be proactive in defusing U.S.-China tensions, fostering a greater Chinese stake in global and regional stability, and encouraging a more open, constructive, and responsible China.

To begin, Washington should remind Beijing that the U.S. alliance system has made a valuable contribution toward maintaining a stable regional security environment in East Asia, a situation that has benefited China enormously. More recently, U.S. alliances and other U.S. military relationships across Eurasia mobilized against the Taliban, al-Qaeda, and other groups to stem terrorist violence is a mutual "good," which benefits China as well as others. Discussions with Chinese counterparts can also refer to the influence Washington wields within its alliances and other political-military relationships to moderate American allies and friends in the region—such as Japan and Taiwan—countries that might otherwise act contrary to Chinese interests and to the interests of regional stability.

This approach must also include the continued strengthening of a military deterrent, or hedging capacity, on the part of the United States in order to maintain regional stability and be better prepared for the uncertainties that still attend China's rise.[1] But the military aspects of this approach need to be balanced with a U.S. security diplomacy that aims to alleviate tensions and mistrust, focuses on shared interests in stability and security, and generates appreciation for the role of the United States and U.S. alliances in maintaining regional stability.

For Washington, five key policy approaches would support and sustain those goals: intensifying bilateral discussions on mutual regional security concerns; maintaining and expanding military-to-military relations; deepening interaction within regional security mechanisms; strengthening coordination with regional friends and allies on issues related to China; and committing to a long-term, nonmilitary resolution to differences between China and Taiwan.

INTENSIFYING BILATERAL REGIONAL SECURITY DISCUSSIONS

The United States and China share an interest in maintaining regional security in Asia and should intensify and sustain their bilateral dialogue on regional security questions. Beijing and Washington would benefit from regularly and thoroughly airing their intentions and interests in South Asia, Central Asia, and the Korean peninsula.

Regional security discussions regarding South Asia and Central Asia grow in importance as both American and Chinese influence and interests in these regions increase with time. In South Asia, both Beijing and Washington have long-standing and variable relationships. Given the South Asian nuclear tests in the spring of 1998, and the post–September 11 international environment, U.S. and Chinese interests and influence in this region have become more critical and sensitive. The reduction and eventual ending of Chinese proliferation-related negotiation with Pakistan must be a top priority on the American agenda. Beijing will seek clarification of the role and intentions of U.S. military and intelligence activities in Pakistan and the strengthening of U.S.-India military and security ties. Both sides should work in tandem to contain and possibly roll back further nuclearization in South Asia, prevent the proliferation of sensitive technologies such as ballistic missiles and nuclear weapons from Pakistan and India to others, ensure the safety of nuclear weapons and materials in India and Pakistan, moderate Pakistan-India tensions to avoid the escalation of conflict, and tackle a range of transnational questions emanating from the region, such as terrorism and drug trafficking. Given China's sensitivity toward developments in South Asia, American concerns in the region, and the ongoing volatility of India-Pakistan relations, Washington and Beijing have a strong interest in working together to curb instabilities and avoid the perception of U.S.-China rivalry in the area. The United States should also foster closer consultations with Beijing with regard to security in Afghanistan—a country bordering on China—not only on terrorism-related issues but also with regard to building a stable and prosperous post-Taliban situation in the country.

Chinese and American interests will come increasingly into contact over the coming years in Central Asia as well, and the two sides would benefit from an intensified dialogue to reassure one another while also identifying new channels of security cooperation. This is increasingly true in the post–September 11 environment, as American interests and presence expand into a region where China has made significant diplomatic, political, and security inroads since the mid-1990s. The United States should seek regular updates on China's activities in the SCO, including military exercises, and come to understand China's long-term intentions for this group. Beijing will want to raise its concerns about the increased American diplomatic and military presence in the region. Chinese leaders and strategists became increasingly concerned with the U.S. role in Eurasia in the wake of the "color revolutions," which in 2004 and 2005 brought dramatic political change to the Ukraine, Georgia, and China's bordering neighbor Kyrgyzstan and in 2005 brought political unrest to Uzbekistan. Such consultations are especially important given the SCO's call in mid-2005 for a timetable for the withdrawal of U.S.-led coalition forces from bases in Central Asia. Both sides are well positioned to share information and views on a range of mutual security challenges in Central Asia, including the stability of local regimes, regional economic development, particularly in the energy sector, and countering terrorism and such activities as drug running and weapons smuggling.

Washington should also continue to engage with China in order to gain Beijing's cooperation in resolving the security challenges posed by North Korea. In particular, Washington should convey to Beijing the risks it takes in not recognizing and acting on the challenges posed by a nuclear North Korea and the benefits that would accrue for China and U.S.-China relations by doing so. For example, Beijing should understand that, at a global level, the weakening and breakdown of international nonproliferation inherent in North Korea's pursuit of nuclear weapons will only encourage others, such as Iran, to consider the nuclear option or still others, such as Pakistan and India, to expand their extant nuclear programs. These countries, being in China's neighborhood for the most part, hold out the prospect for further nuclearization, rather than denuclearization, around China's periphery. Moreover, North Korea has demonstrated its willingness to link with other proliferating states in the spread of nuclear and ballistic missile technologies. Given this record, North Korea must appear very attractive to states and substate actors that seek nuclear weapons and ballistic missiles and that might use them for terrorist purposes.

Washington should remind Beijing that China's own security interests are at stake. North Korea is the fourth nuclear-armed nation directly on China's borders, joining Russia, India, and Pakistan. Not only will this complicate China's relations with its neighbor and ostensible ally and leave Beijing open to nuclear blackmail and coercion, but it will also lower the threshold for possible nuclear weapons use in China's backyard. In addition, North Korea is perhaps the most unstable and weakest regime yet to openly brandish nuclear weapons, raising enormous concerns over materials protection, control and accountability, especially in times of crisis or of any collapse of order in North Korea. Chinese security and economic interests will not benefit from a more disruptive and uncertain regional security environment. Unlike the disarmament situation regarding Iraq and Iran, the North Korea challenge is of immediate strategic concern to Beijing. Moreover, Beijing has provided North Korea with nuclear technology and assistance in missile development in the past, so China bears an enormous responsibility in ensuring a peaceful resolution of this nuclear standoff.

But these cautionary messages from Washington to Beijing need to be leavened with cooperation and consultation. As the regional player best positioned to work with both the United States and North Korea, China should be encouraged in its mediator role, conveying messages and warnings to and from both sides. It should also be encouraged to facilitate a regional dialogue among North Korea, South Korea, Japan, Russia, and China itself. To this end, the United States needs to support such a multilateral and consultative approach, intensifying discussions with China, recognizing China's interests, and offering Beijing (and others) a stake in the process. In taking these measures with regard to North Korea—and similar measures in relation to other key regional areas where their interests overlap, such as Central and South Asia—Washington and Beijing can move in a more positive direction.

MAINTAINING MILITARY-TO-MILITARY RELATIONS

U.S.-China military-to-military relations have gone through many ups and downs since the early 1980s, when the two sides tentatively opened channels of communication between their defense establishments. While current military-to-military relations are at a comparatively low ebb, even previous interactions faced a range of difficulties, unfulfilled expectations, and suspicions.[2] But in spite of these disappointments, frustrations, and problems, Washington should pursue and sustain a military-to-military relationship with China. In addition to gaining close-up information and sharpening perceptions and insights about the Chinese military, discussions between civilian defense officials as well as uniformed personnel can contribute to American interests by lessening mistrust and misperception, by raising the salience of shared interests in stability and security, and by generating a greater understanding of U.S. forces and U.S. alliances as factors in regional and global stability.

China has expanded its military-to-military ties around the world and appears more open to intensifying this kind of dialogue (see chapter 2). Washington should take advantage of this greater openness and implement and sustain military-to-military ties with China on a number of fronts. This would be consistent with the understandings reached between Presidents George W. Bush and Jiang Zemin during their meetings in October 2001, February 2002, and October 2002 and between Presidents Bush and Hu in September and November 2005 and April 2006. To begin, the two sides should move ahead in their efforts to regularize and institutionalize their military-to-military contacts, insulating these contacts from the vicissitudes of U.S.-China relations by making them part of strategic discussions between the two sides. Such contacts should include a strategic dialogue at the defense secretary–defense minister level and subcabinet level, exchange visits between senior civilian and uniformed service leaders, port calls, and academic exchanges between defense education institutions. Regularized, functional meetings on specific issues of mutual concern (such as under the Military Maritime Consultative Agreement) should be strengthened. This model could then be expanded to address other issues between U.S. and Chinese defense establishments, such as counterterrorism, counterpiracy, and nation building.[3]

However, as of this writing, operational and technical exchanges of a more specific nature between the militaries of the United States and China are tightly circumscribed by law. According to the 1999 defense authorization bill, "the Secretary of Defense may not authorize military-to-military exchanges or contact" in a range of stipulated activities if it would "create a national security risk"; the secretary is also required to report annually to Congress on U.S.-China military-to-military exchanges as well as to certify that those contacts did not create a national security risk. The list of proscribed activities are force projection operations, nuclear operations, advanced combined-arms and joint combat operations, advanced logistical operations, chemical and biological defense and other capabilities related to weapons of mass destruction, surveillance and reconnaissance operations, joint war-fighting experiments and other activities related to a transformation in warfare, military space operations and other advanced capabilities of the armed forces, arms sales or military-related technology transfers, release of classified or restricted information, and access to a Department of Defense laboratory.[4]

While remaining within these parameters, U.S.-China military-to-military ties can nevertheless explore ways to expand. In October 2005 U.S. Secretary of Defense Donald Rumsfeld told reporters that his invitation from Beijing to visit China was "a sign of slowly improving military-to-military relations." He added that he would like to see U.S.-China military relations improve in such a way that is "comfortable" for both nations.[5]

More serious consideration should also be given to establishing and sustaining Chinese observer status at certain U.S.-led defense exercises in the Asia-Pacific region. China has increasingly been more open to accepting such invitations, beginning with a Chinese military observer presence at the Rim of the Pacific (Rimpac) exercises in 1998 and the first Pacific Reach 2000, held in October. The latter, a joint search-and-rescue exercise for submarine forces, was hosted by Singapore and included Japan, South Korea, and the United States. In May 2002 six Chinese military personnel were observers at the Cobra Gold military exercises.[6] In June 2006 China sent ten senior military officers to observe Valiant Shield 2006, a major U.S. navy exercise involving 3 U.S. aircraft carrier groups, 30 warships, 280 aircraft, and 22,000 personnel. Beijing and Washington should consider Chinese involvement in other Asia-Pacific multilateral activities, such as the U.S.-led multinational planning augmentation team (MPAT) workshops, which help train officers from around the region to support potential multinational humanitarian and peace enforcement operations in the Asia-Pacific. Now that China has conducted counterterrorism exercises with its neighbor Kyrgyzstan, Washington should strengthen military-to-military cooperation among China, Kyrgyzstan, Kazakhstan, Russia, and the United States. The United States should also consider the possibility of having China observe NATO and U.S. exercises (such as Centrazbat) in the region. Finally, China should be encouraged to continue sending military officers and Ministry of Foreign Affairs officials to executive training courses, seminars, and conferences conducted by the Asia-Pacific Center for Security Studies, a Pentagon-supported research and education facility in Hawaii.

These steps cannot be one-sided—offered by the U.S. side alone—but should be undertaken on the basis of reciprocity and mutual benefit. That said, given the preponderance of American military power in relation to China and the American interest in dispelling misperceptions and misjudgment, in focusing on shared interests in stability, and in gaining China's appreciation and respect for the United States and U.S.-allied presence in the Asia-Pacific region, Washington stands to gain the most from these exchanges. For its part, Beijing should express stronger support for the U.S. alliance system and for the American regional security presence more generally; examples include the stabilizing U.S. role on the Korean peninsula, in Central Asia, and elsewhere around China and the U.S. role in maintaining a peaceful, stable, and prosperous East Asia. The Chinese side should also more transparently discuss questions of strategy, doctrine, preparedness, defense spending, and its long-range military and security intentions while also opening military-related sites on a reciprocal basis to exchange visits with the American side.

Washington should also encourage key military partners to open formalized, regular, and robust bilateral security talks with Beijing. These would include formal security dialogues with Singapore and Indonesia in addition to ongoing security discussions with Australia, Japan, South Korea, Thailand, the Philippines, and the United Kingdom. It is particularly important to encourage the establishment of a more effective China-Japan security dialogue, including discussions to alleviate and avoid potential incidents at sea between their navies, and to consider the formation of China-Japan-U.S. military-to-military relations and security discussions as well. In addition, U.S.-China military-to-military relations and discussions should be embedded in multilateral defense-related activities in the Asia-Pacific region. For example, the unofficial Shangri-la Dialogue, organized in Singapore by the London-based International Institute for Strategic Studies, is a venue where defense ministerial discussions between the United States and China (as well as other countries) can be held in a low-key, informal atmosphere.

DEEPENING INTERACTION WITHIN REGIONAL SECURITY STRUCTURES

China's approach toward regional security mechanisms took a different turn after the late 1990s. Its role in the ARF and the SCO are noted above. In addition, Beijing took a leadership role in ASEAN+3, the China-ASEAN summit, and the East Asia Summit. It also made the extraordinary request for a strategic dialogue with the North Atlantic Treaty Organization. These steps are no doubt attempts by Beijing to bolster its own security, deflect concerns about a China threat, raise questions about the value of U.S.-led alliances, and promote China's new security concept. However, Washington should take advantage of the opportunity to further involve China in constructive behaviors, even while ensuring that Beijing's relationships with these organizations do not weaken American interests or create divisions between the United States and its friends and allies. This is especially the case with the ARF, the six-party talks, and NATO, groups in which the United States already has membership. Washington is best served by using these organizations to encourage a more cooperative China.

In spite of its drawbacks, the ARF remains the best-positioned multilateral organization in the region to generate security consultations consistent with U.S. interests. While it remains too early to know whether the East Asia Summit will take on a more prominent role in regional security affairs, the absence of U.S. participation in that body argues for more, not less, U.S. engagement with the ARF. Washington needs to invest greater diplomatic energy in the ARF, raising the bar of institutional relevance and effectiveness. Specifically, Washington should push the ARF to undertake conflict prevention and consultation measures. ASEAN members with close ties to the United States, such as Singapore and Thailand, could be encouraged to partner with China in establishing an ARF intersessional support group to address transnational crime and illicit activities such as piracy, drug trafficking, and terrorism. Washington could also encourage the ARF to establish a formal secretariat and a strong chairperson (consistent with agreement at the eighth ARF annual meeting in 2001). In addition, Washington should encourage the organization to strengthen its confidence-building and preventive diplomacy capacity by expanding the participation of defense and military establishments in the ARF process, and by creating a regional peacekeeping center. At the same time, Washington should continue its efforts to steadily introduce security-related discussions within the Asia Pacific Economic Cooperation (APEC) forum.

Washington also has a good opportunity to foster more constructive security cooperation from Beijing through the mechanism of the six-party talks. China has taken a high-profile role in these talks and has invested considerable diplomatic and political capital in their success. In the process, Beijing has committed to resolving security issues on the Korean peninsula through peaceful means. The successful rollback of North Korea's nuclear ambitions and the stabilization of the Korean peninsula through diplomacy would reinforce for Beijing the benefits of consultative security mechanisms and the value of working constructively with the United States and its allies to settle regional disputes. In addition, an effective resolution of the outstanding security questions on the Korean peninsula will require even greater Chinese involvement as a responsible guarantor of the settlement. Looking ahead, Washington, Beijing, and other partners will need to consult closely on such issues as disarmament verification and monitoring, removal of fissile materials, demilitarization of borders, and the material and financial support to back an agreement. Failure of Washington to be more engaged with China in this way could result in a lapse or collapse of the talks, with Beijing taking matters even more into its own hands to achieve more narrowly self-interested goals on the Korean peninsula.

NATO stands out as another regional security mechanism through which the two sides can strengthen interaction and cooperation. Encouragingly, China's request to NATO in October 2002 to discuss strategic perceptions, shared security threats, and security activities in Central Asia marks a step in the right direction. Working within a NATO-China framework, Washington could further test Chinese intentions and learn more about Beijing's diplomatic and security interests in Central Asia. Such discussions could also contribute to gaining a greater Chinese acceptance of and respect for the positive role that U.S.-led alliances can play in the post–cold war and post–September 11 world, especially in the volatile parts of Eurasia on China's western frontier, where the United States, NATO, and China have a shared interest in stability and security. By working together to support greater security, certainty, and development in Central Asia, China, the United States, NATO, and their partners in the region can counter problems of terrorism and other political instability. Also important, engaging China as a partner on matters of regional and global security can strengthen Beijing's normative appreciation for security dialogue in general and for the NATO alliance in particular, while fostering more constructive Chinese security policies over the longer term.

A NATO dialogue with China should proceed with due care and realistic expectations. NATO leaders should not let Chinese expectations and concerns form the basis for new tensions within the alliance. China's traditional fear of strategic encirclement may ultimately limit Beijing's openness toward political-military cooperation with Washington and its NATO partners in Central Asia. Beijing will resist co-option, will resist assertive expansion of U.S. and NATO interests in the region, and will unlikely forgo its strategy to extend its political and economic influence in Central Asia. Nevertheless, a NATO-China security dialogue opens a promising channel for Washington to reduce regional tensions and misperceptions with Beijing, identify common interests in Central Asian security, and encourage greater Chinese appreciation for the value of U.S. alliances.

STRENGTHENING CHINA-RELATED COORDINATION WITH REGIONAL ALLIES

Some of the most important work to help dispel misperceptions and misunderstandings between the United States and China, to foster a sense of common U.S.-China purpose to maintain regional stability, and to build a greater understanding about the role and value of U.S. alliances begins closer to home: strengthening coordination with and among key allies with regard to China. This is especially important given the progress China has made in developing economic, political, and security relations with key American allies such as Australia and South Korea and in Europe. Such allied cooperation would include regular debriefings on political, diplomatic, and military-to-military relations with China; assessments of security-related concerns emanating from China; consideration of cross-strait relations and appropriate responses in times of escalating China-Taiwan tensions; intelligence sharing; and coordination on critical messages, public and private, being conveyed to Beijing. Such discussions should take place routinely between the United States and its allies in the region—Australia, Japan, New Zealand, the Philippines, South Korea, and Thailand—as well as with other key military partners in the region, such as Singapore. Washington should also augment the nascent transatlantic dialogue on Asia and China with the European Union in Brussels to include regularized discussions with key capitals such as London, Paris, and Berlin. Moreover, greater efforts should be made to coordinate such discussions among U.S. allies, such as in triangular Australia-Japan-U.S. talks, Europe-Japan-U.S. talks, and Japan-South Korea-U.S. talks.

Of particular importance in the near term is to work closely with Japan to encourage a more stable China-Japan relationship. Deteriorating China-Japan relations are not in U.S. interests. To begin, heightened tensions and the possibility of confrontation or conflict between these two Asian giants would destabilize East Asia, causing calamitous economic damage and setting off the possibility of great power warfare. Even in the absence of outright conflict, U.S. interests are not served when China insists on strictly limiting the role of Japanese defense forces in regional security affairs and stirs up region-wide anxieties about a newly "militarized" Japan. Consultations with Tokyo should recognize these constraints on U.S. and Japanese security goals and consider approaches to China that would alleviate, not exacerbate, them.

Such steps need not aim for the "containment" of China. Indeed, Washington would risk alienating some allies were containment the purpose of closer coordination and consultation. Rather, coordination would benefit regional security by promoting a more common approach among allies on how to manage and respond to China's growing role in Asia and by avoiding alliance divisions, which China could misinterpret or seek to exploit. In short, discrepancies over how to work with China should not become a wedge dividing the United States and its allies. A common theme to emerge from greater consultation should be to remind Beijing of the interests all parties share in continued stability in the Asia-Pacific region, the critical importance of a peaceful resolution to cross-strait differences, and the vital role U.S. alliances can play in maintaining stability in the region. Over time, improved coordination and consultation with allies in the Asia-Pacific region with regard to China should aim to draw Beijing closer to a commonly held vision for regional security and, eventually, lead to closer cooperation between China and the U.S. alliance system in the region.

COMMITTING TO A LONG-TERM, NONMILITARY RESOLUTION TO CROSS-STRAIT DIFFERENCES

For more than five decades, differences between China and the United States with regard to Taiwan have been sensitive, difficult to resolve, and potentially explosive. For China the Taiwan issue brings up profound concerns about territorial integrity, national unity, regional security, and the very legitimacy of China's current rulers. U.S. differences with China over Taiwan are rooted in maintaining regional stability and security, upholding American leadership and credibility, and promoting humanitarian and democratic principles. These differences are stark.

But while a comprehensive and conclusive resolution of these differences remains elusive, it is possible to ease the likelihood of conflict. Because Taiwan Strait issues are so deeply enmeshed in U.S.-China relations, in the role of U.S. alliances, and in the future of regional security, the successful management of these issues has positive implications for other regional and global security questions of interest to the United States and China. As the cross-strait situation becomes more complex, Washington and Beijing will need to integrate their similar interests into their bilateral policy choices.

First, it is important to recall, even though the two sides have often resorted to shows of force around Taiwan to bolster their positions, they have managed to avoid a direct conflict in this theater—and this is true even as the two sides, and Taiwan, have seen a steady increase in the level of armament on each side of the Taiwan Strait and witnessed an increasingly fluid and complex political situation unfold on Taiwan. This is a remarkable achievement given the circumstances. The reason this is possible is that the two sides have recognized a greater shared interest in avoiding a conflict than in precipitating one. Without forswearing the possibility of forceful intervention, the two sides have thus far recognized the critical global, regional, and bilateral stakes at risk—not to mention the security and prosperity of Taiwan itself, one of the world's most important economies and a vibrant example of free markets and democratization in action—were these two major powers, the United States and China, to come into conflict over Taiwan. As a result, Washington and Beijing have remained predominantly committed to seeking a peaceful resolution to differences across the Taiwan Strait.

If anything, this recognition of the global, regional, and bilateral stakes at risk needs to become a more prominent feature of each side's approach to the other. Beijing in particular has steadfastly adhered to the view that the Taiwan issue is an "internal affair" and should remain unconnected to "outside" developments of regional and international affairs. This may have been true more than fifty years ago, when settling accounts with Chiang Kaishek on Taiwan meant concluding the Chinese civil war and preventing the Nationalists and their supporters from launching an attack on mainland China. But many of the forces driving this narrowly internal dynamic have long since faded away. The government on Taiwan formally abandoned its claims to the mainland in the early 1990s. Meanwhile, Taiwan has become an international actor in its own right, whether de jure or de facto. It is the world's fourteenth largest trader internationally and has one of the world's highest per capita GDPs (at over US$14,000) and one of the world's largest foreign exchange reserves (at some US$261.6 billion in late 2006).[7] Taiwan's democratization has also brought it international standing as the first Chinese society to fully embrace and sustain a democratic system.

Mainland Chinese leadership should be reminded that its own international standing will be shaped in part by how it handles its relationship with Taiwan. Beijing must also recognize that regional stability in East Asia—a circumstance from which it benefits enormously—cannot be put at risk without stark and difficult consequences for China. Similar responsibilities come to bear on Washington: the United States, too, must act responsibly, recognizing that deteriorating and openly conflictual relations with China would have a devastating impact on East Asia and the world.

Put simply, all sides have an immense stake in avoiding conflict on questions of sovereignty and intervention, as they pertain to Taiwan, and in finding common ground in maintaining regional security, especially as it pertains to Taiwan. Such a common understanding is consistent with U.S. security commitments in the region, including with the Taiwan Relations Act, with China's strategic requirements for a stable external environment, and with the interests of other parties with a stake in East Asian stability and prosperity. As U.S. Deputy Secretary of State Richard Armitage warned in March 2001, "If there is conflict in the [Taiwan] Strait, we all have failed miserably."[8]

Second, the United States and China share an interest in broadening their perceptual framework of the cross-strait dynamic and in moving beyond a predominantly military orientation. Although defense and deterrence play an important role for all sides and cannot be removed from this equation and its resolution, it is both unwise and quixotic for military approaches to obscure other promising avenues to ease differences and foster their resolution. On the one hand, an overemphasis on military solutions can lead the parties into unnecessary arms buildups, potentially destabilizing offense-defense spirals, and the possibility of well-armed miscalculations and misperceptions. On the other hand, the on-the-ground reality of cross-strait relations has grown well beyond a narrowly military dynamic. Instead, Beijing and Washington share an interest in focusing on a more comprehensive and multivariate approach to cross-strait relations, one that takes into account not just the military dimension of U.S.-China-Taiwan relations but also such other factors as economics, trade, investment, communications, politics, cultural exchanges, and even police matters such as antismuggling and human trafficking in the Taiwan Straits area. Beijing already recognizes the advantages to expanding economic, political, and cultural contact with Taiwan while downplaying the military instrument. But even greater flexibility and openness will need to be demonstrated by Beijing before political conditions are ripe for a peaceful settlement of cross-strait differences. In a word or two, China will need to be a far more attractive and reassuring partner for Taiwan. Restraint in its military buildup opposite Taiwan is a must, to be accompanied by a far greater willingness to treat Taiwan with equality and respect not only in bilateral discussions and negotiations but also in allowing greater international space for Taiwan, where it will make positive contributions to the regional and international communities.

The United States cannot be directly involved in such cross-strait exchanges and dialogue, but it can be more openly supportive of them. Greater restraint by Washington with regard to the military dimension of its relations with Taiwan might also allow it to support nonmilitary spheres of cross-strait interaction. At the end of the day, because Beijing's approach toward Taiwan has become more subtle and multifaceted, it becomes a far more difficult task for Washington to shape favorable outcomes utilizing only the relatively blunt instrument of military deterrence. Greater recognition and encouragement by the United States of those positive aspects of cross-strait relations will contribute to the further enmeshment of China in a peaceful resolution of cross-strait differences and will help ensure that Washington has a voice in that outcome.

Nonproliferation and Arms Control

Fundamental problems between the United States and China on nonproliferation and arms control questions are likely to persist. But more can and must be done with China on these issues in support of the long-term interests of the United States, China, and regional and global security. As discussed in chapter 3, it is possible to gain greater Chinese nonproliferation and arms control cooperation by taking seriously Chinese leaders' aspirations to open constructively to the outside world, especially with the United States, to burnish China's international image, and to participate in more universal norms and practices. The following pages present five important areas where such an approach can be pursued more actively: intensifying the focus on certain persistent problem cases; bolstering China's domestic monitoring and export control capacities; establishing a stable framework for strategic nuclear relations; cooperating on international arms control issues; and recognizing and expanding past successes with China.

INTENSIFYING THE FOCUS ON PERSISTENT PROBLEMS

A 2003 Central Intelligence Agency report found that Chinese entities conducted transactions with Pakistan, Iran, and North Korea that were inconsistent with Beijing's international, bilateral, and domestic regulatory commitments on nonproliferation. The report conceded, however, that in some cases, these transfers might have taken place "without Beijing's knowledge or permission."[9] Iran, for example, actively sought China's assistance in its weapons of mass destruction and missile programs. The report claimed that Chinese (and others') assistance over the years "helped Iran move toward its goal of becoming self-sufficient in the production" of these weapons. In addition, despite October 1997 assurances from Beijing about its nuclear cooperation with Iran, the report stated that "some interactions between Chinese and Iranian entities may run counter to Beijing's bilateral commitments to the United States" and that "Chinese firms are supplying dual-use CW [chemical weapon]-related production equipment and technology to Iran." And in spite of Beijing's 1996 pledge to the United States not to provide assistance to unsafeguarded nuclear facilities such as those in Pakistan, the CIA found that it "cannot rule out . . . some continued contacts subsequent to the pledge between Chinese entities . . . and entities associated with Pakistan's nuclear weapons program." Moreover, while China committed in November 2000 not to assist any country in the development of ballistic missiles capable of delivering nuclear weapons, the CIA report found that "Chinese entities provided Pakistan with missile-related technical assistance during the reporting period." The report also expressed concern about Chinese proliferation-related interaction with North Korea, noting that Pyongyang "continued procurement of raw materials and components for its ballistic missile programs from various foreign sources, especially through North Korean firms based in China." In addition, leaked reports continued to surface alleging Chinese transfers of WMD-related materials and technologies to countries such as Iraq.[10]

However, in spite of these persistent concerns, the U.S.-China bilateral dialogue on nonproliferation has lost its momentum in recent years. Apparent Chinese departures from its commitments to nonproliferation often appear to occur without the knowledge of Chinese government authorities, because the Chinese export control system is not yet adequate to the task and because, in cases such as Pakistan, Beijing maintains long-standing and close strategic and military-technical relations. But Washington should continue to focus on these persistent problems, using sharper tools. First, at all summits as well as major senior-level meetings on nonproliferation and arms control, Washington should seek reaffirmations from Beijing of its continued adherence to all previous bilateral pledges and commitments. Discussions to this end should underscore the fact that China's nonproliferation commitments, or lack thereof, will have a serious effect on U.S.-China relations overall, particularly in the context of the post–September 11 environment and heightened concerns over the possibility of WMD use by terrorists. Second, China's new export control laws and technology control lists provide a documented commitment on the part of the Chinese government, to which Washington should constantly refer in seeking accountability in Beijing to halt proliferation activities.

Third, the two sides need to improve the bilateral mechanism by which specific cases of proliferation concern are raised and addressed, aiming for a more regularized, structured, depoliticized, dependable, and mutually reassuring process. It is critical to pursue this process and to do so at the assistant secretary level or higher. Washington should share specific details as to individuals and entities conducting proliferation-related activities in China;

at the same time, Washington should constantly seek Chinese information about specific individuals and entities of concern to determine their standing in the eyes of the Chinese government and the degree of scrutiny they receive within China's overall nonproliferation process. Part of improving the bilateral dialogue mechanism will also entail greater clarity on specific Chinese pledges. For example, Beijing has committed not to undertake any new nuclear cooperation with Iran once ongoing cooperation is complete; Beijing has also pledged to halt all ballistic-missile-related assistance to all countries. But the United States in its discussions with China must settle lingering uncertainties about "grandfathering" these commitments and bring even preexisting activities to an end (see chapter 3). In the end, Washington should be clear and consistent with the Chinese about U.S. sanctions and penalties and its willingness to impose them when necessary.

Fourth, Washington must also recognize that focusing on remaining problem cases will prove difficult and contentious. To begin with, China's longstanding strategic and military-technical relationship with Pakistan and, to a lesser extent, with Iran and North Korea will be particularly difficult to address. For a variety of conceptual, political, and practical reasons (discussed in chapter 3), Beijing will have a hard time fully halting its military-technical relationship with countries such as Pakistan. Moreover, the nature of current proliferation-related transfers by China has become murkier. Rather than complete systems, such sensitive Chinese exports tend to be subsystems, components, or just plain know-how—and murkier still, dual-use exports—the end uses of which are difficult to monitor and verify. In addition, "perfect" cannot become the enemy of "continued positive progress": Washington should be cautious not to set back continuing improvements in China's nonproliferation record by excessively unhelpful pursuit of compliance.

Finally, in taking these steps on specific problem cases, it should be made clear that Chinese compliance and strengthened export control measures are not considered a favor to the United States. The two sides need to move beyond a kind of horse-trading, quid pro quo, approach to their nonproliferation dialogue. Generally speaking, while specific linkage between Chinese nonproliferation commitments, on the one hand, and American "gifts," on the other, has resulted in some successes, it is a piecemeal approach and too narrowly defines the shared interest the two sides have in stemming the spread of WMD-related systems and technologies. Rather, the working implication should be that the outcome of Chinese and American adherence to nonproliferation and arms control commitments is first and foremost a furthering of the national security of both countries.

BOLSTERING CHINA'S DOMESTIC MONITORING
AND EXPORT CONTROL CAPACITIES

Through its commitments to international treaties and agreements, bilateral pledges to the United States, and the promulgation of domestic laws and regulations, Beijing has taken a number of steps to constrain and prevent the illicit acquisition and transfer of sensitive weapons and technologies. As detailed in chapter 3, China promulgated laws and licensing guidelines over the course of the late 1990s and early 2000s to govern the export of biological-, chemical-, nuclear-, conventional weapon-related and missile-related systems and technologies, including stipulations for punishment in the case of violations. However, although these laws and regulations are on the books, China's capacity to monitor the acquisition and transfer of such materials is in question, particularly on the issue of export controls.[11] Such concerns become more pressing in light of the possibility of terrorist acquisition and the use of WMD and other weapons and materials. As a way to bolster Chinese commitments and contribute to U.S. and Chinese goals of nonproliferation and security more broadly, Washington and Beijing should work to strengthen China's capacity to monitor its domestic stocks of sensitive materials and implement and enforce its export control system. U.S. and Chinese cooperation should proceed on four levels.

First, at the broadest level, the two countries should intensify consultations regarding the development and effectiveness of certain supply-side multilateral export control regimes such as the Nuclear Suppliers Group, the Zangger Committee, the Australia Group, the Missile Technology Control Regime (MTCR), and the Wassenaar Arrangement. Beijing is a member of two of these groups (it has sought membership in the MTCR but has not been approved to join, it has not sought membership in the Wassenaar Arrangement, and it has declined an invitation to join the Australia Group); and China has crafted its relevant export control laws and regulations to be broadly consistent with the aims, guidelines, and control lists advocated by the Nuclear Suppliers Group, the Australia Group, and the MTCR. Regular consultation with Beijing by the United States (and others) about the activities and directions of these groups will reinforce their normative and practical significance for Beijing, especially to the degree that China's rules and enforcement practices fall short of what other major powers in the international community are achieving through multilateral cooperation and coordination. As members of these multilateral export control groups take steps to tighten their national export controls to address specific problems related to terrorism, Washington (and others) can raise these issues bilaterally with Beijing. For example, the Wassenaar Arrangement in December 2002 agreed to review the adequacy of national controls on man-portable air defense systems and consider best-practices guidelines to govern exports of small and light weapons, issues that should be raised bilaterally with Beijing as well.[12] Membership in the Australia Group would be another area for bilateral discussion, and Beijing should be urged to join. Membership in the Wassenaar Arrangement (governing conventional weapons and dual-use goods and technologies) may be less pressing, and membership in the MTCR perhaps the most difficult to achieve. However, Washington should continue to urge Beijing to sign on to the November 2002 International Code of Conduct against ballistic missile proliferation.

Second, Washington-Beijing dialogue on nonproliferation and arms control should spell out more clearly China's new export control system: the bureaucratic mechanisms that make up its export control system, the responsible agencies and individuals involved, and the process by which companies are licensed, approved, and, if necessary, censured. These discussions should also focus on Chinese trigger lists to determine if there are gaps between China's list and the control lists of other countries and international regimes. If there are gaps, Washington should press Beijing to close them.

Third, Washington and Beijing should increase their operational cooperation in strengthening China's domestic export control system. Some work is under way, including exchanges of delegations and Beijing's participation in a regular regional export control seminar sponsored by the United States and Japan. However, more intensive working-level training and technical assistance is needed to strengthen China's licensing procedures, end-use verification, data management, information dissemination and education programs, customs operations, cargo inspection procedures, border- and port-monitoring capacities, and enforcement mechanisms. In addition, the United States should encourage Chinese participation in multilateral export control training and programs offered by the U.S. Department of Commerce and offer bilateral specialized training and seminars as well. Most important, exchanges and assistance should address not only export concerns but also the possibility that China could be used as a transit route for materials coming from and headed to locations outside China. Chinese participation in the Container Security Initiative and the Megaports Initiative (which help countries with major ports monitor the safety of the international supply chain and detect shipments of nuclear and other radioactive materials) is an example of the kind of ongoing U.S.-China cooperation on nonproliferation issues that can be expanded.[13]

Fourth, the United States and China should reengage on matters related to the protection, control, and accounting of nuclear and other sensitive materials that could fall into the hands of terrorists and other substate actors. Often referred to as MPC&A (materials protection, control, and accounting), these are procedures, safety measures, accounting practices, and access control mechanisms designed to prevent the loss, theft, and export of sensitive nuclear materials. A program of cooperation between U.S. national laboratories (Lawrence Livermore National Laboratories, Los Alamos National Laboratories, and Sandia National Laboratories) and China's nuclear weapons laboratories and other nuclear agencies was conducted between 1995 and 1998; the program included conferences, workshops, and demonstrations on nuclear MPC&A, with the expectation of convening training and seminars on fissile material production monitoring, remote sensor monitoring, management of nuclear waste, and nuclear reactor safety. The program also envisioned the possibility of expanding the range of MPC&A activities to include chemical agents. However, this effort was brought to a halt in 1999 by the U.S. Congress over concerns with Chinese nuclear espionage. Given the desirability of ensuring the safety and control of Chinese nuclear materials and other sensitive and potentially dangerous agents, the United States and China should reopen MPC&A exchanges, with appropriate reassurances and intelligence protections as required.

ESTABLISHING A STABLE FRAMEWORK FOR STRATEGIC NUCLEAR RELATIONS

The U.S.-China strategic nuclear relationship is entering fundamentally uncharted territory, both quantitatively and qualitatively, and difficult times between the United States and China may lie ahead over issues of nuclear weapons and strategic stability. Some of this is probably unavoidable, especially as China places a greater reliance on a more robust and modern missile force and nuclear arsenal and the United States increases its reliance on the development and deployment of missile defenses and diminishes the role of nuclear offense. Under such uncertain and unfamiliar conditions, suspicions and lack of transparency, if unchecked, could lead to an offense-defense spiral and an unstable strategic nuclear dynamic in U.S.-China relations. Other, follow-on complications could ensue, such as horizontal proliferation from China and vertical proliferation among China's neighbors.

To check such developments—and to bring a greater degree of stability, predictability, and reassurance to the U.S.-China strategic nuclear relationship—it is essential that the two sides work on measures to alleviate tensions.

It makes little strategic sense for either side simply to acquiesce to a more confrontational and uncertain nuclear relationship. It may be possible for the two sides to reach an acceptable level of mutually assured deterrence and strategic stability, but getting through the transition period while maintaining stability will prove difficult in the absence of good faith efforts to establish confidence-building measures between the two countries. Consistent with China's new security diplomacy and its goal of avoiding overt confrontation with the United States, it is possible to engage Beijing more actively on nuclear weapons issues and to establish a more stable strategic nuclear relationship that favors both U.S. and Chinese interests.

To begin, policymakers and strategists in the United States should recognize and understand the fundamental concepts underlying China's views about nuclear weapons and strategic stability, how those views are changing in the current environment, and how those views will affect future nuclear weapons modernization plans. Most important, for the foreseeable future China should be expected to do what is necessary to maintain, at the very least, a minimal deterrent posture vis-à-vis other nuclear powers, especially the United States. Until and unless the doctrine and deployments of American missile defense, Chinese nuclear weapons modernization, and the overall U.S.-China relationship evolve in way that make Chinese nuclear weapons nearly irrelevant to U.S. national security—a far-off prospect at best—American strategists should accept the present reality of Chinese nuclear weapons and the deterrent they pose—and plan accordingly.

Planning should aim toward four goals: relying upon the overwhelming nuclear force levels of the United States as a deterrent vis-à-vis China; keeping the Chinese nuclear weapons buildup to a minimum; continuing steady development and deployment of missile defenses; and pursuing reassurance measures, bilateral dialogue, and other forms of cooperation on nuclear-weapons-related issues with China to clarify intentions, avoid unfavorable outcomes, and stabilize the U.S.-China nuclear weapons dynamic.

Such steps can succeed if the two sides to make a serious effort to engage in a strategic nuclear dialogue. Such discussions are nearly nonexistent at the official level, limited by a narrow agenda, disrupted by schisms in the U.S.-China relationship, and held hostage to political divisions and debates in Washington and Beijing about the appropriate approach to U.S.-China relations. The leadership on both sides should consider two areas for future action: unilateral statements and bilateral dialogue and exchanges.

Beijing and Washington should consider issuing official, unilateral statements to help clarify intentions and outlooks regarding nuclear weapons and the U.S.-China strategic offense-defense dynamic. When possible, these statements should come from the uppermost leadership, including the presidents of the two countries. Successive U.S. administrations, for example, have sought to reassure China about the purposes of its missile defense plans, and they should continue to do so. President Bill Clinton reiterated the purpose of missile defense as a means to counter "the possibility that a hostile state with nuclear weapons and long-range missiles may simply disintegrate, with command over missiles falling into unstable hands; or that in a moment of desperation, such a country might miscalculate, believing it could use nuclear weapons to intimidate us from defending our vital interests, or from coming to the aid of our allies, or others who are defenseless and clearly in need." He also referred to the problem of terrorists gaining control of nuclear weapons, noting that "in a world where proliferation has complicated the task of preserving the peace . . . we have an obligation to determine the feasibility, the effectiveness, and the impact of a national missile defense."[14] Vice President Al Gore stated that he "would also work to persuade the Chinese that a U.S. [national missile defense] system is not intended to threaten them, and to allay the concerns of our allies," adding that he would "oppose the kinds of missile defense systems that would unnecessarily upset strategic stability and threaten to open the gates for a renewed arms race with Russia and a new arms race with China, including both offensive and defensive weapons."[15]

Likewise, leading officials in the administration of George W. Bush have repeatedly stated that American missile defense plans are not intended for China. The Bush administration has also made indirect comments that might further reassure Beijing about the intentions of American missile defense plans. For example, in early September 2001, the *New York Times* quoted senior Bush administration officials as suggesting American tolerance of a moderate Chinese nuclear weapons buildup in the face of U.S. missile defense plans.[16] Later in 2001, in supporting his decision to withdraw from the Anti-Ballistic Missile Treaty and more vigorously pursue missile defenses, President Bush stated that "the greatest threats to [the United States and Russia] come not from each other, *or other big powers in the world,* but from *terrorists* who strike without warning, or *rogue states who seek weapons of mass destruction.*"[17] China falls outside of this definition of threats to which missile defense should respond both as a "big power" and by the fact that China already has weapons of mass destruction. High-level remarks such as these on the part of the United States, while indirect, can help to alleviate Chinese concerns about missile defense in ways that will limit the Chinese nuclear weapons buildup and other negative outcomes for U.S. interests. Other U.S.

statements might include stronger reassurances about Washington's intentions to continue its moratorium on nuclear testing and, over the longer term, a reconsideration of Comprehensive Test Ban Treaty ratification.

Chinese leaders should also make more open and official statements with the aim of clarifying their perspectives regarding nuclear weapons and the U.S.-China offense-defense dynamic. To begin, Chinese leaders should acknowledge more openly the country's nuclear modernization program, its intention to preserve a basic retaliatory capacity in order to avoid nuclear blackmail, its intention to maintain China's traditional minimal deterrent and no-first-use posture, and its intention to adhere to its moratorium on nuclear testing. Chinese leaders and strategists should also restate findings issued in the past that certain types of missile defense (such as point defenses for the protection of troops and military installations) are acceptable. Beijing should also consider sending more reassuring signals by *not* taking certain steps. For example, not continuing the pace of its missile buildup opposite Taiwan and not deploying those missiles would send an important signal to Washington that Beijing continues to prefer a negotiated, rather than a militarily coerced, solution to differences across the Taiwan Strait. China, through words and action, should seek to operate constructively within a world where missile defenses will become a part of the strategic landscape.

In addition to issuing reassurances unilaterally, Beijing and Washington will need to engage in a bilateral dialogue on questions related to nuclear weapons, missile buildups, missile defenses, and offense-defense ratios. The announcement by President Bush and President Hu in April 2006 that the United States and China should begin a strategic dialogue between the nuclear weapons forces of the two sides was long overdue but a good step forward.[18] It remains to be seen how the two sides will structure these talks. But such discussions could address their respective views about the salience, purpose, and prospects for nuclear weapons, ballistic missiles, and missile defenses. Such discussions would serve to clarify each side's perception of threat, and views could be exchanged on the meaning and purpose of nuclear deterrence in the post–cold war and post–September 11 world. These exchanges could also explain the countries' respective understandings about offense-defense competition and security dilemmas between the countries.

From that broad strategic discussion, the two sides could explain in greater detail their respective nuclear weapons postures and doctrines for nuclear weapons use, including their respective views on missile buildups and the threat of missile proliferation worldwide. These more specific exchanges should also include a discussion of measures taken by each side for the command and control of nuclear weapons, including their protection from the possibility of accidental launches, as well as a discussion of their respective positions on the prospects of nuclear weapons terrorism and the measures each side is taking to prevent terrorist organizations from gaining access to nuclear weapons. Looking further ahead, the two sides could agree to notify one another in the case of missile or missile defense exercises and tests. They could exchange very basic data on their nuclear weapons programs (number of systems and fundamental capabilities) as well as basic briefing information on their missile defense programs (the United States already provides basic briefing information on its missile defense programs; China should consider doing the same).

Over the longer term, it may be possible for the two sides to determine more precisely the parameters for strategic stability between the two sides, discussing appropriate offense and defense balances acceptable to each side and commensurate with each other's strategic interests. Such discussions might include such implicit or explicit understandings as Chinese efforts to limit its nuclear armed missiles, to forgo MRV/MIRV (multiple reentry vehicle and multiple independently targetable reentry vehicle) deployments, and to maintain a land-based nuclear force only; a Chinese withdrawal of or limitations on nuclear-capable missiles in the Taiwan Strait; verifiable agreements that de-alert nuclear forces or otherwise step down from current states of readiness against one another; and discussions as to how the two sides can achieve a stable build down of their nuclear arsenals in the future.

COOPERATING ON INTERNATIONAL ARMS CONTROL

While the two sides made significant progress working together on a range of internationally negotiated arms control and nonproliferation treaties in the early to mid-1990s (concluding the Chemical Weapons Convention and the Comprehensive Test Ban Treaty and permanently extending the Nuclear Nonproliferation Treaty), the United States and China today find themselves deadlocked in the Conference on Disarmament since the late 1990s and at odds over the use of weapons in space. Moreover, the post–September 11 arms control environment (including American decisions to withdraw from the Anti-Ballistic Missile Treaty, to reject the verification protocol to the Biological and Toxin Weapons Convention, to pursue missile defenses more actively, and to bilaterally agree with Russia to achieve new cuts in strategic arsenals) has introduced new complications for the global arms control and nonproliferation agenda. Under these conditions, the United States and China would benefit from a revitalized dialogue on global arms control and nonproliferation issues, which could over time translate into international action with like-minded states. This effort should proceed along two tracks.

First, greater weight needs to be given to adherence, implementation, and enforcement rather than continued negotiation. With this in mind, the two sides should regularly consult on and jointly and publicly declare their continuing and strengthening support for major international arms control and nonproliferation regimes to which they are already parties or whose aims they support. For example, while neither the United States nor China has yet ratified the Comprehensive Test Ban Treaty, they can both express their continuing commitment to maintaining their respective unilateral moratoria on nuclear testing, to supporting the work of the Comprehensive Test Ban Treaty Organization, and to de facto adherence to the treaty. In addition, such regular and public support and focus on implementation should be given to other important regimes (the Nuclear Nonproliferation Treaty and its regular review process and the Chemical Weapons Convention), backed up by joint action in the appropriate international agencies in cases of noncompliance. While neither the United States nor China chose to join the 1997 Ottawa Treaty banning antipersonnel land mines, nevertheless the two could work together in demining efforts along China's southern borders, on the Korean peninsula, and in countries such as Cambodia and Afghanistan.

Second, Washington and Beijing need to come to terms on how to cooperatively address emergent proliferation and arms control challenges on the international scene: restraining formally unacknowledged, de facto nuclear weapons states such as India, Israel, Pakistan, and North Korea; halting new proliferant states such as Iran; and preventing subnational or terrorist use of weapons of mass destruction.

To begin, China and the United States should intensify their dialogue on issues related to Chinese proliferation activities, with special attention to how those activities could contribute to the transfer of dangerous technologies and capabilities to proliferative states and terrorist groups. Washington should test Beijing on its support for the global war on terror and gain unequivocal assurances that the Chinese government is taking every measure to prevent such transfers from taking place, with a special focus on Iran, North Korea, and Pakistan. Given the differences between Beijing and Washington on issues of intervention and the use of force, the two sides risk deep fissures in the relationship if, for example, the United States deems it necessary to take military action against North Korea or Iran to roll back WMD programs in those countries. Instead, the two sides should enter into a process of coordination and action, either regionally or through the United Nations, to restrain and roll back WMD programs in emergent proliferant states. Given China's closer relations with Iran, North Korea, and Pakistan, it makes sense for Washington to consult with Beijing regarding their proliferation activities, including admonitions for current and past transfers of WMD-related technologies and with the prospect for real sanctions and international opprobrium for such transfers in the future.

Because most existing nonproliferation and arms control regimes deal with the behavior of states, China and the United States should work together to sharpen the ability of existing nonproliferation and arms control regimes to prevent, proscribe, and sanction WMD proliferation to and by nonstate actors. Two obvious places to start in this regard would be the work of the International Atomic Energy Agency and the Convention on Physical Protection of Nuclear Material. In a step toward a more effective Biological and Toxin Weapons Convention, the United States and China could formally establish bilateral cooperative efforts to monitor and investigate suspicious disease outbreaks and more tightly regulate their commerce in pathogens, all with an eye to fostering a viable international protocol to prevent the use of biological agents as weapons of war and terror.

The United States should also consider engaging China as a possible partner in the Cooperative Threat Reduction (CTR) program. The CTR program, put in place in 1991, is a highly successful cooperative arms control effort that, among other activities, helps the states of the former Soviet Union in controlling and protecting their nuclear materials and nuclear weapons delivery vehicles, such as missiles, and also contributes to the dismantlement and destruction of nuclear weapons and related delivery systems. A part of this initiative involves a "megatons to megawatts" agreement, which seeks to convert some 500 metric tons of highly enriched uranium, taken from dismantled Russian warheads, into low enriched uranium for use in commercial nuclear reactors in the United States.[19] China, which has extremely ambitious plans to expand its commercial nuclear power facilities but which has only limited supplies of uranium, would benefit from such ready and secure access to suitable nuclear fuels and could become a cooperative partner in one of the world's most important nuclear disarmament activities. China's financial input to the program, paying Russia for the low enriched uranium, would help sustain its important work. China could also be introduced to some of the broader weapons material protection and control activities, key components of the Cooperative Threat Reduction program.[20]

RECOGNIZING AND EXPANDING PAST SUCCESSES

The record of U.S.-China dialogue and engagement on nonproliferation and arms control issues demonstrates that steady progress can be made with China under certain conditions. China has taken positive steps forward when the United States gains a clear international consensus on nonproliferation and arms controls issues and presents it as such to the Chinese. The Chinese have demonstrated their sensitivity to international concerns, and when confronted with such an international consensus, Chinese policymakers typically wish to be seen as supporting its goals. Relatedly, Washington should make a special point of highlighting China's adherence to international arms control and nonproliferation regimes it has already joined (the Nuclear Nonproliferation Treaty, the Chemical Weapons Convention, the Biological and Toxin Weapons Convention, the Nuclear Suppliers Group, and the Zangger Committee) and publicly insist on accountability and explanations when commitments to them may be breached.

U.S. policy should not overlook China's desire to be seen as a constructive international player when it attempts to gain Chinese acceptance of and adherence to nonproliferation and arms control norms and procedures. As Alastair Iain Johnston and Paul Evans put it, "[Chinese] participation in international security institutions has bred further participation. . . . That participation, in conjunction with an evolving Chinese identity as a responsible great power, has generated image costs and benefits that appear to have positively influenced the quality (within limits) of Chinese participation."[21] In seeking these benefits, China in turn gains further incentives for even deeper participation in the regime, as the costs of either dropping out of the regime or opposing it steadily rise. In addition, China has expanded its national laws and regulations on nonproliferation, leading to the necessity for American negotiators to become closely familiar with them—so as to be able to alert China as to where its legal system has been breached. Beijing is increasingly sensitive to its ability to police its own system and will be more likely to take action in cases where it can be shown that its laws are being broken by its citizens and companies.

Constructive Chinese nonproliferation and arms control policies and activities often result from a combination of three factors: explanations of how Chinese proliferation encroaches upon U.S., regional, and ultimately Chinese security interests; effective penalties and sanctions; and positive incentives offered by the United States. With regard to sanctions, U.S. policy over recent years has failed to have the desired effect. Most sanctions have had little more than symbolic effect, are often levied with little to no discussion or negotiation with Beijing, and, most important, have not deterred certain proliferators in China from continuing their activities. If the United States issues sanctions with the goal of stopping Chinese proliferators, it should do so in the context of intensive, persistent, and even irksome consultations with Beijing—and the sanctions should have a real bite.

Incentives might include improved U.S.-China political relations and the opening of trade and investment in advanced technologies, such as civil nuclear cooperation. One of the strongest levers Washington has had to stem Chinese proliferation activities was the promise of improved U.S.-China political relations. A number of key "deliverables" were gained in the run-up to the U.S.-China presidential summit of October 1997, the first between the two countries in Washington since 1985. U.S. leverage also stemmed from China's hope to implement the U.S.-China Peaceful Nuclear Cooperation Agreement (PNCA). This accord had been reached in 1985 during the Reagan administration but could not be initiated until the president could certify to Congress that China was not contributing to nuclear weapons proliferation. As the October 1997 U.S.-China presidential summit approached, implementing the PNCA became an important deliverable for the meeting. As part of the summit agreements, China committed to stop selling cruise missiles to Iran, to bring current civilian nuclear technology cooperation agreements with Iran to a halt, to not initiate any new nuclear cooperation with Iran, and to join and adhere to the commitments of the Zangger Committee.

Washington should recognize—and expand upon—the steady progress over the past decade of introducing international norms and procedures into the Chinese arms control and nonproliferation community and the beneficial effect these procedures have had in the development of nonproliferation and arms control policies and practices on the part of the Chinese. U.S. government and nongovernment programs of research and training, as well as offers of assistance and expertise at the official level, have supported the establishment and growth of a nascent official and unofficial nonproliferation community and culture in China. This process has created greater awareness and understanding of international arms control and nonproliferation norms and practices and should be strongly encouraged to continue.

Sovereignty and Intervention

Chapter 4 describes China's traditional approach to questions of sovereignty and intervention but also shows how, under certain circumstances, Chinese views on these issues are becoming more flexible, pragmatic, and consistent with international norms and U.S. interests. Beijing's more flexible approach to sovereignty and intervention is driven by the fundamental goals of its new security diplomacy: alleviate external tensions in order to address challenges on the domestic front, assure neighbors about a growing China's peaceful intentions, and find ways to balance, but not confront, the United States to achieve Chinese interests more effectively. While the United States and China need not see eye to eye on these questions, the two sides should seek to expand areas of common ground and, where possible, alleviate areas of tension and possible controversy. In dealing with these contrasting viewpoints, policymakers and strategists in both Washington and Beijing should consider measures in three important areas: intensifying dialogue on objectionable and threatening regimes; defining and addressing transnational threats; and encouraging Chinese support and participation in a variety of peacekeeping and nation-building operations.

INTENSIFYING DIALOGUE ON OBJECTIONABLE AND THREATENING REGIMES

Beijing and Washington share an interest in keeping regional instabilities and conflicts to a minimum by ensuring that localized problems do not spill over beyond national boundaries. In many cases, given Beijing's comparatively better diplomatic relations with countries such as Burma, Iran, Sudan, and North Korea, Washington can turn to Beijing to facilitate communication and convey the will of the international community. On the other hand, Beijing has an interest in maintaining stable regional relationships, especially near its borders, in being seen as a responsible great power, and in having a stable and productive relationship with Washington.

The "senior dialogue" launched between the United States and China in August 2005 should help facilitate these kinds of discussion. In addition to addressing issues of specific bilateral concern, the senior dialogue should also take up certain regional and third-party issues, such as finding common ground in approaches toward Burma, Iran, and Sudan while also laying out strategic views toward the Middle East, Latin America, and Central Asia. Subgroup meetings on global regions and on specific cases should be expanded and regularized between the two countries.

DEFINING AND ADDRESSING TRANSNATIONAL THREATS

The two sides need to carry out more concrete discussions and complementary policy actions that accept and address the realities of transnational security threats. Chinese leaders and strategists—traditional guardians of state sovereignty and typically reluctant to consider bilateral or multilateral steps that might meddle in others' internal affairs—have increasingly acknowledged that the spread of transnational security problems has blurred state borders. This is especially important in light of Chinese concerns over questions of sovereignty and intervention. Many of the most challenging issues the Chinese leadership will face over the coming years are transnational in nature: the impact of globalization on China's domestic economy; environmental degradation, water shortages, and energy access; the spread of HIV/AIDS, avian influenza, and other infectious diseases; and what Beijing calls the three evils—terrorism, separatism, and extremism—as well as other types of transborder crime such as drug trafficking, gun running, smuggling, and piracy. Beijing's leaders have noted their concern with these transnational problems and have shown a willingness to work multilaterally in such groups as the SCO to deal with these threats to national sovereignty and regime legitimacy. In July 2002 China's minister of foreign affairs declared that the ARF should focus on nontraditional and transnational security threats in the years ahead.[22]

In focusing on these issues in official discussions with Beijing, Washington can accomplish three goals. First, it can expand areas of common ground with Beijing and enlist Chinese assistance in combating regional and global challenges. Second, to the degree that Beijing addresses transnational threats emanating from within its own borders and seeks Washington's assistance in doing so, American and Chinese interests will benefit. Third, a focus on transnational challenges helps foster a broader, more internationalist, and more interdependent perspective in Chinese leadership circles, which in turn may constrain future unilateralist or nationalist tendencies as China grows stronger.

The opening of a U.S. Federal Bureau of Investigation (FBI) liaison office in the U.S. embassy in Beijing in late 2002 represented a concrete step toward jointly meeting transnational security challenges. Further, since September 11, 2001, Washington and Beijing have initiated a number of regular dialogues on counterterrorism. For example, delegations led by the U.S. State Department's coordinator for counterterrorism and the Chinese Foreign Ministry's director-general of the International Department (including representatives from law enforcement, intelligence, military, diplomatic, and financial agencies) have met on a regular basis since December 2001. In mid-2002 the two sides established a semiannual meeting, focusing on terrorist financing, led by the U.S. Department of the Treasury and the Chinese Ministry of Finance. These exchanges resulted in part in the United States listing the Chinese Uighur East Turkestan Islamic Movement (ETIM) as a terrorist organization and (along with Afghanistan, China, and Kyrgyzstan) requesting the United Nations to do the same. Beijing and Washington also established a U.S.-China Financial Counter-Terrorism Working Group and discussed the possibility of tapping U.S. advice and assistance for event security at the 2008 Beijing Olympic Games.[23] In 2005, joining with Australia, China, India, Japan, and South Korea, the United States helped form the Asia-Pacific Partnership for Clean Development and Climate, aiming to alleviate energy security threats and pollution challenges.[24]

These discussions and agreements should be intensified and sustained, with consideration given to more embassy postings for representatives from other agencies dealing with such issues as drug enforcement, money laundering, piracy, infectious diseases, and human trafficking. Markedly absent from these consultations are regular substantive high-level exchanges between the militaries and defense departments of the two sides. Military-to-military dialogue on counterterrorism questions should be more firmly established between Washington and Beijing.

Even if Washington and Beijing agree on common definitions of transnational security problems and notions of national sovereignty, they can still expect to differ over key issues. On the one hand, Beijing will draw the line at any new definitions and cooperative initiatives that appear to erode its sovereignty claims to places such as Tibet, Xinjiang, and Taiwan. On the other hand, Washington will oppose efforts to define counterterrorism or counterinsurgency in ways that justify inhumane actions against Chinese dissidents and ethnic minorities or that provide a pretext for a military solution to differences across the Taiwan Strait. Perhaps most important, U.S.-China relations will suffer if terrorism and terrorist-related activities emanating from Iran, North Korea, or Sudan threaten U.S. interests and China does little to stem those activities. But overall, there lies a great deal of unexplored common ground between the United States and China, which will expand definitions of sovereignty and intervention in the post–cold war and post–September 11 world. In building on these areas of common ground, Washington could expect a cooperative policy from Beijing incorporating expansive and flexible definitions of sovereignty and intervention.

ENCOURAGING PEACEKEEPING AND NATION BUILDING

Enhanced Chinese participation in peacekeeping can make a dual contribution: fostering China's integration into the global community while at the same time strengthening peacekeeping efforts. As peacekeeping evolves toward "coalitions of the willing," greater Chinese support for and participation in such operations will contribute to their success. Furthermore, as China's military power continues to develop, the international community should encourage China to shoulder greater responsibility for ensuring regional peace and a stable world order.

Greater Chinese involvement in the UN Department of Peacekeeping Operations (DPKO) and in the peacekeeping operations themselves should be encouraged. The DPKO is tasked with planning, managing, and directing all ongoing UN peacekeeping operations, preparing for new missions as needed, and reporting on these activities to the secretary-general and the Security Council. China has in the past had very few officers working for the DPKO, but Chinese participation, particularly in the DPKO's Office of Operations and the DPKO's Best Practices Unit, should be encouraged. The former monitors ongoing missions and includes a situation center, which serves as an information collection point, and a crisis management center. The Best Practices Unit evaluates missions and recommends guidelines for improved action and results. Among its projects are the development of a handbook for peacekeeping and a manual of standard operating procedures for UN forces in the field. Such participation would offer the Chinese leadership, and particularly the People's Liberation Army (PLA), a greater stake in peacekeeping operations. Chinese participation in and support for UN and multinational efforts to address crises in Cambodia (1992–94), East Timor (1999), and Afghanistan (2001) stemmed from China's early involvement in consultations before the dispatch of these missions.

Greater Chinese participation in UN peacekeeping operations might also be encouraged by supporting Beijing's deployment of civilian police abroad. China's increasing emphasis on the provision of civilian police to UN missions could be expanded to provide police training as part of multinational nation-building efforts. China has increasingly invested in this approach in recent years: as of mid-2006, civilian police accounted for over 10 percent of China's contribution to UN peacekeeping forces. Having built up a coterie of internationally experienced civilian police, China should also be encouraged to provide police training as part of postconflict nation-building efforts by the international community. China's programs to provide military and police training as well as 20,000 police uniforms and 50,000 military uniforms for Afghanistan security forces are steps in the right direction and could be expanded in the future.[25]

Over the past two decades, China has dramatically expanded its military-to-military ties as the PLA has become more professional and more internationally aware.[26] Outside observers could build upon this trend in a positive way by encouraging greater cooperation between China and some of the leading peacekeeping contributor states, including Poland, Bangladesh, Austria, Canada, the Scandinavian countries, and Australia. More than eighty countries maintain some form of national peacekeeper training facilities, according to the DPKO, and many of them would have an interest in encouraging greater cooperation and exchanges on peacekeeping affairs with China. British, Canadian, and Australian officials have reportedly expressed interest in cooperating more closely with China on peacekeeping.[27] Britain's efforts bore fruit in June 2000, when China and Britain cohosted a seminar in Beijing on the future of peacekeeping; British Prime Minister Tony Blair and Chinese Premier Wen Jiabao issued a joint statement in May 2005 during Wen's visit to the United Kingdom, in which they declared that "the two sides are committed to expanding co-operation within the framework of UN peacekeeping."[28] Further expanding this policy offers the possibility of multilateral cooperation in engaging China in a low-cost and noncontroversial manner.

The United Nations has rapidly expanded its training programs for peacekeeping operations, which has helped establish some twenty new forces since 1995.[29] A greater number of the training materials could be produced in Chinese and provided to the Chinese peacekeeper training program in Nanjing and the international police training center outside Beijing. Only a few Chinese peacekeepers have been trained at UN centers to date, but with funding assistance and outreach efforts, these numbers could be significantly expanded. Efforts to place foreign officers in Chinese training schools as short-term visiting lecturers might be an effective way to further China's involvement with global peacekeeping training. In addition, the Chinese seat in the UN Department of Peacekeeping Operations Testing and Evaluation Service should be sustained to bolster relations between China and the United Nations. These efforts should not be a one-way street. The Chinese should increase openness and exchanges with other peacekeeping forces and accept a greater degree of transparency toward their peacekeeping activities.

7 | *Looking Ahead*

Motivated by enduring interests to maintain domestic stability and development, reassure neighbors about its "peaceful rise," and avoid an overtly conflictual relationship with the United States, the Chinese leadership has since the late 1990s implemented a new security diplomacy, which is more confident, proactive, and convergent with international norms and, generally speaking, with U.S. interests. This approach is readily apparent in China's more constructive policies across a range of security issues, including such measures as participating in regional security mechanisms and confidence-building measures, expanding its peacekeeping and counterterrorism activities, and improving its nonproliferation and arms control policies at home and abroad. Over the past decade, China's new security diplomacy has solidified into a core aspect of the country's overall national development strategy and looks likely to continue for the years ahead. According to *Liaowang* [Outlook], the Chinese Communist Party weekly general affairs journal:

> Compared with past practices, China's diplomacy has indeed displayed a new face. If China's diplomacy before the 1980s stressed safeguarding of national security and its emphasis from the 1980s to early this century is on the creation of an excellent environment for economic development, then the focus at present is to take a more active part in international affairs and play a role that a responsible power should on the basis of satisfying the security and development interests. In order to

play the role of a responsible power, it is even more necessary to make use of multilateral mechanisms and initiate multilateral diplomacy.[1]

These developments present momentous opportunities and challenges for the international system, regional stability, and U.S. interests. On the one hand, China's global and regional security policies are more and more consistent with international norms, regional expectations and preferences, and U.S. interests. On the other hand, serious differences and uncertainties continue between China and its regional neighbors, particularly between China and the United States, China and Japan, and China and Taiwan. Moreover, concerns persist in Washington and in the region that China may leverage its increased political, diplomatic, and military power to achieve more narrowly self-interested security goals, such as resolving the Taiwan question forcefully, asserting itself more muscularly as a regional political-military power, and seeking to displace the United States as the preeminent power in the western Pacific. Chinese entities continue to proliferate sensitive weapons and technologies to countries such as Iran, North Korea, and Pakistan; and the United States and China remain divided over how best to pursue an effective global arms control agenda. Beijing's narrow interpretation on questions of sovereignty and intervention may encumber appropriate international responses to humanitarian crises or threatening regimes. If not addressed, such differences between the United States and China will increase bilateral tensions, undermine regional and global security relations, and possibly lead to confrontation between the two powers.

In recognizing these stakes, this book outlines China's changing global and regional security diplomacy and explains why it has changed, highlighting the three fundamental interests this diplomacy seeks to realize: to defuse tensions in its external security environment to better focus on domestic challenges, to reassure neighbors about China's rise, and to cautiously balance the United States in a way that accounts for Chinese security interests. The book's core chapters show how China's new security diplomacy works in practice, with a particular focus on Chinese actions in three of the most critical developments shaping global and regional security affairs today: the changing role of alliances and the expansion of regional security mechanisms and confidence-building measures; the growing significance of nonproliferation and arms control, especially as they are linked with counterterrorism; and increasingly flexible approaches to sovereignty and intervention. Chapters 5 and 6 detail the challenges and opportunities that China's new security diplomacy presents to the international community, to regional stability, and to U.S. interests.

For U.S. policy leaders and analysts, the most important conclusions to draw from this work are that although China's new security diplomacy presents serious challenges to the United States, these challenges need not lead to conflict, and equally important, these challenges should not preclude a judicious policy approach to important opportunities for U.S. interests. A balanced, realistic, and strategic approach to China's new security diplomacy will defuse potential challenges, achieve greater benefits for global and regional stability, improve U.S.-China relations, and help realize a more open and constructive China for the future.

However, it remains to be seen whether the United States can formulate and sustain such a policy response. As discussed in chapter 1, Washington has been thwarted from doing so by at least three major constraints: strategic preoccupation with Southwest Asia and the Middle East, a volatile U.S.-China relationship, and the politicized and divisive nature of China policy at home. Yet the American public, its policymakers, and its political leaders can and must debate and develop a more sophisticated and strategic approach toward China. For better or for worse, no bilateral relationship is likely to matter more than that of China and the United States in addressing the strategic challenges of the coming decades: maintaining great power stability, regional security, and global economic growth; stemming weapons proliferation; countering transnational threats such as terrorism, infectious disease, and international crime; ensuring energy security; and dealing with environmental degradation and climate change. The stakes are extremely high to "get China right."

Looking ahead, as U.S.-China relations become more complex and intertwined and as their roles and influence in regional and global affairs likewise grow and intersect, the two countries share a strategic interest in managing differences and acting on opportunities to stabilize and improve global and regional stability overall—and U.S.-China relations in particular. This approach recognizes that the United States and China are unlikely to become close friends, but it realistically demands that statesmen in both countries recognize the high costs of being enemies and to work toward a framework that gives greater weight to what the two countries share in common than to what divides them. But this will not be easy. The achievement of these aims will demand informed realism, astute management, and a nimble, opportunistic diplomacy in Washington.

Informed realism recognizes the broader strategic context in which U.S.-China relations are embedded and the constraints this strategic context places on both sides so that neither side pursues a potentially destabilizing relationship with the other. Informed realism also recognizes that the differences between the United States and China are real and cannot be ignored. At the same time, informed realism understands that China's future is not yet written and that many outcomes, both positive and negative, are possible. Under these conditions, the United States must build bridges of insight and influence to shape the best outcomes while also being positioned to foresee, respond to, and deflect the worst outcomes. Blindly taking a view of either inevitable conflict or trouble-free partnership is a recipe for failure. Looking ahead, the United States and China can share goals consistent with China's new security diplomacy and with U.S. interests: avoiding strategic conflict, maintaining stable and prosperous regional and global conditions, and fostering greater openness and socioeconomic stability in China. But it will take realistic and statesmanlike vision and political courage on both sides to steer the bilateral relationship toward such goals.

Astute management of the U.S.-China relationship demands that American foreign policy leaders, beginning with the president, and especially including those executive branch policymakers and members of Congress who are not primarily China specialists, expend the time and energy necessary to understand and attend to the complex and consequential U.S.-China relationship. Of particular importance, politicians and policymakers need to gain a far greater understanding of what is happening inside China, the remarkable social, economic, and political changes unfolding there, and how those internal developments fundamentally shape China's external behavior. Unfortunately, U.S.-China relations are often highly politicized, leading politicians and policymakers to reach for the easiest answers or to skirt tough details and decisions. Moreover, China remains a mysterious and unfamiliar place for many, with cultural, political, and linguistic differences further fostering misperceptions, misunderstandings, and misjudgments. However, given the strategic interests at stake for the United States in its relationship with China, there is no substitute for a knowledgeable, sophisticated, perceptive, and less-politicized policy process for managing U.S.-China relations. The alternative—leaving China policy to drift or slide unnecessarily into difficulty—is to cede the greater initiative to China, whose pragmatic new security diplomacy helps its strategic outlook.

Finally, a nimble, opportunistic diplomacy toward China will stay alert to and take advantage of emergent opportunities in U.S.-China relations. Recognizing the challenges China poses to the United States should inform and sharpen, not close off, an awareness of how and when promising changes are in train that benefit U.S. interests and the interests of U.S.-China relations overall. Such opportunities are increasingly evident. For example, the post–September 11 environment has helped open new areas of common interests for Washington and Beijing. China's leadership, both under Jiang Zemin and the new "fourth-generation" leaders installed over 2002–03, appears generally committed to establishing a more stable and productive relationship with the United States. In addition, as China's intellectual environment gradually opens, so too emergent debates over U.S.-China relations become more conspicuous, palpable, and visible. While still early, there are clearly outlooks and differences of opinion within China that Washington needs to more attentively interpret, decipher, and test, all with an eye to solidifying positive gains with Beijing. Many aspects of the new security diplomacy itself—a predominately inward focus of attention and energy on the part of Chinese leaders and strategists, appreciation for multilateral diplomacy, preference for peaceful outcomes to disputes, and a desire to avoid confrontation with the United States—present strategic opportunities for the United States, which need to be more fully tested and solidified. Chapter 6 offers an agenda for doing so.

The U.S.-China bilateral relationship appears destined to become more complex and interdependent in the decades ahead. Uncertainties and contention will be an abiding aspect of U.S.-China relations, and the two countries are unlikely to achieve a dramatic and strategic breakthrough. Nevertheless, steady and positive progress in bilateral relations is possible and even necessary. This approach does not discount U.S.-China differences but does recognize the accomplishments of Beijing's new security diplomacy; China's growing influence as a global and regional player in political, economic, and military terms; and the critical role America played and can continue to play in helping shape China's future strategic policy. A richer understanding of China's new security diplomacy and the challenges and opportunities it presents provides the foundation upon which the United States can achieve its long-term interests in a strategically stable and productive relationship with China: neither true friends nor abiding enemies, neither strategic partners nor strategic adversaries, but two of the world's most important powers whose identifiable interests can share common ground.

Appendix. *United States Nonproliferation Sanctions against China, 1987–2006*[a]

Date, sanction, and duration[b]	Description
June 13, 2006 Prohibits all transactions between the designees and any U.S. person and freezes any assets the designees may have under U.S. jurisdiction Ongoing	In accordance with Executive Order 13382 (June 29, 2005), which authorizes the Department of the Treasury to issue financial sanctions against proliferators as well as entities and individuals providing support or services to them, imposed on four Chinese companies and one U.S. company: —Beijing Alite Technologies Company (ALCO) —LIMMT Economic and Trade Company —China Great Wall Industry Corporation (CGWIC) —China Precision Machinery Import Export Corporation (CPMIEC) —G. W. Aerospace (represents CGWIC; located in Torrance, California)
December 23, 2005 Prohibits U.S. government procurement of any goods or services from, or provision of assistance to, or sales of any item on U.S. Munitions List to the sanctioned entities; terminates all sales of any defense articles, defense services, or design and construction services to sanctioned entities; prohibits new export licenses for items controlled by the Export Administration Act of 1979 or the Export Administration Regulations Two years	Pursuant to provisions of Section 3 of the Iran Nonproliferation Act of 2000, imposed on six Chinese entities: —China Aero-Technology Import Export Corporation (CATIC) —China North Industries Corporation (Norinco) —Hongdu Aviation Industry Group (HAIG) —LIMMT Metallurgy and Minerals Company —Ounion (Asia) International Economic and Technical Cooperation —Zibo Chemical Equipment Corporation (Chemet Global)

Date, sanction, and duration[b]	*Description*
December 27, 2004 Sanction and duration same as above	Pursuant to provisions of Section 3 of the Iran Nonproliferation Act of 2000, imposed on seven Chinese entities: —Beijing Alite Technologies Company (ALCO) —China Aero-Technology Import Export Corporation (CATIC) —China Great Wall Industry Corporation (CGWIC) —China North Industries Corporation (Norinco) —Q. C. Chen —Wha Cheong Tai Company —Zibo Chemical Equipment Corporation (Chemet Global)
November 24, 2004 Sanction and duration same as above	Pursuant to provisions of Section 3 of the Iran Nonproliferation Act of 2000, imposed on four Chinese entities: —Liaoning Jiayi Metals and Mineral Company —Wha Cheong Tai Company —Shanghai Triple International —Q. C. Chen
September 23, 2004 Sanction and duration same as above	Pursuant to provisions of Section 3 of the Iran Nonproliferation Act of 2000, imposed on seven Chinese firms: —Beijing Institute of Aerodynamics —Beijing Institute of Opto-Electronic Technology (BIOET) —China Great Wall Industry Corporation (CGWIC) —China North Industries Corporation (Norinco) —LIMMT Economic and Trade Company —Oriental Scientific Instruments Corporation (OSIC) —South Industries Science and Technology Trading Company

Date, sanction, and duration[b]	*Description*
September 20, 2004	
Prohibits U.S. government procurement of any goods, technology, or services from these entities and terminates existing contracts; prohibits providing any assistance and obligating further funds for such purposes to these entities; the secretary of the treasury shall prohibit the importation into the U.S. of any goods, technology, or services produced or provided by these entities, other than information or materials within the meaning of section 203(b)(3) of the International Emergency Economic Powers Act (50 U.S.C. 1702(b)(3))	Pursuant to provisions of Executive Orders 12938 and 13094, imposed on one Chinese company: —Xinshidai Company (China New Era Group)
Two years	
April 1, 2004	Pursuant to provisions of Section 3 of the Iran Nonproliferation Act of 2000, imposed on five Chinese firms:
Same as December 23, 2005, prohibitions	—Beijing Institute of Opto-Electronic Technology (BIOET)
Two years	—China Precision Machinery Import Export Corporation (CPMIEC) —Oriental Scientific Instruments Corporation (OSIC) —Zibo Chemical Equipment Corporation (Chemet Global) —China North Industries Corporation (Norinco)

Date, sanction, and duration[b]	Description
September 19, 2003 Ban on imports, new export licenses, and U.S. government procurement. Declared sanctions apply to any other Chinese state-owned entities engaged in activities related to development of any missile equipment, electronics, space systems or equipment, and military aircraft. However, sanction on missile technology–related imports would be waived for a period of one year for reasons "essential to the national security of the United States." Two years	Imposed sanctions for a third time in one year on China North Industries Corporation (Norinco) for alleged "missile technology proliferation activities."
July 24, 2003 Same as September 20, 2004, prohibitions Duration not specified, until otherwise waived by the secretary of state	Pursuant to provisions of Executive Orders 12938 and 13094, imposed on China Precision Machinery Import/Export Corporation (CPMIEC) for transfer of missile technology, including ban on U.S. government procurement and any imports of CPMIEC goods into the United States
July 3, 2003 Same as December 23, 2005, prohibitions Duration of two years or until otherwise waived by the secretary of state	Pursuant to Section 3 of the Iran Nonproliferation Act of 2000, imposed on one North Korean and five Chinese entities: —Changgwang Sinyong Corporation (North Korea) —Taian Foreign Trade General Corporation —Zibo Chemical Equipment Corporation (Chemet Global) —Liyang Yunlong (Liyang Chemical Equipment Company) —China North Industries Corporation (Norinco) —China Precision Machinery Import/Export Corporation (CPMIEC)

Date, sanction, and duration[b]	*Description*
May 23, 2003 Same as September 20, 2004, prohibitions Duration of two years or until otherwise waived by the secretary of state	Pursuant to provisions of Executive Orders 12938 and 13094, imposed on China North Industries Corporation (Norinco), including ban on U.S. government procurement and any imports of Norinco goods into the United States
July 9, 2002 Prohibition of U.S. government procurement of any goods or services from the sanctioned entities; prohibition of any export licenses by or to the sanctioned entities Two years	Pursuant to Iran-Iraq Arms Non-Proliferation Act of 1992, imposed for weapons proliferation–related activities with Iran on certain Chinese companies, one Chinese citizen, and one Indian citizen: —Jiangsu Yongli Chemicals and Technology Import Export Corporation —Q. C. Chen —China Machinery and Equipment Import Export Corporation —China National Machinery and Equipment Import Export Corporation —CMEC Machinery and Electric Equipment Import and Export Corporation —CMEC Machinery and Electrical Import Export Corporation —China Machinery and Electric Equipment Import Export Company —Wha Cheong Tai Company —China Shipbuilding Trading Company —Hans Raj Shiv
July 9, 2002 Same as above Period of at least one year until further notice	Pursuant to Arms Export Control Act and Export Administration Act of 1979, imposed for weapons proliferation activities with Iran on certain Chinese companies and one Chinese citizen: —Jiangsu Yongli Chemicals and Technology Import Export Corporation —China Machinery and Equipment Import Export Corporation —China National Machinery and Equipment Import Export Corporation —CMEC Machinery and Electric Equipment Import Export Company —CMEC Machinery and Electrical Import Export Company —China Machinery and Electric Equipment Import Export Company —Wha Cheong Tai Company —Q. C. Chen

Date, sanction, and duration[b]	Description
May 9, 2002 Same as December 23, 2005, prohibitions Two years unless otherwise determined by the secretary or deputy secretary of state	Pursuant to Iran Nonproliferation Act of 2000, imposed for weapons exports to Iran (probably chemical- and missile-related) on Chinese, Armenian, and Moldovan companies, and Chinese, Armenian, and Moldovan citizens: —Liyang Yunlong (Liyang Chemical Equipment Company) —Zibo Chemical Equipment Corporation (Chemet Global) —China National Machinery and Electric Equipment Import Export Company —Wha Cheong Tai Company —China Shipbuilding Trading Company —China Precision Machinery Import Export Corporation (CPMIEC) —China Aero-Technology Import Export Corporation (CATIC) —Q. C. Chen —Lizen Open Joint Stock Company (Armenia) —Armen Sargsian (Armenia) —Cuanta, SA (Moldova) —Mikhail Pavlovich Vladov (Moldova)
January 16, 2002 Same as December 23, 2005, prohibitions Two years unless otherwise determined by the secretary or deputy secretary of state	Pursuant to Iran Nonproliferation Act of 2000, imposed for chemical weapons–related exports to Iran on two Chinese companies and one Chinese citizen: —Liyang Yunlong (Liyang Chemical Equipment Company) —China Machinery and Electric Equipment Import Export Company —Q. C. Chen
September 1, 2001 Prohibition of U.S contracts and exports relating to Missile Technology Control Regime Annex–controlled items to the sanctioned entities; practical effect of banning licenses for U.S. satellite exports to China Two years; sanctions against Pakistani entity lifted in wake of September 11 terrorist attacks	Pursuant to the Arms Export Control Act and the Export Administration Act of 1979, imposed for missile-related exports to Pakistan on one Chinese company and one Pakistani entity: —China Metallurgical Equipment Corporation —National Development Complex (Pakistan)

Date, sanction, and duration[b]	*Description*
June 14, 2001 Same as December 23, 2005, prohibitions Two years unless otherwise determined by the secretary of state	Pursuant to Iran Nonproliferation Act of 2000, imposed for "proliferation activities," reported to be chemical weapons–related exports to Iran, on one Chinese company: —Jiangsu Yongli Chemicals and Technology Import Export Corporation
May 21, 1997 Prohibition of U.S. government procurement of goods or services from the sanctioned entities or persons; prohibition of the importation into the United States of any products produced by the sanctioned entities One year; subsequently reimposed against some entities; see above	Pursuant to the Chemical and Biological Weapons Control and Warfare Elimination Act of 1991, imposed for export of dual-use chemical precursors and/or chemical production equipment and technology to Iran on five Chinese individuals, two Chinese companies, and one Hong Kong company: —Nanjing Chemical Industries Group —Jiangsu Yongli Chemicals and Technology Import Export Corporation —Cheong Yee (Hong Kong company) —Liao Minglong, Tian Yi, and Chen Qingchang (a.k.a. Q. C. Chen), Pan Yongming, and Shao Xingsheng (Chinese citizens)
August 24, 1993 Prohibition of the export of Missile Technology Control Regime (MTCR) items; prohibition of U.S. government contracts for goods and services with the sanctioned entities Waived November 1, 1994; sanctions on Pakistani Ministry of Defense expired August 1995	Pursuant to Missile Technology Control Act of 1990, imposed for missile technology proliferation activities on Chinese and Pakistani entities: —Ministry of Aerospace —China Precision Machinery Import Export Corporation (CPMIEC) —China National Space Administration —China Aerospace Corporation —China Great Wall Industry Corporation (CGWIC) —Chinese Academy of Space Technology —Beijing Wan Yuan Industry Corporation —China Haiying Company —Shanghai Astronautics Industry Bureau —China Chang Feng Group —Ministry of Defense (Pakistan)

Date, sanction, and duration[b]	*Description*
May 25, 1991 Prohibition of the export of missile-related computer technology and satellites to sanctioned entities	Pursuant to Missile Technology Control Act of 1990, imposed for missile-related proliferation activities on Chinese and Pakistani entities: —China Precision Machinery Import Export Corporation (CPMIEC) —China Great Wall Industry Corporation (CGWIC) —Space and Upper Atmosphere Research Commission (SUPARCO) (Pakistan)
Waived March 23, 1992; sanctions against SUPARCO expired	
October 22, 1987 Suspension of high-tech liberalization for exports to China	Imposed on Chinese cruise missile–related sales to Iran
Lifted March 9, 1988	

a. Revised and updated from information compiled by the East Asia Nonproliferation Program, Center for Nonproliferation Studies, Monterey Institute of International Studies (www.nti.org/db/china/sanclist.htm). See also Dianne E. Rennack, *China: Economic Sanctions* (Washington: Congressional Research Service, updated February 1, 2006).

b. Status as of June 2006.

Notes

Chapter One

1. See, for example, China's Information Office of the State Council, *China's National Defense* (Beijing: July 1998), p. 1.

2. Portions of this section are updated and revised from Bates Gill, "China's Evolving Regional Security Strategy," in *Power Shift: China and Asia's New Dynamics*, edited by David Shambaugh (University of California Press, 2005).

3. China's Information Office of the State Council, *China's National Defense in 2000* (Beijing: October 2000), p. 8.

4. The five principles are mutual respect for sovereignty and territorial integrity, mutual nonaggression, mutual noninterference in each other's internal affairs, equality and mutual benefit, and peaceful coexistence.

5. China's Information Office of the State Council, *China: Arms Control and Disarmament* (Beijing: November 1995).

6. China's Information Office of the State Council, *China's National Defense*, pp. 34–35.

7. See "Promote Disarmament Process and Safeguard World Security," speech by Jiang Zemin before the UN Conference on Disarmament, Geneva, March 26, 1999 (www.china-un.org/eng/zghlhg/cj/unga/t29298.htm); the full text can be found at *People's Daily*, November 8, 2002 (http://english.people.com.cn/200211/18/eng20021118_106985.shtml). The principles are reiterated in China's Information Office of the State Council, *China's National Defense in 2000*, p. 8. See also an early presentation of the concept in China's Information Office of the State Council, *China's National Defense*, pp. 6–7. David M. Finkelstein provides an excellent early analysis in "China's New Security Concept: Reading between the Lines," *Washington Journal of Modern China* 5, no. 1 (1999): 37-49.

8. *People's Daily*, November 8, 2002.

9. One of the earliest discussions of China as a "responsible great power" to appear in English was Xia Liping, "China: A Responsible Great Power," *Journal of Contemporary China* 10, no. 26 (2001): 17–25. A more recent and detailed discussion of the concept is in Tang Shiping and Zhang Yunling, "Zhongguo de diqu zhanlue" [China's Regional Strategy], *Shijie Jingji yu Zhengzhi* [World Economics and Politics], no. 6 (2004): 8–13. A slightly revised version of this article appears in English in David Shambaugh, ed., *Power Shift: China and Asia's New Dynamics* (University of California Press, 2005), pp. 48–68.

10. China's Information Office of the State Council, *National Defense in 2000*, p. 1.

11. Evan S. Medeiros and M. Taylor Fravel, "China's New Diplomacy," *Foreign Affairs* (November–December 2003): 22–35.

12. Zheng Bijian was vice president of the Chinese Communist Party Central Party School. One of the first major explanations of the concept came in his speech "New Path for China's Peaceful Rise and the Future of Asia," Bo'ao Forum, Bo'ao, Hainan Island, November 3, 2003 (http://history.boaoforum.org/english/E2003nh/dhwj/t20031103_184101.btk). He also expressed some early formulations of the concept at a conference convened by the Center for Strategic and International Studies in Washington, November 13, 2003, and further detailed these views during the Bo'ao Forum of April 2004 at a special workshop, "China's Peaceful Rise and Economic Globalization." Wen Jiabao, the Chinese premier, addressed China's peaceful rise in a speech in the United States in December 2003: "Working Together to Write a New Chapter in China-US Relations" (Washington, December 9, 2003) (www.fmprc.gov.cn/eng/wjdt/zyjh/t55971.htm). See also "China's Peaceful Rise: A Road Chosen for the Rejuvenation of a Great Nation," *People's Daily*, February 18, 2004 (http://english.peopledaily.com.cn/200402/18/eng20040218_135155.shtml#); Evan Medeiros, "China Debates Its 'Peaceful Rise' Strategy," *YaleGlobal*, June 22, 2004; Zheng Bijian, "China's 'Peaceful Rise' to Great-Power Status," *Foreign Affairs* (September–October 2005): 18–24; China's Information Office of the State Council, *China's Peaceful Development Road* (Beijing: December 2005) (FBIS, CPP2005122078042).

13. "China's Peaceful Rise: A Road Chosen."

14. Robert G. Sutter, *China's Rise in Asia: Promises and Perils* (New York: Rowman and Littlefield, 2005), chap. 12. See also Medeiros, "China Debates Its 'Peaceful Rise' Strategy."

15. Hu Jintao, "China's Development Is an Opportunity for Asia," speech at the Bo'ao Forum for Asia 2004 annual conference, April 24, 2004 (http://english.people.com.cn/200404/24/eng20040424_141419.shtml); Wen Jiabao's remarks are summarized in "The 10th Conference of Chinese Diplomats Stationed Abroad Held in Beijing," available at the website of the Chinese Ministry of Foreign Affairs, www.fmprc.gov.cn/eng/zxxx/t155418.htm.

16. Discussions and interviews with leading Chinese foreign policy analysts and strategists, Beijing, Shanghai, and Washington, in January 2001, February, May, and July 2002, and August 2004. Recent expressions of "new thinking" include Tang and

Zhang, "Zhongguo de diqu zhanlue." Shi Yinhong, a professor of international relations at Renmin University in Beijing, usefully summarizes some of these debates and arguments in "The Rising China: Essential Disposition, Secular Grand Strategy, and Current Prime Problems," seminar transcript, Asian Voices: Promoting Dialogue between the United States and Asia, Sasakawa Peace Foundation, Washington, February 12, 2002. Deng Yong also identifies a number of Chinese strategic perspectives, some arguing for the acceptance of a unipolar world for the foreseeable future: Deng Yong, "Hegemon on the Offensive: Chinese Perspectives on U.S. Global Strategy," *Political Science Quarterly* 116, no. 3 (2001): 343–65. See also essays in Zhang Yunling, ed., *Huoban haishi duishou: tiaozheng zhong de Zhong Mei Ri E guanxi* [Partners or Adversaries: China-United States-Japan-Russia Relations in Flux] (Beijing: China Academy of Social Sciences Press, 2000); Zi Zhongyun, "Weile minzu de zuigao liyi, weile renmin de changyuan fuzhi" [For the Supreme Interests of the Nation, for the Long-term Welfare of the People], *Taipingyang Xuebao* [Pacific Journal] (December 1999): 10–15.

17. Liu Jianfei, "The Building of Democratic Politics in China and Sino-U.S. Relations," *Zhanlue yu Guanli* [Strategy and Management], no. 2 (March 2003): 76–82 (FBIS, CPP20030506000226).

18. The author is indebted to Iain Johnston, Harvard University, for his insights into the community of "new thinkers" in Chinese academic and policy circles. E-mail correspondence with Iain Johnston, August 2004.

19. See Peter Hays Gries's incisive account of the intellectual and public debate toward Japan in the early 2000s in "China's 'New Thinking' on Japan," *China Quarterly* 184 (2005): 831–50.

20. China's Information Office of the State Council, *China's National Defense in 2002*, p. 1.

21. Wang Jisi, "China's Search for Stability with America," *Foreign Affairs* (September–October 2005): 39–48.

22. Avery Goldstein outlines a similar set of motivations guiding China's grand strategy. See his *Rising to the Challenge: China's Grand Strategy and International Security* (Stanford University Press, 2005).

23. See, for example, Aaron L. Friedberg, "The Future of U.S.-China Relations: Is Conflict Inevitable?" *International Security* 30, no. 2 (2005): 7–45; David M. Lampton, *Same Bed, Different Dreams: Managing U.S.-China Relations, 1989–2000* (University of California Press, 2001); Bates Gill, "Limited Engagement," *Foreign Affairs* (July–August 1999): 65–76; David Shambaugh, "Containment or Engagement of China? Calculating Beijing's Responses," *International Security* 21, no. 2 (1996): 180–209.

24. In his insightful essay, Friedberg, "The Future of U.S.-China Relations," table 1, categorizes China analysts into two broad camps—optimists and pessimists—with each camp falling into three subcategories. On the one hand are liberal optimists, realist optimists, and constructivist optimists; on the other are liberal pessimists, realist pessimists, and constructivist pessimists. He writes, "the most common manifestation

of the debate over the future of U.S.-China relations is the disagreement between liberal optimists and realist pessimists," p. 10, which probably gives too much credit to the liberal optimists. Within the Washington policy community the debate is mostly engaged between what he terms "realist pessimists" (my term is "China hawks") and "realist optimists" (roughly equivalent to my "engager-hedgers"). In any event, he notes the likelihood that "the fundamentally mixed character of the U.S.-China relationship will not change very much . . . with periodic shifts toward greater cooperation or increased competition, but without a clear trend in either direction," p. 43.

25. Details on this incident are drawn from U.S. Department of State, Office of the Spokesman, "State Department Report on Accidental Bombing of Chinese Embassy" (July 6, 1999), which includes the oral explanation given by Undersecretary of State Thomas Pickering on June 17, 1999, to the Chinese government. Also see the remarks of George Tenet, director of the Central Intelligence Agency, and John Hamre, deputy secretary of defense, in "Hearing on the Bombing of the Chinese Embassy," U.S. House of Representatives Permanent Select Committee on Intelligence, July 22, 1999.

26. See Observer, "We Urge Hegemonism Today to Take a Look at the Mirror of History," *People's Daily*, June 22, 1999 (FBIS, *Daily Report: China*).

27. Both quotes are from U.S. Secretary of State Colin L. Powell, "Remarks at The Elliot School of International Affairs," September 5, 2003 (www.state.gov/secretary/rm/2003/23836.htm).

28. U.S. Secretary of State Colin L. Powell, "Remarks at Conference on China-U.S. Relations," November 5, 2003 (www.state.gov/secretary/rm/2003/25950.htm).

29. Robert B. Zoellick, "Whither China: From Membership to Responsibility?" remarks to the National Committee on U.S.-China Relations, New York, September 21, 2005 (www.state.gov/s/d/rem/53682.htm).

30. Drawing from his September 2005 speech (ibid.), Zoellick, along with Chinese Vice Foreign Minister Dai Bingguo, launched the U.S.-China Senior Dialogue to discuss critical issues between the two countries. The group met twice in 2005. See, for example, Robert B. Zoellick, "Statement on Conclusion of the Second U.S.-China Senior Dialogue" (www.state.gov/r/pa/prs/ps/2005/57822.htm). See also *NBR Analysis* 16, no. 4 (2005) (www.nbr.org/publications/analysis/pdf/vol16no4.pdf).

Chapter Two

1. The Nine Power Pact, signed as part of the Washington Naval Conference of 1921–22 by Belgium, China, France, Japan, Italy, the Netherlands, Portugal, the United Kingdom, and the United States, affirmed China's sovereignty, independence, and territorial integrity. The Kellogg-Briand Pact, a U.S. initiative, sought to renounce war as an instrument of national policy. China and some sixty-one other nations were party to this treaty.

2. Harry Harding finds that Beijing has sought three kinds of cooperative relations: "links with wealthier and more powerful *benefactors*, its strategy and economic

ties to smaller and weaker *clients*, and its more equal but less intense relationships with a larger number of foreign *partners.*" See Harry Harding, "China's Co-operative Behaviour," in *Chinese Foreign Policy: Theory and Practice,* edited by Thomas W. Robinson and David Shambaugh (Oxford, U.K.: Clarendon, 1994), p. 376 (emphasis in original).

3. For a more comprehensive examination of Sino-Soviet and Sino-American relations and the Korean War, see Sergei N. Goncharov, John W. Lewis, and Xue Litai, *Uncertain Partners: Stalin, Mao, and the Korean War* (Stanford University Press, 1995); Chen Jian, *China's Road to the Korean War: The Making of the Sino-American Confrontation* (Columbia University Press, 1996).

4. Treaty of Friendship, Cooperation, and Mutual Assistance between the People's Republic of China and the Democratic People's Republic of Korea, Peking, 11 July 1961, in *Documents on International Affairs 1961,* edited by D. C. Watt (Oxford University Press, 1965), pp. 258–59.

5. Preceding quotes from ibid., articles 2 and 3.

6. The Chinese Foreign Ministry statement at the time: "All the facts show that the Albanian leadership has decided to pursue the anti-China course, deliberately abandoned the agreements signed between the two sides providing Chinese aid to Albania, slandered and tried to fabricate charges against Chinese experts, and sabotaged the economic and military cooperation between China and Albania in a planned and systematic way, making it impossible for our aid work to go on while you have blocked the way to a solution of the problems through consultation. . . . The disruption of the economic and military cooperation between China and Albania is wholly the making of the Albanian side, which must bear the full responsibility." Quoted in Elez Biberaj, *Albania and China: A Study of an Unequal Alliance* (Boulder, Colo.: Westview, 1986), pp. 135–36.

7. In 1986 the United States abrogated its alliance responsibilities to New Zealand under the Australia–New Zealand–United States (ANZUS) alliance because of a disagreement over New Zealand's decision to no longer allow nuclear-powered or nuclear-armed vessels in its waters. However, New Zealand has not formally withdrawn from the alliance, and the ANZUS treaty is still in effect. SEATO was in effect from September 1954 to June 1977 and included Australia, France, the United Kingdom, New Zealand, Pakistan, the Philippines, Thailand, and the United States. Following the end of SEATO, the U.S.-Thailand alliance continues to be governed by the SEATO Manila Pact and the 1962 Thanat-Rusk Communiqué. CENTO, in which the United States was an associate member, lasted from August 1959 to September 1979; full members at its founding were Iran, Iraq, Pakistan, Turkey, and the United Kingdom.

8. See David Shambaugh, "China Engages Asia: Reshaping the Regional Order," *International Security* 29, no. 3 (2003–04): 64–99, esp. p. 70.

9. These quotes are drawn, respectively, from China's Information Office of the State Council, *China's National Defense* (Beijing: July 1998), p. 5, and China's Information Office of the State Council, *China's National Defense in 2000* (Beijing: October 2000), pp. 6–7.

10. U.S. Department of Defense, *Annual Report to Congress on the Military Power of the People's Republic of China*, June 22, 2000 (www.defenselink.mil/news/Jun2000/china06222000.htm).

11. As examples, see, "PRC Journal Ascertains Bush Administration's New Military Strategy," *Contemporary International Relations* 11, no. 5 (2001): 12–16 (FBIS, CPP20010614000176); "Shanghai Paper Views US Asia-Pacific Security Strategy, China Containment," *Shanghai Liberation Daily*, June 16, 2001 (FBIS, CPP20010619000003); "Renmin Ribao Views U.S. Military Presence in Central Asia," *People's Daily*, March 22, 2002 (FBIS, CPP20020322000057).

12. Bonnie Glaser, "Face to Face in Shanghai: New Amity amid Perennial Differences," *Comparative Connections*, January 2002 (www.csis.org/pacfor/cc/0104Qus_china.html). See also Shambaugh, "China Engages Asia," p. 91.

13. "Text: Guidelines for U.S.-Japan Defense Cooperation," September 23, 1997 (www.fas.org/news/japan/97092302_epo.html). See also analyses on the 1997 U.S.-Japan Defense Guidelines in Michael Green, *Japan's Reluctant Realism: Foreign Policy Challenges in an Era of Uncertain Power* (New York: Palgrave, 2001), pp. 90–108; Avery Goldstein, *Rising to the Challenge: China's Grand Strategy and International Security* (Stanford University Press, 2005), pp. 105–09.

14. "PRC FM Spokesman: China Resolutely Opposes US-Japan Statement on Taiwan Issue," Xinhua, February 20, 2005 (FBIS, CPP20050220000055).

15. "Kyodo: China Indicates Australia-U.S. Pact Should Not Cover Taiwan," Kyodo, March 8, 2005 (FBIS, JPP20050308000089).

16. "PRC FM Spokesman: Military Alliances Should Not Go beyond Bilateral Scope," Xinhua, March 8, 2005 (FBIS, CPP20050308000174).

17. The ARF evolved from a less formal political and security dialogue group known as the ASEAN Post-Ministerial Conference (PMC). Established in 1979, the ASEAN PMC at that time included ASEAN plus seven "dialogue partners": Australia, Canada, the European Community, Japan, New Zealand, the Republic of Korea, and the United States. China and Russia joined the ASEAN PMC as observers in 1991, and Laos and Vietnam joined as observers in 1992.

18. The first ARF meeting in 1994 brought together foreign ministers from Australia, Brunei, Canada, China, the European Union (presidency), Indonesia, Japan, Laos, Malaysia, New Zealand, Papua New Guinea, the Philippines, the Republic of Korea, Russia, Singapore, Thailand, the United States, and Vietnam. The ARF's membership now includes Cambodia (1995), India (1996), Burma (1996), Mongolia (1999), and the Democratic People's Republic of Korea (2000). See the Australian Department of Foreign Affairs and Trade website, www.dfat.gov.au/arf/arf_members.html.

19. Extensive ARF information and documentation can be found at the official website of the ASEAN Secretariat, www.aseansec.org.

20. Yan Xuetong, "China's Security after the Cold War," *Contemporary International Relations* 3, no. 5 (1993): 1–16, esp. p. 15.

21. Ding Kuisong, "ASEAN Regional Forum: Its Role in Asian Pacific Security Cooperation," *Contemporary International Relations* 8, no. 7 (1998): 14–27, quotations on pp. 20–21, 24–25.

22. Wu Peng, "Shilun woguo yatai diqu anquanguan ji fazhan" [A Treatise on China's Security Concept for the Asia-Pacific Region and Development], *Shijie Jingji yu Zhengzhi* [World Economy and Politics], no. 5 (1999): 12–16, esp. p. 13.

23. "China's Position on Asia-Pacific Security," *Beijing Review,* August 8-14, 1994, p. 21–22.

24. "'Text' of Qian Qichen Speech to ARF," Xinhua, August 7, 1997 (FBIS, *Daily Report: China,* August 8, 1997).

25. "'Text' of Chinese FM Tiang [sic] Jiaxuan's Speech at the 7th ARF Meeting" (FBIS, *Daily Report: China,* July 28, 2000).

26. Amitav Acharya, *The ASEAN Regional Forum: Confidence Building* (Ottawa: Department of Foreign Affairs and International Trade, 1997), pp. 16–17.

27. Banning Garrett and Bonnie Glaser, "Multilateral Security in the Asia-Pacific Region and Its Impact on Chinese Interests: Views from Beijing," *Contemporary Southeast Asia* 16, no. 1 (1994): 14–34, esp. p. 14.

28. Garrett and Glaser, "Multilateral Security," pp. 14–15.

29. These points drawn from Mely Caballero-Anthony, "ASEAN-China Relations Turn the Corner," *PacNet Newsletter,* December 12, 2002 (www.csis.org/pacfor/pac0252.htm).

30. Rosemary Foot, "China in the ASEAN Regional Forum: Organizational Processes and Domestic Modes of Thought," *Asian Survey* 38, no. 5 (1998): 425–40, esp. p. 426. See also China's Information Office of the State Council, *China's National Defense in 2004* (Beijing: December 2004), chapter 9.

31. "Chinese Delegation Submits Position Document on New Security Concept to ASEAN Forum" (FBIS, CPP20020801000128).

32. For a summary of the November 2003 intersessional meeting, see www.dfat.gov.au/arf/intersessional/report_interses_03_04.html. See also "FM Stresses Asian Security Issues in ASEAN Forum," Xinhua, June 19, 2003 (www.china.org.cn/english/international/67429.htm).

33. "Dong meng daibiao guanmo Zhongguo tezhong budui fan jiechi yanlian" [ARF Delegation Observes Chinese Special Forces Counterterror Drill], Xinhuanet, November 7, 2004 (http://news.xinhuanet.com/mil/2004-11/07/content_2186478.htm).

34. China's Information Office of the State Council, *China's National Defense in 2004,* chapter 9.

35. "Joint Statement on East Asian Cooperation," November 28, 1999 (www.asean sec.org/5469.htm); *Toward an East Asian Community: Region of Peace, Prosperity and Progress,* Report of the East Asia Vision Group, October 31, 2001 (www.aseansec.org/pdf/east_asia_vision.pdf).

36. Eric Teo Chu Cheow, "E. Asia Summit's Birthing Pains," *Straits Times,* February 22, 2005 (www.siiaonline.org/et_st220206).

37. U.S. Department of State official, e-mail correspondence with author, November 23, 2005.

38. See also P. Parameswaran, "US Says Not Ready to Accede to ASEAN Nonaggression Pact," Agence France-Press, October 5, 2005. The Treaty of Amity and Cooperation has been signed by all ten ASEAN nations, as well as China (2003), India (2003), Japan (2004), Pakistan (2004), South Korea (2004), Russia (2004), Australia (2005) and New Zealand (2005).

39. Lu Jianren, "East Asia Summit: A New Platform for Regional Cooperation," *People's Daily*, December 14, 2005 (http://english.people.com.cn/200512/14/eng20051214_228024.html).

40. "Kuala Lumpur Declaration on the East Asia Summit," December 14, 2005 (www.aseansec.org/18098.htm).

41. "ASEAN and China Cooperative Operations in Response to Dangerous Drugs (ACCORD)," October 13, 2000 (www.aseansec.org/645.htm).

42. Joint Declaration of ASEAN and China on Cooperation in the Field of Non-Traditional Security Issues, 6th ASEAN-China Summit, November 4, 2002 (www.aseansec.org/13185.htm).

43. Declaration on the Conduct of Parties in the South China Sea, November 4, 2002 (www.asseansec.org/13163.htm).

44. Instrument of Accession to the Treaty of Amity and Cooperation in Southeast Asia, October 8, 2003 (www.aseansec.org/15271.htm); Treaty of Amity and Cooperation in Southeast Asia, February 24, 1976 (www.aseansec.org/1217.htm).

45. Joint Declaration of the Heads of State/Government of the Association of Southeast Asian Nations and the People's Republic of China on Strategic Partnership for Peace and Prosperity, October 8, 2003 (www.aseansec.org/15265.htm).

46. "Chairman's Statement of the 8th ASEAN + China Summit," Vientiane, November 29, 2004 (www.aseansec.org/16749.htm).

47. ASEAN Workshop on Earthquake-Generated Tsunami Warning, Beijing, China, January 25–26, 2005 (www.aseansec.org/17249.htm).

48. Yang Yanyi, "A New Approach: China's Perception and Policy on Security Dialogue and Cooperation," *Foreign Affairs Journal*, no. 68 (June 2003): 17–26, quotation on p. 26. At the time of this article, Yang was the deputy director of policy planning in the Ministry of Foreign Affairs.

49. Except for China, all members of the Shanghai Five and its follow-on organization, the Shanghai Cooperation Organization, are concurrently members of NATO's Partnership for Peace. Shanghai Five members Kazakhstan, Kyrgyzstan, and Russia all joined Partnership for Peace in 1994; Tajikistan joined Partnership for Peace in 2001. The Shanghai grouping expanded to six countries in 2001 with the inclusion of Uzbekistan, which had joined Partnership for Peace in 1994.

50. China's Information Office of the State Council, *China's National Defense*, p. 35.

51. In July 1998 China and Kazakhstan reached a final agreement resolving remaining border disputes along their 1,700-kilometer (about 1,000-mile) border,

the first full border dispute resolution between China and one of its Shanghai Five partners. "China: Jiang Zemin on Nuclear Arms Race, Sino-Kazakh Border Pact" (FBIS, *Daily Report: China*, July 6, 1998). The July 2000 quote is from "Xinhua: 'Full Text' of Dushanbe Statement of 'Shanghai Five'" (FBIS, CHI-2000-0705, July 7, 2000).

52. "Xinhua: 'Full Text' of Dushanbe Statement of 'Shanghai Five'"; "Shanghai Five States Issue Bishkek Declaration" (FBIS, *Daily Report: Central Eurasia*, August 25, 1999).

53. "Xinhua: 'Full Text' of Dushanbe Statement of 'Shanghai Five.'"

54. "'Shanghai Five' Nations Sign Joint Statement," *People's Daily*, July 6, 2000 (http://english.peopledaily.com.cn/200007/06/eng20000706_44803.html).

55. "Xinhua: 'Full Text' of Dushanbe Statement of 'Shanghai Five.'"

56. Dushanbe Declaration of the Heads of State of the People's Republic of China, the Republic of Kazakhstan, the Kyrgyz Republic, the Russian Federation and the Republic of Tajikistan, p. 3, conveyed to the United Nations General Assembly as document A/55/133-S/2000/682, July 11, 2000 (www.un.org/documents/ga/docs/55/a55133.pdf).

57. This and following quotes from Declaration on the Creation of the Shanghai Cooperation Organization, signed at Shanghai, China, June 15, 2001 (www.sectsco.org/news_detail.asp?id=88&LanguageID=2).

58. "Shanghai Cooperation Organization Approves Center of Anti-Terror," *China Daily*, June 8, 2002 (www.china.org.cn/english/FR/34120.htm); "Russia: Shanghai Group Aims to Increase Economic Cooperation," Radio Free Europe/Radio Liberty, June 12, 2002 (www.rferl.org/nca/features/2002/06/12062002134601.asp).

59. "Presidents of the Six Member Countries Highly Evaluate the St. Petersburg Summit of SCO," June 11, 2002, Ministry of Foreign Affairs of the PRC (www.fmprc.gov.cn/eng/gjhdq/dqzzywt/2633/2634/2636/t15568.htm).

60. "Shanghai Cooperation Organization Issues Charter," Xinhua, June 8, 2002 (FBIS, CEP20020710000381).

61. The description of this exercise is drawn from "China Ends War Games with Kyrgyzstan," Associated Press, October 11, 2002; "China, Kyrgyzstan Hold Joint Antiterror Military Exercise," Xinhuanet, October 12, 2002; "Joint War Games Boost Terror Fight," *South China Morning Post*, October 12, 2002.

62. SCO Secretary General Zhang Deguang and senior staff, interview, Beijing, April 2004. Additional information available at the Chinese Foreign Ministry website, www.fmprc.gov.cn/eng/topics/sco/t57970.htm.

63. Interviews with officials at the Shanghai Cooperation Organization secretariat, Beijing, China, April 2004.

64. "Fifth SCO Summit Held in Astana; Hu Jintao Gives 'Important Speech,'" Xinhua, July 5, 2005 (FBIS, CPP20050705000256).

65. See "Astana Brings New Horizons for Shanghai Cooperation Organization" (www.kazind.com/newsarchives/newsvol33.html).

66. "China Vows to Promote Security Cooperation within SCO," Xinhua, November 16, 2005 (FBIS, CPP2005116302004).

67. "PRC Defense Ministry Officer Says SCO Military Cooperation No Threat to Any Country," Xinhua, November 7, 2005 (FBIS, CPP20051107052017).

68. Joint Communiqué of the Meeting of the Council of Heads of Member States of the Shanghai Cooperation Organization, June 15, 2006; see website of the Secretariat of the Shanghai Cooperation Organization, www.sectsco.org.

69. Declaration on Fifth Anniversary of Shanghai Cooperation Organization, June 15, 2006; see website of the Secretariat of the Shanghai Cooperation Organization, www.sectsco.org.

70. Joint Statement by the Ministers of Foreign Affairs of the Member States of the Shanghai Cooperation Organization, Beijing, January 7, 2002 (http://missions.itu.int/~kazaks/eng/sco/sco06.htm).

71. "Russia Has Misgivings about Shanghai Cooperation Organization," *Eurasia Insight*, June 27, 2001 (www.eurasianet.org/departments/insight/articles/eav062001.shtml).

72. See the joint statement in "Text of PRC-Russia Statement Released," Xinhua (FBIS, *Daily Report: China*, April 26, 1996). On the evolution of China-Russia relations, see also Goldstein, *Rising to the Challenge*, pp. 136–43.

73. "Text of Sino-Russian Joint Statement," Xinhua (FBIS, *Daily Report: China*, April 23, 1997).

74. The December 10, 1999, Sino-Russian joint statement is at www.fmprc.gov.cn/eng/3804.html.

75. "Full Text of Sino-Russian 18 July Declaration," Xinhua (FBIS, *Daily Report: China*, July 19, 2000).

76. Treaty of Good Neighborly Friendship and Cooperation between the People's Republic of China and the Russian Federation, Xinhua, July 16, 2001 (FBIS, CPP20010716000104).

77. Ibid., chapter 9.

78. Text of Putin-Hu Jintao Joint Declaration, Russian Ministry of Foreign Affairs, May 28, 2003 (FBIS, CEP20030528000286).

79. Text of Sino-Russian Premiers' Meeting Communiqué, Xinhua, September 24, 2004 (FBIS, CPP20040924000233).

80. China-Russia Border Agreement, Xinhuanet, October 14, 2004.

81. "Chinese, Russian Presidents Meet Press after Talks," Xinhua, July 1, 2005 (httpp://news.xinhuanet.com/english/2005-07/01/content_3164428.htm).

82. "China, Russia Pledge Efforts to Boost Economic, Cultural Coop," Xinhua, July 3, 2005 (http://news.xinhuanet.com/english/2005-07/03/content_3169570.htm).

83. "China, Russia to Promote Military Cooperation," Xinhua, July 3, 2005 (http://news.xinhuanet.com/english/2005-07/03/content_3169571.htm).

84. Full Text of China-Russia Joint Statement on 21st Century World Order, Xinhua, July 1, 2005.

85. "PRC Expert: Hu, Putin Joint Statement 'Symbolic Action' against US Unilateralism," *Beijing Review*, July 15, 2005 (FBIS, CPP20050715000128).

86. Alexander Lukin, *The Bear Watches the Dragon: Russia's Perceptions of China and the Evolution of Russian-Chinese Relations since the Eighteenth Century* (Armonk, N.Y.: M. E. Sharpe, 2003).

87. Watt, *Documents on International Affairs 1961.*

88. "ROK's Yonhap: China, N. Korea to Expand Military Ties: Chinese Defense Minister," Yonhap, November 6, 2004 (FBIS, KPP20041106000001).

89. "It Is the Firm Stand of the Party and Government of China to Further Develop the Sino-Korean Friendship," *KCNA*, November 6, 2004 (FBIS, KPP20041106 000024).

90. See trade statistics at the website of the Korea Economic Insitute (www.keia.org/4-Current/NorthKorea.ppt#32,1,Slide 1); Robert Marquand, "North Korea's Border Trade Getting Busier," *Christian Science Monitor*, April 14, 2005 (www.csmoniotor.com/2005/0414/p01s04-woap.html).

91. According to the treaty, formal withdrawal comes into effect ninety days after an announcement of intent to withdraw. However, North Korea did not consider itself bound by this waiting period, arguing that in 1993 it already announced its intent to withdraw from the treaty and had only "suspended" this intention awaiting the outcome of agreements reached with the United States at that time.

92. Glenn Kessler, "N. Korea Says It Has Nuclear Arms," *Washington Post*, April 25, 2003, p. A1.

93. Joint Declaration of the Denuclearization of the Korean Peninsula, January 20, 1992 (www.globalsecurity.org/wmd/library/news/rok/1992/appendix17.htm).

94. "ROK Chief Negotiator: China's Role 'Outstanding' in Six-Party Talks," *People's Daily*, September 20, 2005 (http://english.people.com.cn/200509/20/eng20050920_209460.html).

95. See "DPRK FM Clarifies Stand on New Measure To Bolster War Deterrent," Korea Central News Agency (Pyongyang), October 3, 2006 (FBIS, KPP20061003 971124).

96. Information on China–North Korea nuclear-related cooperation from the Monterey Institute's Center for Nonproliferation Studies database, available at the Nuclear Threat Initiative website, www.nti.org. The *Washington Times*, on December 17, 2002, citing leaked intelligence information, reported that China exported some twenty tons of tributyl phosphate to North Korea, a chemical substance with commercial applications that can also be used in the extraction of fissile material from spent nuclear fuel.

97. In December 2003 Ning Fukui, who served as the Chinese Foreign Ministry's vice director of Korean affairs from 1995 until 2000, was appointed special ambassador in charge of the nuclear issue on the Korean peninsula. See "Ambassador for Nuke Issue Named," *China Daily*, December 12, 2003 (www.chinadaily.com.cn/en/doc/2003-12/19/content_291649.htm).

98. See, for example, Pang Zhongying, "Building a Regional Security Mechanism," PacNet, April 5, 2004 (www.csis.org/pacfor/pac0413A.pdf). Pang at the time of the

publication was director of the Institute of Global Issues at Nankai University. See also Yuan Peng, "Advancing the Second Round of Development of Sino-US Relations," *Global Times*, December 27, 2004 (FBIS, CPP20050113000200). Yuan at the time of the publication was deputy director, Division of American Studies, China Institute of Contemporary International Relations.

99. David M. Finkelstein, "China's New Security Concept: Reading between the Lines," *Washington Journal of Modern China* 5, no. 1 (1999): 37–49, quotations on p. 41.

100. For discussions advocating bilateral over multilateral security approaches, see, for example, Bao Wei, "Lianmeng zhanlue de yunyong yu fazhan" [The Application and Development of Alliance Strategy], in *Gouji Zhanlue Lun* [The Theory of International Strategy], edited by Yu Qifen (Beijing: Academy of Military Sciences, 1998); Yu Xiaoqiu, "Ou-Ya doubian anquan jizhi zhi bijiao fenxi" [A Treatise on China's Security Concept for the Asia-Pacific Region and Development], *Shijie jingji yu zhengzhi* [World Economics and Politics], no. 6 (1999): 9–11; Yan Xuetong, "Orientation of China's Security Strategy," *Contemporary International Relations* 6, no. 2 (1996): 1–15; Yan Xuetong, "Security Cooperation in Asia-Pacific: Bilateralism vs. Multilateralism," paper presented at Georgia Tech's Center for International Strategy, Technology, and Policy, 1999 (www.gatech.edu/cistp/rpt99/Yan.html).

101. Liu Jiangyong, "International Partnerships Facing Challenges," *Contemporary International Relations* 9, no. 4 (1999): 1–12. Liu, a leading East Asia specialist with the China Institute for Contemporary International Relations, specifically contrasts the military alliance building of the United States with China's advocacy of partnership building. Liu writes that China's partnerships are not directed at any other nation and emphasize regular visits and enhanced political-, economic-, and security-related contacts as important confidence-building measures. According to Liu, partnerships can resolve differences through dialogue and promote equal cooperation on shared concerns, with the goal of promoting mutual benefit while minimizing hostility.

102. Mure Dickie and Shawn Donnan, "Jakarta in Missile Deal with Beijing," *Financial Times*, August 1, 2005, p. 1.

103. "EU Becomes China's Largest Trade Partner," *People's Daily Online*, January 7, 2005 (www.chinadaily.com.cn/English/doc/2005-01/07/content_406961.htm).

104. Joint Statement of the China-EU Summit, December 9, 2004, Chinese Foreign Ministry website (www.fmprc.gov.cn/eng/wjb/zzjg/xos/xwlb/t174512.htm).

105. European Commission news release, "EU and China Are Set to Collaborate on GALILEO, the European Global System of Satellite Navigation," IP/03/1226, September 18, 2003.

106. "Foreign Minister Li Zhaoxing Speaks on Hu Jintao's 'Fruitful' Four-Nation Trip," Xinhua, November 19, 2005 (FBIS, CPP20051119063024).

107. "Xinhua: Wen Jiaobao Ends 'Highly Successful' India Visit," Xinhua, April 12, 2005 (FBIS, CPP2005041200013).

108. "China, India to Hold First-Ever 'Strategic Dialogue' in India on 24 Jan," Xinhua, January 23, 2005 (FBIS, CPP20050123000031).

109. "XNA Roundup: China-India Relations Enter Comprehensive Development Period," Xinhua, April 8, 2005 (FBIS, CPP20050408000096).

110. "Chinese, Indian Military Leaders Underscore Bilateral Ties," Xinhua, December 28, 2004 (FBIS, CPP20041228000171).

111. "Xinhua: Wen Jiabao Ends 'Highly Successful' India Visit."

112. "SCMP Editorial Views Sino-Indian Meetings as Milestone to Reconciliation," *South China Morning Post,* April 13, 2005 (FBIS, CPP20050413000159).

113. "India, China to Avoid Large-Scale Military Exercises Near LAC," *Hindu,* April 11, 2005, p. 1.

114. "Xinhua: Wen Jiabao Ends 'Highly Successful' India Visit."

115. "Delhi TV: Chinese Envoy Says Beijing to Support Delhi's Candidature for UN Seat," New Delhi Doordarshan DD News Channel, April 19, 2005 (FBIS, SAP20050419000090).

116. Japan was also given observer status to the group, and Afghanistan gained full membership. See "China Accorded SAARC Observer Status" (http://english.gov.cn/2005-11/14/content_97525.htm). On reported Indian opposition to Chinese observer status, see "Scholar Analyzes Chinese 'Challenge' to India's Leadership Potential in SAARC," *Indian Express,* November 7, 2005 (FBIS, SAP20051108378014); see also "Pakistan: 'Main Objection' to China's Status in SAARC Said Raised by India," *News,* November 12, 2005 (FBIS, SAP20051112033002).

117. See China's Information Office of the State Council, *China's National Defense in 2004,* chapter 9; "China's Military Diplomacy in 2003," *PLA Daily,* December 29, 2003 (http://english.pladaily.com.cn/english/pladaily/2003/12/29/20031229001013_MilitaryNews.html). For an excellent background on Chinese military diplomacy, see Kenneth W. Allen and Eric A. McVadon, *China's Foreign Military Relations* (Washington: Henry L. Stimson Center, October 1999).

118. "China, Pakistan Hold Joint Antiterror Drill," *People's Daily Online,* August 7, 2004 (http://english.people.cn.com/200408/07/eng20040807_152120_htm).

119. "China Launches Military Exercise 'Iron Fist-2004,'" *People's Daily Online,* September 26, 2004 (http://english.peoopledaily.com.cn/200409/25/eng20040925_158268.html).

120. "Sino-Tajik Exercises Promote Friendship," *China Daily,* September 25, 2006 (http://english.people.com.cn/200609/25/eng20060925_306138.html).

121. "Chinese Ships Arrive for Wargame," *Dawn,* November 22, 2005 (www.dawn.com/2005/11/22/top4.htm); "China-India Joint Naval Exercises Staged in Indian Ocean, *People's Liberation Army Daily,* December 2, 2005 (http://english.chinamil.com.cn/site2/news-channels/2005-12/02/content_352773.htm); "First Sino-Thai Joint Naval Exercise Held in Gulf of Thailand," *People's Liberation Army Daily,* December 14, 2005 (http://english.chinamil.com.cn/site2/news-channels/2005-12/14/content_362133.htm).

122. "Chinese, Australian Navies Hold Maritime Exercises," *People's Daily Online,* October 15, 2004 (http://english.people.com.cn/200410/15/eng20041015_160260.htm).

123. "Foreign Observers Attend Chinese War Games for the First Time," Xinhuanet, August 25, 2003 (http://news.xinhuanet.com/english/2003-08/25/content_1044252.htm).

124. "China Launches Military Exercises," Xinhuanet, September 25, 2004 (http://news.xinhuanet.com/english/2004-09/25/content_2020144.htm).

125. "China Conducts Military Drills in Inner Mongolia, Foreign Observers Attend," Xinhua, September 28, 2005 (FBIS, CPP20050927055010).

126. Cobra Gold is held annually by the United States, Thailand, and Singapore and is the largest multinational exercise and movement of peacetime forces in the Pacific. In 2004 troops from the Philippines and Mongolia were added to the exercise, bringing its total strength to 18,500. Observers of the exercise include Australia, Cambodia, China, France, India, Indonesia, Japan, Malaysia, Mongolia, the Philippines, Russia, South Korea, Sri Lanka, and Tonga.

127. China's Information Office of the State Council, *China's National Defense in 2004*, chapter 9.

128. "Full Text of Jiang Zemin's Speech Delivered at 'Shanghai Five' Summit," Xinhua (FBIS, *Daily Report: China*, July 6, 2000).

129. "ROK Daily: Imports from China Outpaced U.S. Imports," *Chungang Ilbo*, January 13, 2005 (FBIS, KPP20050112000182).

130. "China's Trade Performance," US-China Business Council (www.uschina.org/statistics/foreigntrade_2004.html).

131. "Full Text of Jiang Zemin's Speech Delivered at 'Shanghai Five' Summit."

132. Hu Yumin, "Conventional Arms Control in the Past 10 Years and in the Future," *International Strategic Studies*, no. 4 (1999): 22–30, quotations on p. 27.

133. Xu Tao, "Promoting 'Shanghai Five' Spirit for Regional Cooperation," *Contemporary International Relations* 11, no. 5 (2001): 14–24, quotations on p. 20.

134. Statement of the Chinese Delegation on TMD, Bangkok, March 3–5, 1999 (http://cns.miis.edu/research/neasia/notes.htm#99); "'Text' of Chinese FM Tiang [sic] Jiaxuan's Speech at the 7th ARF Meeting," Xinhua (FBIS, *Daily Report: China*, July 28, 2000).

135. Wu Xinbo, "Integration on the Basis of Strength: China's Impact on East Asian Security," report prepared for the Asia/Pacific Research Center, Institute for International Studies, Stanford University, February 1998, p. 10.

136. Foot, "China in the ASEAN Regional Forum," p. 435.

137. Xie Wenqing, "Observing U.S. Strategy of U.S. Global Hegemony from NATO's Use of Force against FRY," *International Strategic Studies*, no. 3 (July 1999): 1–9, esp. pp. 7–8.

138. Li Zhongcheng, "The Role of an Emerging China in World Politics," *Contemporary International Relations* 8, no. 2 (1998): 1–8, esp. p. 2.

139. Alastair Iain Johnston and Paul Evans, "China's Engagement with Multilateral Security Institutions," in *Engaging China: The Management of an Emerging Power*, edited by Alastair Iain Johnston and Robert S. Ross (New York: Routledge, 1999), p. 237.

Chapter Three

1. China's record as an arms exporter before the 1990s is analyzed in R. Bates Gill, *Chinese Arms Transfers: Purposes, Patterns, and Prospects in the New World Order* (Westport, Conn.: Praeger, 1992).

2. Other authors have examined the interesting and generally positive evolution of China's approach to nonproliferation and arms control policy. Two outstanding works in this regard are Wendy Frieman, *China, International Arms Control and Non-Proliferation* (London: RoutledgeCurzon, 2004); and Evan S. Medeiros, *Shaping Chinese Foreign Policy: U.S. Diplomacy and the Evolution of China's Nonproliferation Policies and Practices, 1980–2004* (Stanford University Press, forthcoming).

3. Li Changhe, quoted in Conference on Disarmament, "Final Record of the Eight Hundred and Twenty-Fifth Plenary Meeting," May 27, 1999 (CD/PV.825), p. 17.

4. Wang Zhenxi and Zhao Xiaozhou, "Lengzhan hou meiguo junkong yu caijun zhengce de tiaozheng" [Revisions in US Post-Cold War Arms Control and Disarmament Policies], *Guoji Zhanlue Yanjiu* [International Strategic Studies], no. 2 (1998): 16–22, quotations on pp. 18, 20.

5. Li Changhe, Ambassador for Disarmament Affairs of the People's Republic of China, "Statement at the Plenary Meeting of the Conference on Disarmament," Geneva, May 27, 1999 (www.nti.org/db/china/engdocs/lich0599.htm).

6. The motivations, evolution, and implications of China's arms transfer policies are covered in Evan Medeiros and Bates Gill, "Chinese Arms Exports: Policy, Players, and Process," occasional paper, Strategic Studies Institute (Carlisle, Pa.: U.S. Army War College, 2000); Alastair Iain Johnston and Paul Evans, "China's Engagement with Multilateral Security Institutions," in *Engaging China: The Management of an Emerging Power*, edited by Alastair Iain Johnston and Robert S. Ross (New York: Routledge, 1999), esp. pp. 235–56; Jing-dong Yuan, "Culture Matters: Chinese Approaches to Arms Control and Disarmament," *Contemporary Security Policy*, no. 1 (April 1998): 85–128; Zhu Mingquan, "The Evolution of China's Nuclear Nonproliferation Policy," *Nonproliferation Review* 4, no. 2 (1997): 40–48; Wu Yun, "China's Policies toward Arms Control and Disarmament: From Passive Responding to Active Leading," *Pacific Review* 9, no. 4 (1996): 577–606; Alastair Iain Johnston, "Learning versus Adaptation: Explaining Change in Chinese Arms Control Policy in the 1980s and 1990s," *China Journal*, no. 35 (January 1996): 27–61; Gill, *Chinese Arms Transfers*; John W. Lewis, Hua Di, and Xue Litai, "Beijing's Defense Establishment: Solving the Arms-Export Enigma," *International Security* 14, no. 4 (1991): 87–109.

7. "Iran, China Sign Arms Technology Pact," *Washington Times*, January 22, 1990, p. 2; James Bruce, "Iran and China in $4.5 Billion Partnership," *Jane's Defence Weekly*, September 11, 1996, p. 3; "Sino-Iranian Arms Deal," *Jane's Defence Weekly*, September 18, 1996, p. 13.

8. Elaine Sciolino, "CIA Report Says Chinese Sent Iran Arms Components," *New York Times*, June 22, 1995, p. A1; Jeffrey Smith and David Ottaway, "Spy Photos Suggest China Missile Trade," *Washington Post*, July 3, 1995, p. 1.

9. Bill Gertz, "China Sold Iran Missile Technology," *Washington Times*, November 21, 1996, p. 1.

10. For a detailed discussion of Iran's nuclear-related imports, see Andrew Koch and Jeanette Wolf, "Iran's Nuclear Procurement Program: How Close to the Bomb?" *Nonproliferation Review* 5, no. 1 (1997): 123–35.

11. This section relies in part on the extensive resources and information compiled by the East Asia Nonproliferation Program, Center for Nonproliferation Studies, Monterey Institute of International Studies, and is available at http://cns.miis.edu.

12. For example, over the twenty years 1966 to 1985, China provided more than 34 percent of Pakistan's arms imports, compared to about 26 percent each from the United States and France. Calculations based on figures in Michael Brzoska and Thomas Ohlson, *Arms Transfers to the Third World, 1971–1985* (Oxford University Press, 1987), app. 7.

13. U.S. Central Intelligence Agency, "Unclassified Report to Congress on the Acquisition of Technology Relating to Weapons of Mass Destruction and Advanced Conventional Munitions, 1 January through 30 June 2000," February 2001 (www.cia.gov/cia/publications/bian/bian_feb_2001.htm).

14. "Libyan Arms Designs Traced Back to China," *Washington Post*, February 15, 2004, p. 1.

15. U.S. Central Intelligence Agency, "Unclassified Report to Congress on the Acquisition of Technology Relating to Weapons of Mass Destruction and Advanced Conventional Munitions, 1 July through 31 December 2000," September 2001 (www.cia.gov/cia/publications/bian/bian_sep_2001.htm#10).

16. U.S. Central Intelligence Agency, "Unclassified Report to Congress on the Acquisition of Technology Relating to Weapons of Mass Destruction and Advanced Conventional Munitions, 1 January through 30 June 2001," January 2002 (www.cia.gov/cia/publications/bian/bian_jan_2002.htm); U.S. Central Intelligence Agency, "Unclassified Report to Congress on the Acquisition of Technology Relating to Weapons of Mass Destruction and Advanced Conventional Munitions, 1 July through 31 December 2003," January 2004 (www.cia.gov/cia/reports/721_reports/july_dec2003.html#15).

17. *Report of the Commission to Assess the Ballistic Missile Threat to the United States* (Rumsfeld Commission Report), pursuant to Public Law 201, 104th Congress, July 15, 1998.

18. Sha Zukang, "US Missile Defense Plans: China's View," *Disarmament Diplomacy* 43 (January-February 2000) (www.acronym.org.uk/dd/dd43/43usnmd.htm).

19. China's Information Office of the State Council, *China's National Defense in 2004* (Beijing: December 2004), chap. 10.

20. Article 4 of the Nuclear Nonproliferation Treaty reads: "(1) Nothing in this Treaty shall be interpreted as affecting the inalienable right of all the Parties to the Treaty to develop research, production and use of nuclear energy for peaceful purposes without discrimination and in conformity with Articles I and II of this Treaty. (2) All the Parties to the Treaty undertake to facilitate, and have the right to participate in,

the fullest possible exchange of equipment, materials and scientific and technological information for the peaceful uses of nuclear energy. Parties to the Treaty in a position to do so shall also co-operate in contributing alone or together with other States or international organizations to the further development of the applications of nuclear energy for peaceful purposes, especially in the territories of non-nuclear-weapon States Party to the Treaty, with due consideration for the needs of the developing areas of the world."

21. The author is indebted to Evan Medeiros for drawing attention to this point.

22. China's Information Office of the State Council, *China's National Defense* (Beijing: July 1998), pp. 53–54. The same principles were set out in China's first white paper on arms control, China's Information Office of the State Council, *China's Arms Control and Disarmament* (Beijing: November 1995). See also China's Information Office of the State Council, *China's Nonproliferation Policy and Measures* (Beijing: December 2003).

23. This discussion of Chinese export controls draws from the East Asia Nonproliferation Project, Center for Nonproliferation Studies, Monterey Institute of International Studies (http://cns.miis/edu); Jing-dong Yuan, Phillip C. Saunders, and Stephanie Lieggi, "Recent Developments in China's Export Controls: New Regulations and New Challenges," *Nonproliferation Review* 9, no. 3 (2002): 153–67; Medeiros and Gill, "Chinese Arms Exports"; Fu Cong, "An Introduction of China's Export Control System," paper presented at Tokyo Workshop on Nonproliferation Export Control Regimes, Tokyo, Japan, December 11–12, 1997.

24. For a translation of these regulations, see FBIS, *Daily Report: China*, January 17, 1999; see also "China Approves New Export Controls on Sensitive Technology," Reuters, December 2, 1998.

25. Regulations of the People's Republic of China on Export Control of Missiles and Missile-Related Items and Technologies, August 22, 2002 (www.fmprc.gov.cn/eng/33980.html); Missiles and Missile-Related Items and Technologies Export Control List, August 22, 2002 (www.fmprc.gov.cn/eng/33981 html).

26. For two analyses of the Chinese missile export control regulations, one by a Chinese and one by an American, see Phil C. Saunders, "Preliminary Analysis of Chinese Missile Technology Export Control List," September 6, 2002 (http://cns.miis.edu/cns/projects/eanp/pub/prc_msl.pdf); and Li Bin, "Comments on the Chinese Regulation on Missile Technology Export Control," August 26, 2002 (http://learn.tsinghua.edu.cn/homepage/S00313/eexctl.htm). See also Yuan, Sanders, and Lieggi, "Recent Developments in China's Export Controls," esp. pp. 160–62.

27. Regulations of the People's Republic of China on Export Control of Missiles and Missile-Related Items and Technologies, article 3.

28. Yuan, Sanders, and Lieggi, "Recent Developments in China's Export Controls," pp. 160–62.

29. *SIPRI Yearbook 1997: Armaments, Disarmament, and International Security* (Oxford University Press, 1997), table 9.1; *SIPRI Yearbook 2002: Armaments, Disarmament, and International Security* (Oxford University Press, 2002), table 8A.2. According

to these data, the United States ranked as the number-one supplier of conventional weapons over the period 1996–2001, capturing approximately 28.1 percent of the conventional arms market in 2001, and 44.5 percent of the market over the period 1997–2001. Also see *SIPRI Yearbook 2005,* appendix 10A (www.sipri.org/contents/armstrad/app10A2005.pdf).

30. Richard F. Grimmett, "Congressional Conventional Arms Transfers to Developing Nations, 1996–2003" (Washington: Congressional Research Service, August 26, 2004), p. 77.

31. For a comprehensive open-source study of Chinese arms exports, which analyzes and substantiates these trends, see Medeiros and Gill, "Chinese Arms Exports."

32. "Foreign Ministry Holds Regular News Conferences on Nuclear Cooperation with Iran," Irna Tehran (FBIS, CHI-96-008, January 9, 1996).

33. "China Agrees to End Nuclear Trade with Iran when Two Projects Completed," *NuclearFuel,* November 3, 1997, pp. 3–4.

34. White House news release, Secretary of State Madeleine Albright and National Security Adviser Sandy Berger, October 29, 1997; R. Jeffrey Smith, "China's Pledge to End Iran Nuclear Aid Yields U.S. Help," *Washington Post,* October 30, 1997, p. 1.

35. White House news release, "Fact Sheet: Accomplishments of the U.S.-China Summit, October 30, 1997"; see also Steve Erlanger, "U.S. Says Chinese Will Stop Sending Missiles to Iran," *New York Times,* October 18, 1997.

36. U.S. Department of State, "Text: U.S.-China Joint Statement on South Asia" (http://usinfo.state.gov/regional/ea/uschina/sasia.htm).

37. Embassy of the People's Republic of China, "Sino-U.S. Joint Statement on South Asia," June 27, 1998 (www.china-embassy.org/eng/zmgx/zysj/kldfh/t36228.htm).

38. Quotations in this paragraph from "PRC FM Spokesman on Non-Proliferation Issue," Xinhua, November 21, 2000 (FBIS, CPP20001121000110).

39. Alan Sipress, "Chinese Arms Firm Faces U.S. Sanctions," *Washington Post,* September 1, 2001. For more details, see U.S. Department of State Public Notice 3774, *Federal Register,* September 11, 2001, p. 47256.

40. Regulations of the People's Republic of China on Export Control of Missiles and Missile-Related Items and Technologies; Missiles and Missile-Related Items and Technologies Export Control List.

41. For more details on China and the CTBT, see Bates Gill, "Two Steps Forward, One Step Back: The Dynamics of Chinese Nonproliferation and Arms Control Policy-Making in an Era of Reform," in *The Making of Chinese Foreign and Security Policy in the Era of Reform, 1978–2000,* edited by David M. Lampton (Stanford University Press, 2001).

42. Of the five major nuclear powers, China and the United States have not ratified the CTBT. France and the United Kingdom ratified the treaty on April 6, 1998. The Russian Federation ratified the treaty on June 30, 2000.

43. "China Airs Stand on Nuclear Testing," *Beijing Review,* October 18–24, 1993, p. 4.

44. The Soviet Union's last test was in 1990, and Russia has not tested since. The last test by the United Kingdom was in 1991, and the United States last tested in 1992.

France suspended testing between late 1991 and late 1995 but carried out its last round of testing between September 1995 and January 1996. In contrast, China conducted six tests during the CTBT negotiations.

45. Ragnhild Ferm, "Nuclear Explosions, 1945–98," in *SIPRI Yearbook 1999* (Oxford University Press, 1999), table 12B.2.

46. Quotations in this paragraph from *China's Position on and Suggestions for Ways to Address the Issue of Prevention of an Arms Race in Outer Space at the Conference on Disarmament*, February 8, 2000, reprinted in part in "Chinese CD PAROS Working Paper," *Disarmament Diplomacy*, no. 43 (January-February 2000) (www.acronym.org.uk/dd/dd43/43paros.htm).

47. Wade Boese, "Chinese Concession Fails to End UN Disarmament Conference's Stalemate," *Arms Control Today*, October 2003 (www.armscontrol.org/act/2003_10/CD.asp).

48. Wade Boese, "Fissile Material Treaty Dispute Prolongs Conference on Disarmament Deadlock," *Arms Control Today*, March 2005 (www.armscontrol.org/act/2005_03/CD.asp).

49. Evan Medeiros demonstrates the critical influence of the United States in shaping China's approach to nonproliferation in his book *Shaping Chinese Foreign Policy*.

50. Johnston and Evans, "China's Engagement with Multilateral Security Institutions," p. 254 and, more generally, pp. 235–54.

51. U.S. Central Intelligence Agency, "Unclassified Report to Congress on the Acquisition of Technology Relating to Weapons of Mass Destruction and Advanced Conventional Munitions, 1 July through 31 December 2003."

52. See ibid.; also see U.S. Central Intelligence Agency, "Unclassified Report to Congress on the Acquisition of Technology Relating to Weapons of Mass Destruction and Advanced Conventional Munitions, 1 January through 30 June 2001"; U.S. Central Intelligence Agency, "Unclassified Report to Congress on the Acquisition of Technology Relating to Weapons of Mass Destruction and Advanced Conventional Munitions, 1 January through 30 June 2000."

Chapter Four

1. Kofi A. Annan, "Two Concepts of Sovereignty," *Economist*, September 18, 1999, pp. 49–50. This article introduces the concepts Annan presented on sovereignty, human rights, and intervention in his General Assembly speech on September 20, 1999. See "Secretary-General Presents His Annual Report to the General Assembly," September 20, 1999 (SG/SM/7136 GA/9596).

2. For a more comprehensive examination of China's new sovereignty debate and how and why China's approach to sovereignty is changing in the face of domestic and international pressures, see Allen Carlson, *Unifying China, Integrating with the World: Securing Chinese Sovereignty in the Reform Era* (Stanford University Press, 2005).

3. Samuel S. Kim, "Sovereignty in the Chinese Image of World Order," in *Essays*

in Honor of Wang Tieya, edited by R. St. J. Macdonald (London: Kluwer Academic, 1993), pp. 429, 442.

4. Moving clockwise from its southeast, China borders on Vietnam, Laos, Myanmar, India, Bhutan, Nepal, Pakistan, Afghanistan, Tajikistan, Kyrgyzstan, Kazakhstan, Russia, Mongolia, and North Korea. South Korea, Japan, and the Philippines are in close maritime proximity, as is the forward-deployed presence of U.S. forces in the Western Pacific. Data on China's land borders and bordering countries from www.cia.gov/cia/publications/factbook/geos/ch.html.

5. Michael H. Hunt, *The Genesis of Chinese Communist Foreign Policy* (Columbia University Press, 1996); Michael D. Swaine and Ashley J. Tellis, *Interpreting China's Grand Strategy* (Santa Monica, Calif.: Rand, 2000), esp. chaps. 2, 3.

6. Cao Xufei, "Tupo zhanzheng bianyuan: sikao yu chaoyue" [The Breakthrough in the Brink of War: Thinking and Transcending], *Shijie jingji yu zhengzhi* [World Economy and Politics], no. 6 (1999): 29–35.

7. Kim, "Sovereignty in the Chinese Image of World Order," p. 429.

8. For an excellent analysis of the new security concept, see David M. Finkelstein, "China's New Security Concept: Reading between the Lines," *Washington Journal of Modern China* 5, no. 1 (1999): 37–49. See also the broader discussion in chapter 1 of this volume.

9. China's Information Office of the State Council, *China's National Defense in 2000* (Beijing: October 2000), p. 6.

10. Ibid., pp. 8, 13.

11. Guo Longlong and others, *Lianheguo Xinlun* [New Theories about the United Nations] (Shanghai: Shanghai Jiaoyu Chubanshe, 1995), pp. 14–15.

12. Wang Junli, "China's National Interests and the Guiding Principles of International Strategy," in *Guoji zhanlue lun* [The Theory of International Strategy], edited by Yu Qifen (Beijing: Junshi Kexue Yuan Chubanshe, 1998), pp. 422–24.

13. Kim, "Sovereignty in the Chinese Image of World Order," p. 430.

14. Guo and others, *Lianheguo Xinlun,* p. 17. On the other hand, the phrase "new international economic order" (*xin guoji jingji zhixu*) has been used to point with favor toward a more equitable and desirable global distribution of income, contrary to what Chinese officially term the current "old, unfair, and irrational . . . economic order." For example, see Pan Sen, "Guanyu Minzu Zizhiquan de Yixie Sikao" [Some Thoughts on the Right of National Self-determination], *Guoji Wenti Yanjiu* [International Studies], no. 2 (1997): 37–45, quotations on pp. 37, 41. See also China's Information Office of the State Council, *China's National Defense in 2000,* p. 6.

15. Ma Ling, "US Strategy for the 21st Century as Viewed From China," *Ta Kung Pao,* an interview with Colonel Yao Youzhi, a strategist with the People's Liberation Army Academy of Military Sciences (FBIS, *Daily Report: China,* May 3, 1999).

16. Zi Zhongyun, "Weile minzu de zuigao liyi, weile renmin de changyuan fuzhi" [For the Supreme Interests of the Nation and for the Long-term Welfare of the People], *Taipingyang Xuebao* [Pacific Journal], December 1999, quotations on p. 13.

17. Statement by President Jiang Zemin of the People's Republic of China at the Millennium Summit of the United Nations, September 7, 2000 (www.fmprc.gov. cn/english). Chinese analysts also argue that in providing basic food, shelter, and national stability, Chinese leaders are making a valuable contribution to peace, development, and human rights. See, for example, Li Tiecheng, "Jianchi yu hongyang lianheguo xianzhang zongzhi he yuanze" [Uphold and Carry Forward the Principles and Aims of the UN Charter], *Guoji Wenti Yanjiu* [International Studies], no. 1 (1997): 20.

18. Yan Xuetong, "China's Security after the Cold War," *Contemporary International Relations* 3, no. 5 (1993): 1–16, quotation on p. 12.

19. Wu Peng, "Shilun woguo yatai diqu anquanguan ji fazhan" [A Treatise on China's Security Concept for the Asia-Pacific Region and Development], *Shijie Jingji yu Zhengzhi* [World Economy and Politics], no. 6 (1999): 12–17, quotation on pp. 13–14.

20. Kim, "Sovereignty in the Chinese Image of World Order," p. 443.

21. For a comprehensive analysis of China's approach to these issues, see Pan Shen, "Guanyu minzu zijuequan de yixie sikao" [Some Thoughts on the Right of National Self-Determination], *Guoji Wenti Yanjiu* [International Studies], no. 2 (1997): 37–45, quotation on p. 37.

22. Yan Xuetong, "China's Security after the Cold War."

23. See, for example, Guo and others, *Lianheguo Xinlun*, p. 16.

24. Pan, "Guanyu minzu zijuequan de yixie sikao," pp. 39–42.

25. Guo and others, *Lianheguo Xinlun*, pp. 119, 125.

26. Ibid., p. 120.

27. Ibid., pp. 117–18.

28. UN document S/PV/3868 (March 31, 1998); UN document S/RES/1160 (March 31, 1998).

29. "Renmin Ribao Commentator on Embassy Bombing," *People's Daily* (FBIS, *Daily Report: China*, May 9, 1999); Observer, "On the New Developments of US Hegemonism," *People's Daily* (FBIS, *Daily Report: China*, May 27, 1999); Observer, "We Urge Hegemonism Today to Take a Look at the Mirror of History," *People's Dialy* (FBIS, *Daily Report: China*, June 22, 1999).

30. Erik Eckholm, "Bombing May Have Hardened China's Line," *New York Times*, May 18, 1999.

31. David Zweig, *Internationalizing China: Domestic Interests and Global Linkages* (Cornell University Press, 2002), p. 268.

32. Yan Xuetong, *Zhongguo guojia liyi fenxi* [Analysis of China's National Interests] (Tianjin: Tianjin People's Press, 1996), p. 217.

33. Li Shaojun, "Guoji anquan moshi yu guojia de anquan zhanlue xuanzhe" [National Security Models and Options for National Security Strategy], *Shijie jingji yu zhengzhi* [World Economics and Politics], no. 6 (1996): 4–9, quotation on p. 7.

34. Zi Zhongyun, "Weile minzu de zuigao liyi, weile renmin de changyuan fuzhi" [For the Supreme Interests of the Nation and for the Long-term Welfare of the

People], *Taipingyang Xuebao* [Pacific Journal] (December 1999): 10–15, quotation on p. 13.

35. Wu Peng, "Shilun woguo zai yatai dichu anquan jincheng zhong ying jianchi de yuanze yu shishe [An Exploratory Study on the Principles and Measures China Should Persist In Amid the Security Process of the Asia-Pacific Region], *Shijie Jingji yu Zhengzhi* [World Economy and Politics], no. 7 (1999): 47–51, quotation on p. 48; Yan, *Zhongguo guojia liyi fenxi*, p. 192.

36. Guo and others, *Lianheguo Xinlun*, p. 15; Wu, "Shilun woguo zai yatai," p. 50.

37. See, for example, Chen Dezhao, "Jingji quanqiuhua dui zhongguo de jiyu yu tiaozhan" [The Opportunities and Challenges for China Posed by Economic Globalization], *Guoji Wenti Yanjiu* [International Studies], no. 3 (1999): 7–12, esp. p. 9; Yan Xuetong, *Zhongguo guojia liyi fenxi*, pp. 130ff.

38. Yan Xuetong, "China's Security after the Cold War," *Contemporary International Relations* 3, no. 5 (1993): 1–16, quotation on p. 9.

39. Yan, *Zhongguo guojia liyi fenxi*, p. 131.

40. Chen, "Jingji quanqiuhua dui zhongguo de jiyu yu tiaozhan," p. 11.

41. M. Taylor Fravel, "Regime Insecurity and International Cooperation: Explaining China's Compromises in Territorial Disputes," *International Security* 30, no. 2 (2005): 46–83, quotations on p. 46. I am grateful to Dr. Fravel for bringing earlier versions of this work to my attention.

42. Parts of the following section are drawn from Bates Gill and James Reilly, "Sovereignty, Intervention, and Peacekeeping: The View from Beijing," *Survival* 42, no. 3 (2000): 41–60. For a comprehensive and analytically rich look at China's approach to peacekeeping, see the excellent study by Stefan Staehle, "China's Participation in the United Nations Peacekeeping Regime," master's thesis, Elliott School of International Affairs, George Washington University, May 21, 2006.

43. Guo and others, *Lianheguo Xinlun*, p. 15. See also Zhang Jian, "Lianheguo weihe xingdong de lishi yu xianzhuang" [The History and Current State of United Nation Peacekeeping Operations], *Guoji Wenti Yanjiu* [International Studies], no. 4 (1994): 7–16, esp. p. 14.

44. Guo and others, *Lianheguo Xinlun*, p. 121.

45. These quotations are drawn, respectively, from Zhang, "Lianheguo weihe xingdong de lishi yu xianzhuang," p. 14; and Zhou Bing, "Xianzhe lianheguo zai xinde guoji zhengzhi jingji xingshi xia de zuoyong," [A Preliminary Analysis for the Role of the United Nations in the New International Political and Economic Situation], *Shijie Jingji yu Zhengzhi* [World Economy and Politics], no. 2 (1999), pp. 43–46, quotation from p. 44.

46. Quotations from China's Information Office of the State Council, *China's National Defense in 2000*, pp. 57–58. See also Guo and others, *Lianheguo Xinlun*, p. 122; Zhang, "Lianheguo weihe xingdong de lishi yu xianzhuang," p. 9; Shao Zhongwei, "Peacekeeping on Agenda," *China Daily*, June 27, 2000.

47. Guo and others, *Lianheguo Xinlun*, p. 121.

48. See, for example, Guo and others, *Lianheguo Xinlun*, pp. 121–23; Sun Wei, "Peace-Keeping or Peace Enforcing?" *Beijing Review*, July 24, 1995, p. 20.

49. According to the UN peacekeeping website, in September 2006 China contributed 168 civilian police, 67 military observers, and 1,413 troops, for a total of 1,648 (www.un.org/Depts/dpko/dpko). Unless otherwise noted, data and information on Chinese participation in UN peacekeeping operations are drawn from this site.

50. The twenty-four UN missions are MINURSO (Mission for the Referendum in Western Sahara), MINUSTAH (Stabilization Mission in Haiti), MONUC (Organization Mission in the Democratic Republic of the Congo), ONOMOZ (Operations in Mozambique), ONUB (Operations in Burundi), UNAMA (Assistance Mission in Afghanistan), UNAMIC (Administration Mission in Cambodia), UNAMSIL (Mission in Sierra Leone), UNIFIL (United Nations Interim Force in Lebanon), UNIKOM (Iraq-Kuwait Observer Mission), UNMEE (Mission in Ethiopia and Eritrea), UNMIBH (Mission in Bosnia-Herzegovina), UNMIK (Interim Administration Mission in Kosovo), UNMIL (Mission in Liberia), UNMIS (United Nations Mission in Sudan), UNMISET (Mission in Support of East Timor), UNOCI (Operation in Côte d'Ivoire), UNOMIL (Observer Mission in Liberia), UNOMSIL (Observer Mission in Sierra Leone), UNOTIL (United National Office in Timor-Leste), UNTAC (Transitional Authority in Cambodia), UNTAET (Transitional Administration in East Timor), UNTAG (Transition Assistance Group, Namibia), and UNTSO (Truce Supervision Organization, Golan Heights and Lebanon).

51. One was a military observer serving in the Iraq-Kuwait Observer Mission (UNIKOM) in Kuwait. The rest were soldiers: three serving in the Transition Authority in Cambodia (UNTAC), one serving in the Transition Assistance Group (UNTAG) in Namibia, two serving in the United Nations Mission in Liberia (UNMIL), one serving in the United Nations Truce Supervision Organization (UNTSO) in Lebanon, and one serving in the Organization Mission in the Democratic Republic of the Congo (MONUC).

52. "Chinese Riot Police Head for Haiti Mission," *China Daily*, November 22, 2004.

53. Data from the UN peacekeeping website (www.un.org/Depts/dpko/dpko/index.asp). These data represent Chinese contributions for the month of September 2006. Contributions change month to month, as peacekeepers are rotated in and out, missions are expanded or disbanded, or new missions are established.

54. M. Taylor Fravel, "China's Attitude toward U.N. Peacekeeping Operations since 1989," *Asian Survey* 36, no. 11 (1996): 1102–22.

55. UN Security Council, September 15, 1999 (S/RES/1264).

56. "Spokesman on Joining UN East Timor Special Mission," Xinhua (FBIS, *Daily Report: China*, September 16, 1999).

57. UN Security Council, October 25, 1999 (S/RES/1272).

58. UN Security Council, September 12, 2001 (S/RES/1368).

59. "Text of 4 December Transcript of Foreign Ministry Press Conference: 'Foreign Ministry Spokesperson Zhang Qiyue Answers Questions from Reporters at Press Conference,'" December 4, 2001 (FBIS, CPP20011204000109).

60. Kabul Bakhtar News Agency, July 24, 2002 (FBIS, IAP20020724000097); "Statement by Ambassador Wang Yingfan, Permanent Representative of China to the United Nations, at the Security Council on the situation in Afghanistan," March 26, 2002 (www.china-un.org/eng/27765.html).

61. See, for example, UN Security Council, December 20, 2001 (S/RES/1386); UN Security Council, May 23, 2002 (S/RES/1413); UN Security Council, November 27, 2002 (S/RES/1444).

62. See, for example, UN Security Council, December 12, 1996 (S/RES/1088); UN Security Council, June 21, 2000 (S/RES/1305); UN Security Council, June 21, 2001 (S/RES/1357); UN Security Council, July 12, 2002 (S/RES/1423).

63. UN Security Council, November 8, 2002 (S/RES/1441).

64. China's Information Office of the State Council, *China's National Defense in 2002*, p. 35.

65. "Full Text of UN Permanent Five Summit Document," *People's Daily*, September 8, 2000 (www.fmprc.gov.cn/eng/4906.html).

66. UN Security Council, June 13, 2001 (S/RES/1353).

67. See, for example, Barbara Crossette, "UN Mission Is Reprieved," *New York Times*, March 1, 1996, p. A8. See also UN document, February 25, 1999 (S/PV.3982); Deborah Kuo, "MOFA's Wu Stresses Taiwan-Macedonia Ties Firm, Solid," Taiwan Central News Agency, February 22, 1999 (FBIS, *Daily Report: China,* February 22, 1999).

68. "China to Send Anti-Riot Peacekeepers for Haiti," Xinhuanet, June 4, 2004 (www.chinaview.cn); "Chinese Riot Police Head for Haiti Mission," *China Daily,* November 22, 2004.

69. PLA officials, interviews with author, New York City, January 2000.

70. Information on Chinese peacekeeping training from www.un.org/Depts/dpko/training/CUNPK.htm.

71. This information is drawn in part from Chinese military officials based at the United Nations, interviews with author, New York, January 2000.

72. Information on the new facility is from "China to Build Asia's Largest UN Police Training Center," Xinhuanet, August 20, 2002 (http://news.xinhuanet.com/english/2002-08/20/content_530614.htm).

73. Information on Chinese civilian police training is from www.un.org/Depts/dpko/training/CUNPK.htm.

74. Chinese military officers cited the case of Cambodia, where two soldiers and one officer died, as an instance where such fears were realized. Chinese military officials, interviews with author, New York, January 2000.

75. As of April 2005, fifty countries—including several of China's neighbors such as Malaysia, Singapore, Nepal, Bangladesh, Kyrgyzstan, Mongolia, Pakistan, and Russia—have provided this memorandum of understanding Level 3 commitment to the United Nations. The information on the standby arrangements system is drawn from the UN peacekeeping website, www.un.org/Depts/dpko/milad/fgs2/unsas_files/status_report/statusreport.htm.

76. Quoted from the UN peacekeeping website, www.un.org/Depts/dpko.

77. The incentives for Chinese officers to participate in peacekeeping operations are mixed. Once they leave their unit, they lose their position. This means that they

are not only missing promotion opportunities but also could lose their job in the PLA, due to ongoing force reductions. However, many officers appreciate the opportunity to travel abroad, meet foreigners, and practice their English. Most notably, they get to keep their UN pay (about US$160 a day in Cambodia; the UN now pays approximately US$1,000 a month per person). Regular troops do not get to keep their UN pay but receive instead their regular PLA salary. Chinese military officials, interviews with author, New York, January 2000.

78. Chinese officer, interview with author, New York, June 2000.

79. This section draws in part from Bates Gill and Melissa Murphy, "China's Evolving Approach to Counterterrorism," *Harvard Asia Quarterly* 9, nos. 1, 2 (2005): 21–32.

80. "SCMP Cites PRC Media on Osama bin Ladin Connection to Uyghur Separatists," *South China Morning Post*, July 25, 2002 (FBIS, CPP20020725000061).

81. U.S. Congressional Research Service, "U.S.-China Counterterrorism Cooperation: Issues for U.S. Policy," Report for Congress, updated May 2005 (www.fas.org/sgp/crs/row/RS21995.pdf).

82. U.S. Department of State, *Country Reports on Terrorism 2004* (April 27, 2005), chap. 6 (www.state.gov/s/ct/rls/45394.htm).

83. R. Bates Gill, *Chinese Arms Transfers: Purposes, Patterns, and Prospects in the New World Order* (Westport, Conn.: Praeger, 1992), p. 40.

84. Ibid., p. 60.

85. Barry Rubin, "China's Middle East Strategy," *Middle East Review of International Affairs* 3, no.1 (1999): 46-54.

86. Guang Pan, "China's Success in the Middle East," *Middle East Quarterly* 4, no. 4 (December 1997) (www.meforum.org/article/373).

87. Yezid Sayigh, "The Foreign Policy of the PLO," Palestinian Academic Society for the Study of International Affairs (ww.passia.org/seminars/96/foreign_policy_plo.html).

88. Yasser Arafat, quoted in the *Peking Review*, March 27, 1970, p. 5.

89. Pan, "China's Success in the Middle East."

90. In 2002, following the discovery of Chinese-made weapons in Afghanistan, some media outlets reported suspicions that China's military had supported the Taliban and al-Qaeda. U.S. Defense Secretary Donald Rumsfeld downplayed the reports, noting that Afghanistan is "filled with weapons" from every country. See U.S. Congressional Research Service, "U.S.-China Counterterrorism Cooperation."

91. For more detail concerning China and its far west, see, for example, S. Frederick Starr, ed., *Xinjiang: China's Muslim Borderland* (New York: M. E. Sharpe, 2004).

92. Joshua Kurlantzick, "The Unsettled West," *Foreign Affairs* (July-August 2004): 136–43.

93. U.S. Congressional Research Service, "China's Relations with Central Asian States and Problems with Terrorism," Report for Congress, updated October 7, 2002.

94. U.S. Congressional Research Service, "China's Relations with Central Asian States and Problems with Terrorism."

95. Ibid.

96. For these descriptions, see "Commentary on Ethnic Separatism, Religious Activities," *Xinjiang Ribao*, May 7, 1996 (FBIS, FTS1996050700002).

97. "PRC Foreign Minister Tang Reaffirms Support for US in Fight against Terrorism," Xinhua, September 21, 2001 (FBIS, CPP20010921000079).

98. U.S. Department of State, "U.S., China Stand against Terrorism," October 19, 2001 (www.state.gov/s/ct/rls/rm/2001/5461.html).

99. "Afghanistan-China Relations Excellent—Karzai," *People's Daily*, March 27, 2002 (http://english.people.com.cn/200203/26/eng20020326_92826.shtml).

100. "China Offers US$15 Million in Aid to Afghanistan," *China Daily*, January 4, 2004 (www.chinadaily.com.cn/english/doc/2004-04/01/content_319880.htm).

101. U.S. Congressional Research Service, "U.S.-China Counterterrorism Cooperation."

102. U.S. Congressional Research Service, "China's Relations with Central Asian States and Problems with Terrorism."

103. "12 UN Conventions on Terrorism" (www.unodc.org/unodc/terrorism_conventions.html).

104. Memorandum of Understanding between the Governments of the Member Countries of the Association of Southeast Asian Nations (ASEAN) and the Government of the People's Republic of China, January 10, 2004 (www.aseansec.org/15647.htm).

105. APEC, "Counterterrorism" (www.apecsec.org.sg/content/apec/apec_groups/som_special_task_groups/counter_terrorism.html).

106. "China Pledges Efforts in Fight against Terrorism, Corruption," *People's Daily Online*, November 19, 2004 (http://english.people.com.cn/200411/19/end20041119_164463.html).

107. "China, EU Issue Joint Statement after Summit (full text)," September 10, 2006 (http://news.xinhuanet.com/english/2006-09/10/content_5071239.htm).

108. Fravel, "Regime Insecurity and International Cooperation," pp. 49–50.

109. Ibid., pp. 78–81.

110. Samuel S. Kim, "China and the Third World," in *China and the World: China's Foreign Relations in the Post–Cold War Era*, edited by Samuel S. Kim, 3d ed. (Boulder, Colo.: Westview, 1994), pp. 132–33; see also Fravel, "China's Attitude toward U.N. Peacekeeping Operations," p. 1121; Nigel Thalakada, "China's Voting Pattern in the Security Council, 1990–1995," in *The Once and Future Security Council*, edited by Bruce Russett (New York: St. Martin's, 1997), pp. 86–87.

111. Cao Xufei, "Tupo zhanzheng bianyuan: sikao yu chaoyue" [The Breakthrough in the Brink of War: Thinking and Transcending], *Shijie jingji yu zhengzhi* [World Economy and Politics], no. 6 (1999): 29–36, quotation on p. 34.

112. Chinese military officials, interviews with author, New York and Beijing, January 2000 and April 2004.

113. "Vietnamese PM Addresses ASEAN Summit, Citing New Challenges, Fighting Terrorism," Vietnam News Agency, November 4, 2002 (FBIS, SEP20021105000067). In November 2002 China and ASEAN signed the Declaration on the Conduct of Parties in the South China Sea, in which the parties concerned "undertake to resolve their territorial and jurisdictional disputes by peaceful means, without resorting to the threat or use of force, through friendly consultations and negotiations by sovereign states directly concerned, in accordance with universally recognized principles of international law, including the 1982 UN Convention on the Law of the Sea" (www.aseansec.org/13163.htm).

114. "India, China Hoping to 'Reshape the World Order' Together," *Washington Post,* April 12, 2005 (www.washingtonpost.com/wp-dyn/articles/A43053-2005Apr11.html).

115. Quoted in "China to Send Antiriot Peacekeepers for Haiti," Xinhuanet, June 4, 2004 (www.chinaview.cn).

Chapter Five

1. Thomas J. Christensen, "Have Old Problems Trumped New Thinking? China's Relations with Taiwan, Japan, and North Korea," *China Leadership Monitor,* no. 14 (Spring 2005) (www.chinaleadershipmonitor.org/20052/tc.html).

2. The nature of Chinese claims to Taiwan, the Taiwan view of these claims, and American involvement in the Taiwan question over the past sixty years compose an extremely complex set of historical, legal, political, and security issues. See Richard C. Bush, *At Cross Purposes: U.S. Taiwan Relations since 1942* (New York: M. E. Sharpe, 2004); Alan Romberg, "Rein in at the Brink of the Precipice: American Policy toward Taiwan and U.S.-PRC Relations" (Washington: Henry L. Stimson Center, 2003); Nancy Bernkopf Tucker, *China Confidential: American Diplomats and Sino-American Relations, 1945–1996* (Columbia University Press, 2001). For the Chinese official perspective, see China's Information Office of the State Council, *The One China Principle and the Taiwan Issue* (Beijing: February 2000); China's Information Office of the State Council, *The Taiwan Question and Reunification of China* (Beijing: Taiwan Affairs Office, August 1993).

3. "Full Text of Anti-Secession Law," *People's Daily,* March 14, 2005 (http://english.people.com.cn/200503/14/eng20050314_176746.html). The language comes from article 8.

4. See "The 8-Point Proposition Made by President Jiang Zemin on China's Reunification," January 30, 1995 (www.china-embassy.org/eng/7126.html).

5. "PRC's Qian Qichen Says Taiwan Independence 'Dangerous Road'" (FBIS, CHI-2000-0825). See also "Qian Qichen's Speech at Reception Marking 51st Anniversary of PRC's Founding" (FBIS, CHI-2000-0929); "PRC's Qian Qichen Urges Cross-Strait Reunification" (FBIS, CHI-2001-0122).

6. Macabe Keliher and Craig Meer, "Taiwan and China: Too Close for Comfort?" *Asia Times*, October 24, 2003 (www.atimes.com/atimes/China/EJ24Ad01.html). See also U.S. Department of State, "Background Note: Taiwan," Bureau of East Asian and Pacific Affairs, December 2005 (www.state.gov/r/pa/ei/bgn/35855.htm).

7. On the continuing challenges of China-Japan and China-Taiwan relations, see Thomas J. Christensen, "Have Old Problems Trumped New Thinking? China's Relations with Taiwan, Japan, and North Korea," *China Leadership Monitor*, no. 14 (Spring 2005) (www.chinaleadershipmonitor.org/20052/tc.html).

8. Michael J. Green and Thomas J. Christensen, eds., *The U.S.-Japan Alliance: Past, Present, and Future* (New York: Council on Foreign Relations, 1999); Thomas J. Christensen, "China, the U.S.-Japan Alliance, and the Security Dilemma in East Asia," *International Security* 23, no. 4 (1999): 49–80.

9. "Japan-U.S. Joint Declaration on Security: Alliance for the 21st Century," April 17, 1996 (www.mofa.go.jp/region/n-america/us/security/security.html).

10. Jin Linbo, "Meiri tongmeng zaidingyi de beijing, guocheng, jiqi yingxiang" [The Background, Process, and Other Effects of the Redefinition of the U.S.-Japan Alliance], *Guoji Wenti Yanjiu* [International Studies], no. 1 (1999): 35–40.

11. The incoming administration's strategy toward the U.S.-Japan alliance was best articulated in what became known as the Armitage Report; Institute for National Strategic Studies, "The United States and Japan: Advancing toward a Mature Partnership" (Washington: National Defense University, October 11, 2000). Persons contributing to this report who assumed influential positions in the first Bush administration included Deputy Secretary of State Richard Armitage, Deputy Secretary of Defense Paul Wolfowitz, Senior Director for Asian Affairs on the National Security Council Torkel Patterson, Assistant Secretary of State for Asia and Pacific Affairs James Kelly, Director for Asian Affairs on the National Security Council Michael Green, and Special Adviser to the Undersecretary of State for Global Affairs Robert Manning.

12. Japan Defense Agency, "National Defense Program Guideline for FY2005 and After," December 10, 2005 (www.jda.go.jp/e/index_.htm).

13. Ministry of Foreign Affairs of the People's Republic of China, "Foreign Ministry Spokeswoman Zhang Qiyue's Comment on Japan's New Outline for National Defense," December 14, 2004 (www.fmprc.gov.cn/eng/xwfw/s2510/t174804.htm).

14. Japan Defense Agency, "Joint Statement of U.S.-Japan Security Consultative Committee," February 19, 2005 (www.jda.go.jp/e/index_.htm).

15. "Xinhua Cites Japan Spokesman on Taiwan, Reiterates PRC Policy Statements," February 25, 2005 (FBIS, CPP20050225000227).

16. Chinese authorities put a stop to the demonstrations after several weeks.

17. "China-Japan Disputes," *CBC News Online*, July 15, 2005 (www.cbc.ca).

18. "Stalemate Threatens as China Says Ties with Japan at 30-Year Low," Agence France-Press, April 18, 2005 (FBIS, CPP2005041800005).

19. This section draws in part from Bates Gill and Andrew Thompson, "A Test for

Beijing: China and the North Korean Nuclear Quandary," *Arms Control Today* 33, no. 4 (2003): 12–14.

20. "Xinhua: 'Full Text' of Dushanbe Statement of Shanghai Five" (FBIS, *Daily Report: China*, July 7, 2000).

21. "'Shanghai Five' Nations Sign Joint Statement," *People's Daily*, July 6, 2000 (http://english.peopledailyu.com.cn/200007/06/end20000706_44804.html).

22. "Xinhua: 'Full Text' of Dushanbe Statement of Shanghai Five"; "Declaration on the Creation of the Shanghai Cooperation Organization, signed at Shanghai, China, June 15, 2001" (www.sectsco.org/news_detail.asp?id=88&LanguageID=2).

23. "Declaration of Heads of Member States of Shanghai Cooperation Organisation," Astana, July 5, 2005 (www.sectsco.org).

24. See IRIN Asia, November 25, 2005 (www.irinnews.org/report.asp?ReportID=50319&SelectRegion=Asai&SelectCountry=CENTRAL_ASIA); *Pravda*, November 21, 2005 (http://newsfromrussia.com/world/2005/11/21/68151.html).

25. U.S. Department of State official, e-mail correspondence with author, November 23, 2005.

26. "China's Power Play," *Wall Street Journal*, August 4, 2005 (http://online.wsj.com/article/SB112311916239104637.html). See also "China Opposes U.S. Joining East Asia Summit: Newsweek," Kyodo, September 26, 2005 (www.findarticles.com/p/articles/mi_m0WDQ/is_2005_Oct_3/a1_n15662856).

27. Axel Berkofsky, "Tokyo Lacking Community Spirit," *Asia Times*, October 5, 2005 (www.atimes.com/atimes/Japan/GJ05Dh04.html).

28. "Malaysia's Abdullah Urges Building East Asian Community on Win-Win Formulas," *Bernama*, April 23, 2005 (Open Source Center SEP2005043000020).

29. "Wu Jianmin Says EAC 'Roadmap' Not Yet Reached; US Not Excluded," Xinhua, October 31 2005 (Open Source Center CPP2005103105204).

30. "PRC Foreign Ministry Official Sees 'Stronger' Role for US in Regional Unity," *South China Morning Post*, February 5, 2005 (Open Source Center CPP20050205 000038).

31. Media conference, Beijing, August 17, 2004 (www.foreignminister.gov.au/transcripts/2004/040817_ds_beijing.html).

32. "President Welcomes Prime Minister of Australia to the White House," July 19, 2005 (www.whitehouse.gov/news/releases/2005/07/20050719.html).

33. Hugh White, "Handling China Delicately," *The Age* [Melbourne], August 18, 2005 (www.theage.com.au/news/hugh-white/handling-china-delicately/2005/08/17/1123958129532.html).

34. Ivan Cook, *Australians Speak 2005: Public Opinion and Foreign Policy* (Sydney: Lowy Institute for International Policy, 2005; www.lowyinstitute.org). Similarly favorable views of China and more cautious views of U.S. policy were expressed to the author in October 2005 by Australian businesspersons, politicians, and policy analysts in Perth, Melbourne, Canberra, and Sydney.

35. *Global Views 2006: Comparative Topline Reports* (Chicago: Chicago Council on

Global Affairs, October 11, 2006), pp. 69, 71, 96 (www.thechicagocouncil.org/UserFiles/File/2006%20Comparative%20Topline.pdf).

36. Polling information in this and the previous paragraph is drawn from Pew Global Attitudes Project, "International Public Concern about North Korea; but Growing Anti-Americanism in South Korea," August 22, 2003 (http://pewglobal.org/commentary/display.php?AnalysisID=67); Kisuk Cho, senior secretary to the president of the Republic of Korea for public relations, "Understanding Public Opinion in Korea," November 4, 2005 (www.korea.net/News/News/NewsView.asp?serial_no=20051104015&part=111&SearchDay=).

37. Eric V. Larson and others, *Ambivalent Allies? A Study of South Korean Attitudes toward the U.S.* (Santa Monica, Calif.: Rand, March 2004), esp. pp. 63–64 (www.rand.org/pubs/technical_reports/2005/RAND_TR141.pdf).

38. *Global Views 2006.*

39. European Union officials and parliamentarians, discussions with author, Brussels, October 2005; French government officials, discussions with author, Paris, October 2005; German government officials, discussions with author, Berlin, October 2005.

40. Quoted from "China Warns Australia on Taiwan Stance," *The Age* [Melbourne], March 8, 2005 (www.theage.com.au/news/National/China-warns-Australia-on-Taiwan-stances/2005/03/08/1110160778362.html).

41. U.S. Central Intelligence Agency, "Unclassified Report to Congress on the Acquisition of Technology Relating to Weapons of Mass Destruction and Advanced Conventional Munitions, 1 July through 31 December 2003," January 2004 (www.cia.gov/cia/reports/721_reports/july_dec2003.htm#15). Earlier CIA reports are U.S. Central Intelligence Agency, "Unclassified Report to Congress on the Acquisition of Technology Relating to Weapons of Mass Destruction and Advanced Conventional Munitions, 1 January through 30 June 2001," January 2002 (www.cia.gov/cia/publications/bian/bian_jan_2002.htm); U.S. Central Intelligence Agency, "Unclassified Report to Congress on the Acquisition of Technology Relating to Weapons of Mass Destruction and Advanced Conventional Munitions, 1 January through 30 June 2000," February 2001 (www.cia.gov/cia/publications/bian/bian_feb_2001.htm).

42. Evan S. Medeiros, *Shaping Chinese Foreign Policy: U.S. Diplomacy and the Evolution of China's Nonproliferation Policies and Practices, 1980–2004* (Stanford University Press, forthcoming).

43. "China's Position on and Suggestions for Ways to Address the Issue of Prevention of an Arms Race in Outer Space at the Conference on Disarmament," February 8, 2000, reprinted in part in "Chinese CD PAROS Working Paper," *Disarmament Diplomacy*, no. 43 (January-February 2000): 45–46.

44. "China, Russia Propose New Instrument on Security of Outer Space," Xinhua, June 28, 2002 (www.china.org.cn/english/2002/Jun/35773.htm).

45. "China, Myanmar, Hold First Joint Committee Meeting on Economic, Trade Cooperation," *People's Daily*, June 8, 2005 (http://english.people.com.cn/200506/08/eng20050608_189071.html).

46. China-Iran relations are summarized in Sharif Shuja, "Warming Sino-Iranian Relations: Will China Trade Nuclear Technology for Oil?" *China Brief* (2005) (www.jamestown.org/publications_details.php?volume_id=408&issue_id=3344&art icle_id=2369793).

47. U.S. Department of State, "Sudan," in *Country Reports on Human Rights Practices 2004*, February 28, 2005 (www.state.gov/g/drl/rls/hrrpt/2004/41628.htm).

48. For a good overview of China-Sudan relations, see Yitzhak Shichor, "Sudan: China's Outpost in Africa," *China Brief* 5, no. 21 (2005): 9–11.

49. For an overview of China-Zimbabwe relations, see Joshua Eisenman, "Zimbabwe: China's African Ally," *China Brief* 5, no. 15 (2005): 9–11.

50. U.S. Department of State, "Zimbabwe," in *Country Reports on Human Rights Practices 2004*, February 28, 2005 (www.state.gov/g/drl/rls/hrrpt/2004/41634.htm).

51. The following paragraphs draw in part from Bates Gill and Melissa Murphy, "China's Evolving Approach to Counterterrorism," *Harvard Asia Quarterly* 9, nos. 1, 2 (2005): 21–32.

52. "Statement by H. E. Mr. Wang Yingfan, Ambassador and Permanent Representative of the People's Republic of China to the United Nations at the 56th Session of the General Assembly of United Nations on Item 166: Measures to Eliminate International Terrorism," October 3, 2001 (http://un.fmprc.gov.cn/eng/21700.html).

53. Pan Zhenqiang, "China's National Defense Policy into the 21st Century," *Foreign Affairs Journal*, no. 70 (December 2003): 25–36. See also Chinese concerns expressed in Council on Foreign Relations, "Terrorism Q&A" (www.cfrterrorism.org/coalition/china_print.html).

54. "President Lagos Opens APEC Summit; China Urges Action against Terrorism," Xinhua, November 21, 2004; BBC Monitoring (www.nexis.com/research/search/submitViewTagged).

55. The following points come from "CIISS and HIIR Co-Sponsored International Symposium on International Counterterrorism Situation and Cooperation," *International Strategic Studies*, no. 3 (July 2004): 65–68.

56. Xiong Guangkai, "International Counterterrorism Situation and Its Features since 9.11," *International Strategic Studies*, no. 3 (July 2004): 1–9.

Chapter Six

1. Evan S. Medeiros, "Strategic Hedging and the Future of Asia-Pacific Stability," *Washington Quarterly* 29, no. 1 (2005–06): 145–67.

2. Ann Scott Tyson, "Admiral Tries to Revive Chinese Ties: Military Contacts Have Eroded, Pacific Command Chief Says," *Washington Post*, September 23, 2006, p. A14. See also Kurt Campbell and Richard Weitz, "The Limits of U.S.-China Military Cooperation: Lessons from 1995–1999," *Washington Quarterly* 29, no. 1 (2005–06): 169–86; David Shambaugh, *Modernizing China's Military: Progress, Problems, Prospects* (University of California Press, 2004), esp. chap. 8; David M. Finkelstein,

"U.S.-China Military Relations: The Time Is Right to Deepen the Dialogue," *Freeman Report,* October 2005 (www.csis.org/media/csis/pubs/frv05v10.pdf).

3. The Military Maritime Consultative Agreement, the first formalized confidence-building measure between China and the United States, was signed during the visit of U.S. Secretary of Defense William Cohen to China in January 1998. Working group meetings were held in 1998 and 1999 but were disrupted with the inadvertent U.S. bombing of the Chinese embassy in Belgrade in May 1999. The two sides resumed the dialogue in May 2000. Upon entering office, the Bush administration announced the suspension and review of all U.S.-China military-to-military contacts, which were to proceed on a case-by-case basis. The collision of a Chinese jet fighter and a U.S. EP-3 surveillance plane in April 2001 spurred the two sides to resume annual senior-level meetings and more frequent working-level meetings.

4. National Defense Authorization Act for FY2000, Public Law 106-65, October 5, 1999, section 1201.

5. U.S. Department of State, "Rumsfeld Visit Is Sign of Improved U.S.-China Military Ties" (http://usinfo.state.gov/eap/Archive/2005/Oct/20-94351.html).

6. Cobra Gold is held annually by the United States, Thailand, and Singapore and is the largest multinational exercise and movement of forces in the Pacific. See "Chinese Military Says Seeing U.S. War Games 'Positive' for Ties" (www.defensenews.com/story.php?F=1885497&C-assiapac).

7. "Emerging-market indicators," *Economist,* October 14–20, 2006, p. 106.

8. "Hearing of the Senate Foreign Relations Committee, Nomination for Deputy Secretary of State," *Federal News Service,* March 15, 2001 (www.fnsg.com/transcripta.htm?id=20010315t6398&query=).

9. U.S. Central Intelligence Agency, "Unclassified Report to Congress on the Acquisition of Technology Relating to Weapons of Mass Destruction and Advanced Conventional Munitions, 1 July through 31 December 2001," January 2003 (www.cia.gov/cia/publications/bian/bian_jan_2003_htm). Quotations in this paragraph are from this report.

10. For example, see Bill Gertz, "Chinese Sold Iraq 'Dual-Use' Chemical," *Washington Times,* March 15, 2003 (http://nucnews.net/nucnews/2003nn/0303nn/030315nn.htm#300); Bill Gertz, "N. Korea Using China to Obtain Missile Supplies," *Washington Times,* January 22, 2003 (http://nucnews.net/nucnews/2003nn/0301nn/030122nn.htm#031).

11. See the excellent study on China's export control system, Evan Medeiros, *Chasing the Dragon: Assessing China's System of Export Controls for WMD-Related Goods and Technologies* (Santa Monica, Calif.: Rand, 2005) (www.rand.org/pubs/monographs/2005/RAND_MG353.sum.pdf).

12. On the December 2002 Wassenaar Arrangement meeting, see www.wassenaar.org/docs/public_statement_021212.htm.

13. See U.S. Department of State, "U.S., China to Cooperate on Detecting Illicit Nuclear Material; Agreement Part of U.S. Megaports Initiative to Enchance Ocean-

Shipping Security," Bureau of International Information Programs, November 22, 2005 (http://lists.state.gove/archives/us-china.html).

14. Office of the White House Press Secretary, "Remarks by the President on National Missile Defense," Georgetown University, Washington, September 1, 2000.

15. Al Gore is quoted in Charles Babington, "Missile Defense Is Elevated as Campain Issue," *Washington Post*, September 1, 2001, p. A1.

16. David E. Sanger, "U.S. to Tell China It Will Not Object to Missile Buildup," *New York Times*, September 2, 2001, p. A1.

17. "Remarks by the President on National Missile Defense," December 13, 2001 (www.whitehouse.gov/news/releases/2001/12/20011213-4.html; emphasis added).

18. For text, see the U.S. Department of State website, www.state.gov/r/pa/ei/bgn/18901.htm.

19. Details on the Cooperative Threat Reduction program can be found at the website of the Nuclear Threat Initiative, www.nti.org/db/nisprofs/russia/forasst/nunn_lug/overview.htm.

20. The author is grateful to John Hamre for bringing my attention to this policy proposal.

21. Alastair Iain Johnston and Paul Evans, "China's Engagement with Multilateral Security Institutions," in *Engaging China: The Management of an Emerging Power*, edited by Alastair Iain Johnston and Robert S. Ross (New York: Routledge, 1999), p. 254; see, more generally, pp. 235–54.

22. Foreign Minister Tang Jiaxuan, speech at the annual ARF foreign ministers meeting, July 31, 2002 (www1.chinadaily.com.cn/news/2002-07-31/80220.html).

23. On U.S.-China counterterrorism cooperation, see U.S. Department of State, Office of the Spokesman, "Designation of the Eastern Turkistan Islamic Movement under UNSC Resolutions 1267 and 1390," September 11, 2002 (http://usinfo.state.gov/regional/ea/uschina/etim1.htm); U.S. Department of State news release, "Joint Press Release of the United States of America and the People's Republic of China," June 21, 2002 (http://usinfo.state.gov/regional/ea/uschina/uschintr.htm); U.S. Department of the Treasury, Office of Public Affairs, "The United States and China Meet to Discuss Terrorist Financing," May 30, 2001, PO-3139 (http://uninfo.state.gov/regional/ea/uschina/terrfinan.htm).

24. Office of the White House Press Secretary, "Fact Sheet: The Asia-Pacific Partnership on Clean Development and Climate," January 11, 2006 (www.whitehouse.gov/news/releases/2006/01/20060111-8.html).

25. Kabul Bakhtar News Agency, July 24, 2002 (FBIS, IAP20020724000097); "Statement by Ambassador Wang Yingfan, Permanent Representative of China to the United Nations, at the Security Council on the Situation in Afghanistan," March 26, 2002 (www.china-un.org/eng/27765.html).

26. Kenneth W. Allen and Eric A. McVadon, "China's Foreign Military Relations" (Washington: Henry L. Stimson Center, October 1999).

27. Ibid., p. 27.

28. Shao Zhongwei, "Peacekeeping on Agenda," *China Daily*, June 27, 2000; "UK-China Joint Statement," May 10, 2005 (www.dfid.gov.uk/countries/asia/China/joint-statement.asp).

29. Harvey J. Langholtz, "The Training and Assessment of UN Peacekeepers with Distance-Education Pedagogy," *Peaceworks*, no. 29 (July 1999): 37–38. This periodical is published by the United States Institute of Peace and is available from its website, www.usip.org.

Chapter Seven

1. "PRC: Liaowang Article Sees PRC's 'New Diplomacy' Stress on 'More Active' International Role," *Liaowang*, July 11, 2005 (FBIS, CPP20050719000118, July 19, 2005).

Index